The Marketing Primer

The Marketing Series is one of the most comprehensive collections of textbooks in marketing and sales available from the UK today.

Published by Heinemann Professional Publishing on behalf of the Chartered Institute of Marketing, the series has been specifically designed, developed and progressively updated over a number of years to support students studying for the Institute's certificate and diploma qualifications. The scope of the subjects covered by the series, however, means that it is of equal value to anyone studying other further or higher business and/or marketing related qualifications.

Formed in 1911, the Chartered Institute of Marketing is now the largest professional marketing management body in Europe with over 21,000 members and 20,000 students located worldwide. Its primary objectives are focused on the development of awareness and understanding of marketing throughout UK industry and commerce and in the raising of standards of professionalism in the education, training and practice of this key business discipline.

Other titles in the series

The Strategy of Distribution
Management
Martin Christopher

Marketing Communications
C. J. Coulson-Thomas

The Marketing of Services
D. Cowell

Marketing Research for Managers
S. Crouch

Case Studies in International
Marketing
P. Doyle and N. A Hart

The Principles and Practice of
Selling
A. Gillam

Essentials of Statistics in Marketing
*C. S. Greensted, A. K. S. Jardine and
J. D. Macfarlane*

The Practice of Advertising
N. A. Hart and I. O'Connor

Glossary of Marketing Terms
N. A. Hart and J. Stapleton

The Principles and Practice of
Export Marketing
E. P. Hibbert

The Practice of Public Relations
W. Howard

Legal Aspects of Marketing
J. L. Livermore

Economics: an introduction for
students of business and marketing
F. Livesey

Mini Cases in Marketing
*L. Massingham and
G. Lancaster*

How to sell a service: Guidelines for
effective selling in a service
business
*Malcolm H. B. McDonald with
John Leppard*

Marketing Plans: how to prepare
them; how to use them
Malcolm H. B. McDonald

Case Studies in Marketing,
Advertising and Public Relations
C. McIver

International Marketing
S. J. Paliwoda

Business Analysis for Marketing
Managers
L. A. Rogers

Effective Sales Management
J. Strafford and C. Grant

Profitable Product Management
J. Ward

Behavioural Aspects of Marketing
Keith C. Williams

Business Organization
R. J. Williams

The Fundamentals and Practice of
Marketing
J. Wilmshurst

The Fundamentals of Advertising
J. Wilmshurst

Management Controls and
Marketing Planning
R. M. S. Wilson

Bargaining for Results
J. Winkler

Pricing for Results
J. Winkler

The Marketing Primer

Key issues and topics explained

GEOFF LANCASTER

*Reader in Marketing, Huddersfield Polytechnic
and Senior Examiner to the Chartered Institute of
Marketing and Chief Examiner to the London
Chamber of Commerce and Industry*

and

LESTER MASSINGHAM

*Principal at MTMS Limited and Senior
Examiner to the Chartered Institute of Marketing*

Published on behalf of the
Chartered Institute of Marketing

Heinemann Professional Publishing

Heinemann Professional Publishing Ltd
Halley Court, Jordan Hill, Oxford OX2 8EJ

OXFORD LONDON MELBOURNE AUCKLAND
SINGAPORE IBADAN NAIROBI GABORONE KINGSTON

First published 1988
Reprinted 1990

British Library Cataloguing in Publication Data

Lancaster, Geoff A.
  The marketing primer.
  1. Marketing
  I. Title II. Massingham, Lester III. Series
  658.8

ISBN 0 434 91092 9

Typeset by Inforum Ltd, Portsmouth
Printed in Great Britain by
Richard Clay Ltd, Chichester

Contents

List of illustrations   vii
Preface   ix

1   Preparing for examinations   1
Objective setting   1
The revision process   2
Information retention   3
Application   4
Sitting examinations   5
Extracts from a number of examiners' reports   5

2   Listing of questions answered in the text   10

3   Questions and answers   15
Questions 1–5, relating to the wider remit of marketing   17
Questions 6–8, relating to buyer behaviour   40
Questions 9–12, relating to market research and related
    issues   54
Questions 13–16, relating to products (or services)   79
Questions 17–19, relating to pricing   102
Questions 20–4, relating to promotion (advertising, selling
    and public relations)   115
Questions 25–30, relating to distribution (channels and
    logistics)   138
Questions 31–3, relating to international marketing and
    exporting   163
Questions 34–8, relating to strategic issues   181
Questions 39–40, relating to more specific marketing issues   201

4   Mini case studies   212
International marketing: Exotic Siam Ltd   213
Planning and control: 'Gabrielle'   221
Marketing communications: the Arthur Morrison Group   231

Index   238

To Norman Waite and Bill Betts at the Chartered Institute of Marketing who so generously gave us access to examiners' reports and indeed provided the impetus for the text to be written in the first place. In addition our thanks must go to Richard Pearson, Export Manager of Drake Fibres Ltd who, as a personal friend, provided many practical pointers and indeed acted as a constructive critic as the text was being written.

Illustrations

1   Micro environment   23
2   Influences of the total environment   27
3   Diffusion: distribution and classification of adopter categories   48
4   Relationship between diffusion theory and the PLC   49
5   MkIS – the information process   66
6   The relation between cost and product development   84
7   Total assembly of company products   86
8   The product life cycle   90
9   Use of PLC concept   95
10 Determination of target price   112
11 The components of a control system   186

Preface

Marketing is a subject that occurs as a separate syllabus in a number of examining bodies' examinations. It also features strongly in more general business studies syllabuses. Professional examinations, such as those of the accountancy and commercial bodies, the Institute of Purchasing and Supply, the Institute of Export and of course the Chartered Institute of Marketing, require the study of marketing as a separate subject area. It is a single subject in the London Chamber of Commerce and Industry and Royal Society of Arts examinations. It is prominent at the National and Higher levels of the Business and Technician Education Council examinations and in Advanced Level Business Studies. It also forms a significant part of undergraduate and post-graduate degree programmes in business studies.

This text does not pretend to be a self-contained instructional manual. In fact it is assumed that a basic marketing textbook or course of instruction will be followed concurrently with this text. The aim of this book is to complement other forms of study. Clearly, different levels of examination will require different 'depths' and 'applications' of knowledge, to suit the requirements of differing educational needs. This 'marketing primer' leads the reader along the appropriate path, and, where relevant, gives pointers to further reading and study at a suitable level for the examination being attempted.

The essentials of marketing are covered through the questions and answers. Although it is not possible within the confines of this text to cover all the issues that might arise in marketing, all the major areas are dealt with. The text starts with marketing's wider remit and then becomes more specific, examining marketing research, the product (or service), pricing, promotion (including advertising, selling and public relations), distribution (including channels and logistics), retailing, international marketing, and marketing strategy, and concludes with questions and answers on ethics in marketing and industrial marketing.

The answers given to each individual question are comprehensive, and it is *not* expected that an examination candidate will be able to cover the points in the same detail within the confines of, say, a 30-minute answer period. However, because marketing is mainly a behaviourally based subject, questions can be answered well in a number of different ways – making marketing a 'richer' and more interesting subject to study. The answers are thus designed to cover the main conceivable approaches, and the student will tailor these to suit the individual examination circumstances.

The question and answer approach adopted for this text is therefore invaluable to students at any level, as it gives the framework and content of an answer. It shows what essay and examination questions are asking for, as well as giving detailed information upon the content matter that should be included in the answer. So many students, although able to learn the information required in syllabuses, are not able to apply this knowledge when answering examination questions. Existing model answer books simply give a suggested answer to a question without discussing the implications of the way the question is asked and developing the appropriateness of alternative lines of approach.

As well as covering questions and answers relating to marketing, this book also gives constructive advice upon how to prepare for examinations. This covers such matters as advice on studying, revision techniques and how to cope with the stress of such preparation. It advises upon examination technique, and gives pointers upon what examiners tend to look for in answers from candidates, backed up with extracts from marketing examiners' reports.

Where appropriate, pointers are given at the end of questions as to how the student can explore the subject matter of the question in greater detail. In some cases specific textbooks or journal articles are quoted. However, the point is also made that marketing is taking place all around, and students should be encouraged to take 'current affairs' into consideration when answering questions. Some answers are also dealt with at greater length than others. This is not to say that these longer answers are necessarily more important than the shorter ones, but that giving all the answers detailed treatment would have produced a text of unmanageable proportions, and this would have destroyed the real purpose of a 'marketing primer'.

This text must be viewed as being somewhat 'different' from a traditional marketing textbook. It is a learning and revision aid, and will be invaluable for those students studying for, and taking examinations in, the subject of marketing.

ONE

Preparing for examinations

A number of potentially successful students fail to achieve their full potential in examinations because they are unable to appreciate 'examination technique'. This section is designed to help such students in practical terms. It should help to instill a positive way of thinking to give them confidence in their own abilities through being adequately prepared in terms of subject knowledge and indeed 'attitude' towards the examination itself.

Only very exceptional students will be able to complete a course of study and then pass an examination with very limited revision. Most students need to plan their work and revision rigorously and set themselves objectives.

Objective setting

It seems to be an obvious maxim that one should plan and organize work before an examination, but the reality is that many students fail to do this in any logical and planned way. Instead 'panic' often sets in as the examination approaches, with students being ill-prepared, not having revised the essentials. The sad thing is that these are often quite capable students who have worked hard during their course, but because of an inability to organize their revision schedule effectively they under-perform in the examination.

An obvious stage in this planning process is to obtain a copy of the appropriate syllabus, especially if the examination is for an external body, as opposed to being an internally set examination. External syllabuses are usually very detailed and are usually prefaced with a statement of objectives relating to individual subjects. Such objectives should give an indication of the level of ease or difficulty that can be expected, and also the level of generality or detail to be expected. Following the objectives, a good syllabus should break down the subject into a number of logical sub-divisions.

The next logical stage in the planning process is to obtain past examination papers, while checking whether or not there have been any syllabus changes from one past examination paper to the other. You will then be able to ascertain the time available to answer a range of questions, and be able to practise completing answers to questions within time limits. In fact many students fail examinations not through lack of knowledge but simply owing to bad time management, i.e. spending too much time on earlier questions and then running out of time on later questions. Specimen examination answers are available from most examination bodies, and the best ones are clearly those that are written by the examiners themselves. Do not be too 'put off' when reading these, because they normally provide very comprehensive answers that students could not really be expected to replicate under normal examination timings and conditions. However, they are useful, especially if written by the examiner, because they do at least give some insight into his or her thinking.

The date and time of the examination is clearly very important, and you should find this out as soon as possible, even if it is only for ensuring that you are entered for the examination in good time. More to the point, knowing the date will enable a revision timetable to be drawn up in good time. The most sensible approach to revision is 'little and often', rather than leaving it to the 'last minute'. It is in these latter circumstances that 'panic' can set in as the examination approaches and the realization dawns that complete revision cannot be undertaken because of insufficient time.

Once the revision timetable has been drawn up, you should ensure that it covers all the topics on the syllabus. It is also a good idea to look through previous examination papers to see if there is any trend in 'regularly asked' questions. However, to attempt a forecast of examination questions is rather dangerous, because it does not follow that certain questions will come up at certain times, and there is no reason to suppose that a particular question will not come up in a slightly different form in sequential examinations. It is very rarely that anybody can stick rigidly to an examination timetable, and the reality is that you will fall behind. The maxim must therefore be to ensure that revision starts well before the examination date, and to ensure that 'contingency' time (or 'slack') is built into the revision schedule for 'catching up'. Some people tend to work better in the morning and others can revise more effectively late at night. You should know whether you are a 'morning' or a 'night' person, but the important thing to ensure is that you obtain sufficient sleep and relaxation immediately before the examination. If not, your performance and even your health could become impaired.

The revision process

There are no clear rules about when to start revising, but a good guideline is about 8 weeks before the examination. In practice it is not usually possible to start earlier than this, because the course of study will probably not have finished before then. A good number of students leave less time than this, a procedure that can lead to superficial revision or heavy reliance upon certain 'banker' questions that have been forecast to appear on the examination paper (or 'question spotting', as it is commonly termed).

When revising, it is important that you engage in 'active learning'. It is possible to spend hours revising without actually understanding or remembering much. The best way therefore is to take brief key notes of the topic being revised. These notes should include appropriate sources of information relevant to the topic being revised, such as lecture notes, textbooks, correspondence course material, your own ideas, etc. When writing these notes, note the key points and space the notes out so you can find topics quickly at a later date nearer the examination. Quite often it is useful to put as many diagrams and illustrations as possible into such notes, as they are invaluable as aids to memory. Many students find it useful to condense their notes at each successive revision session, starting out with relatively detailed ones and ending up with a few basic statements and key words which provide 'leads' into the main aspects of the problem.

Progress tests are also useful every few days during the revision programme. Such progress tests should cover the areas being revised and should be devised before the start of the revision period. A useful source for such questions is previous examination papers or questions that appear at the back of chapters in marketing textbooks. It is of course important that the time allocated to the test closely matches the time available in an actual examination. Upon completion, self-evaluation of the test is important, but the opinion of fellow students, tutors or others with knowledge of the subject can also be very helpful.

A revision aid that was pioneered by the Open University is that of 'self-help' groups, or studying with other students who are revising for the same examination, which provides a medium for pooling information, questioning ideas and evaluating performance. Such groups can take the form of 'brainstorming' sessions, individual presentations on selected topics, informal discussion of questions, 'mock' examinations, etc. The principal benefit of this group approach is that it encourages participants to be brief and to the point, while at the same time providing a comprehensive answer to the problem under review.

Information retention

Spending hours 'rote' learning is not the way to success. Note-taking and reading 'around' a subject are more effective methods. Reading speed is also important, and it is well known that some people have perfected the skill of 'skim' reading. Providing skim reading can be combined with information retention and understanding, the process of revision can be very effective. It is not the purpose of this section to attempt to teach such skills, but the following guidelines may be of help:

PREPARING FOR EXAMINATIONS

1 Approach revision with a positive attitude rather than regarding it as an unpleasant task.
2 Sit in a comfortable position behind a desk or table with a good light.
3 Revise in sections, e.g. whole sentences/paragraphs, rather than dwelling on each word: the aim is to obtain an appreciation of the meaning of what is being said.
4 When revising in this quick manner, it is important not to spend too long before taking a break. About half an hour is the optimum time to spend before taking 5 minutes off. Such a break allows time for reflection, and it is also something to look forward to when one is covering a lot of revision ground very quickly.
5 The importance of note-taking cannot be emphasized enough. Remember to include points that are not fully understood, in order to pursue them later, rather than spending excessive time pondering over such points while revising.
6 For key concepts that have to be committed to memory, try to take the first letters and make these into a sentence or word, no matter how meaningless such a sentence or word may be, e.g. *Richard Of York Gave Battle In Vain* – ROYGBIV – for remembering the colours of the spectrum. Remember that wide reading improves vocabulary and this is clearly an asset when sitting an examination.

Application

One of the most common causes of examination failure is that students simply do not answer the question set. They seem determined to give a potted version of their notes instead of attempting to apply such knowledge to the question itself. If questions are purely descriptive, then this should pose less of a problem, but at higher levels of examination it is more likely that questions will be more conceptually based and the student will be expected to apply skills of understanding and analysis.

Descriptive questions usually begin with 'explain', 'define', 'outline', 'state' or 'describe'. When answering such questions, remember to include explanations and definitions. Better answers will also include hypothetical or practical examples to reinforce the points made. Analytical questions, which are more difficult to answer, usually begin with 'analyse', 'criticize', 'assess', 'evaluate' or 'discuss'. (Both types of question, however, require the student to demonstrate that the question has been fully comprehended.) It is important to put forward differing viewpoints and to support them with appropriate examples in order to show an awareness of criticisms that can be levelled at a particular viewpoint. Such an answer should end with a conclusion that summarizes the key issues and presents the student's own judgement of the subject.

Such careful revision and preparation as has been described should reduce any 'nerves' that might be present before the examination. For those still prone to stress, it is a good idea to talk it over with family, fellow-students or counsellors. Such discussion usually helps to reduce anxiety. Examinations are stressful, but, when viewed in a positive manner, such stress will not be harmful. It is also sensible to allow enough time to compose oneself at the beginning of an examination (up to 5 minutes if necessary), since it can be unrewarding to start writing in other than a calm and detached fashion.

Sitting examinations

Once the questions have been distributed it is important to read and re-read all instructions and questions most carefully. Questions should then be rated in terms of whether they can be answered adequately. Only thus can any choice be effectively used. It should then be possible to list the order in which the selected questions are to be answered, starting with the one where the subject-matter is best known. This will build up self-confidence to attempt what seem to be the more difficult questions later.

After thinking about each question to be answered, prepare an essay plan, consisting of brief notes made at the beginning of the answer book, giving the main points and structure of the essay. Such a plan gives direction to an answer, making it easier to compose. It is better to start the actual answer on a new page and, when the answer is finished, lightly cross out the essay plan. Other obvious points are to write legibly and to number all answers correctly and clearly, making sure that additional sheets have your name or number on them and these are attached to the answer book in chronological sequence.

Budget your time in order to complete the number of questions to be attempted: this normally means, when marks are equal, spending equal time on each answer. Some papers are sectionalized with disproportionate marks to each part (like the mini-case papers followed by a section of formal questions); here you should pay particular attention to the mark apportionment and the guidelines given. Remember that time is at a premium, so do not waste it by repeating the examination question or the same words or phrases. Finally, remember to write enough; too many candidates fail through giving embryonic answers with too little application or embellishment to score a pass mark.

Advice upon how to tackle different types of question is given throughout the text, so it is not repeated here. However, the following section contains extracts from examiners' reports noting common faults made by candidates and common causes of failure.

Extracts from a number of examiners' reports

The purpose of this section is to give a brief overview of what marketing examiners think about the work presented by candidates. It is not meant to be a comprehensive listing, but does provide pointers to the most usual causes of failure.

- The overall standard of the entry was disappointing, with most candidates seeming to have very little knowledge or understanding of the subject. This was shown by the number of wild guesses that were offered, showing that candidates were unfamiliar with the subject, presumably because they had done little reading.
- The first general observation is that candidates must write clearly the number of the question being attempted. In many cases it was unclear whether candidates were making points within a question they had started to answer, or whether their points related to a new question. Candidates should use the left hand margin for question numbers only and should leave a space of at least three lines between questions.
- Many candidates who failed did so because they misjudged time and concentrated too long on certain questions. When the question calls for 'notes' or 'brief' explanation, then the candidates should abide by these instructions.
- Some candidates could offer no more than sketchy answers to some questions. Frequently, candidates failed to grasp the purpose of the question: their answers were concerned with what they thought they knew rather than what was asked for in the question.
- The overall performance of candidates was low because of their inability to present five adequate answers. It was apparent that preconceived answers were produced rather than a considered response to the questions set.
- The general standard of candidates was disappointing: most candidates were ill prepared for an examination at this standard. Many answers were too short, providing a few basic bits of information, but in a number of cases, such information was quite unrelated to the question set. Most candidates had obviously had very little guidance in their studies.
- It was incredible how many detailed answers had nothing whatever to do with the questions. Most of the candidates seemed to be on the very fringes of marketing. While modern marketing and marketing research techniques may not be practised in third world countries, the object in taking an examination in marketing is surely to show that candidates have learned something about the subject.
- A surprising feature of this examination was the number of candidates who wrote long answers which had nothing to do with the questions allegedly being answered. Others thought it sufficient to draw a line down the centre of the page and scribble some scrappy notes on either side of it, setting out pros and cons.
- The marketing world is in a state of constant change and both tutors and

candidates should be aware of newer developments, such as direct response marketing.

- The major general comment is that too many candidates do not read and answer the set questions. Candidates cannot expect good results when they treat every question as if it reads 'Write all you know about . . .'.
- Candidates answered the questions they wanted to answer, rather than the questions they were required to answer.
- The principal reason for failure was mis-reading or misunderstanding of the questions.
- A large number of candidates gave no indication of which question they were attempting and some even ran one answer into another with no clear indication of where one question ended and the other began.
- There is still evidence of insufficient preparedness in terms of quite basic knowledge: students would do well to consult some of the recommended texts more often. Some did not seem to be able to balance their answers very well and produced, for example, two very long answers then three answers of inadequate length.
- Some candidates had obviously been tutored in terms of examples to use. This indicates a lack of imagination: candidates should be encouraged to read widely and to take their own examples from currently reported business events from newspapers, journals, television, etc., and to quote marketing examples of what they see around them.
- The old excuse of being a student with no practical experience to draw upon should no longer pertain: marketing is happening all around us and it takes only imagination to work relevant happenings into examination answers.
- Many students who failed this examination did not necessarily fail through lack of knowledge, but because of the fact that they failed to read the question thoroughly and did not answer the questions set.
- There is now sufficient case material documented in textbooks and the press for students to be able to cite this; the excuse of being unable to quote examples because of lack of practical experience should no longer apply. Thus, students should be encouraged to use everyday examples, even if their knowledge of these is only second-hand. It goes without saying that this will help students whose arts of expression are not so strong, and quite often the use of a relevant case example can save a lengthy and tedious explanation.
- A point that really should not have to be made is that this whole paper is about the *International* aspects of Marketing; low marks were awarded, for instance, to students who answered the 'standardization' and 'centralization' questions without any reference to overseas situations.
- (With regard to a mini-case set of answers) a more serious fault for a relatively considerable number of students lay in their attempts to outline a marketing plan. Irrespective of the actual proposals made, there are several

approaches which could have been used; and it was distressing at this stage to observe the ignorance shown by inability to present a marketing plan and its constituent parts. While the examiners appreciate the time constraint, students at this stage of their course should be able to outline a plan logically, covering the main stages in sequence, and making brief proposals under each heading, so that the whole hangs together coherently, and would be a workable proposition.

- One glaring problem, which is continually referred to in comments on individual questions, is that candidates are seldom aware of the practical application of behavioural knowledge and lose marks in consequence.
- The main deficiencies were lack of comprehension, inadequate preparation and little practice in answering questions under examination conditions. Presentation was often poor and the language far from being precise. Many candidates did not answer the question asked and it is suggested that they read the questions more carefully and confine their answers to the information required.
- Every year, one fundamental point must be repeated – for students to appreciate the necessity of reading the question to determine exactly what the examiner is seeking to test and then framing the answer accordingly. In most questions, there is a key word or phrase which indicates the point(s) required.
- Candidates who score high marks in this examination will be those who, in addition to demonstrating a basic understanding, distinguish themselves on a combination of one or more of the following factors:
  - Appropriate use of relevant practical examples and an appreciation of reality.
  - Evidence of ability to think creatively or originally about a topic or problem, i.e. placing less of an emphasis on textbook content, merely using it to support their own ideas.
  - Answers which adhere to the specific question set and are clear, concise and objective.
- The typical question in this paper falls into two parts, in which Part one opens up some topic usually directing the candidate's attention to some aspect of the topic and inviting him or her to set out theoretical and institutional knowledge bearing on that topic. This is the bit which can be got out of any of the better texts. The second part of the question is normally designed to thrust the candidate into explanation or discussion of the wider experience of marketing as it is practised in the candidate's environment, and this is where the examiner is looking to see whether, from personal experience, discussions with colleagues, teachers and fellow marketers, and overall knowledge of the marketing scene (as expressed in, say, well known contemporary advertising campaigns), the candidate appears to have a minimum awareness and understanding of what is going on in the

world in which he or she is following a career. It is in this second area that the majority of candidates still fail to do justice to themselves.

The reports from which these observations are taken are of course very much longer than the extracts produced above, but a good cross-section of what marketing examiners say about poor candidates' papers is provided. It hardly needs any more comment or elaboration to see where most of the mistakes lie. The point that should be taken is not to fall into the same traps yourself nor to suppose that examiners do not discriminate in favour of candidates who communicate, accurately and fully, exactly what *is* required. They do!

TWO

Listing of questions answered in the text

Questions relating to the wider remit of marketing

1 The meaning of the term 'marketing' remains an area of confusion in the minds of many. As a marketing practitioner, explain the implications and real meaning of marketing. Show how this can be distinguished from 'selling'.
2 Business activity does not take place in a vacuum. Describe a manufacturing or service company in relation to a simple marketing system and discuss the influence of wider environmental forces.
3 Explain the principal functional elements of marketing management. Illustrate your answer with reference to a product or service with which you are familiar.
4 Discuss the problems associated with a firm's transition from being sales-oriented to being marketing-oriented.
5 Describe the principal elements of market structure for *either* an industrial market *or* a consumer market of your own choice.

Questions relating to buyer behaviour

6 One precept of economic theory holds that the consumer is an essentially rational being. What influences are at work on the consumer which would tend to contradict this?
7 Describe the theory of the diffusion of innovations and critically examine its relevance to marketing management.
8 Discuss the role and behaviour of the industrial purchaser in comparison with the domestic consumer. Would you agree that the industrial purchase is devoid of all but economic considerations?

Questions pertaining to marketing research and related issues

9 Write notes on FOUR of the following:
    (i)   Latin square design

(ii) Consumer panels
(iii) Quota sampling
(iv) Random (probability) sampling
(v) Test marketing

10 What do you understand by the term 'Marketing Information System'? How does it differ from Marketing Research?

11 Describe and comment upon 'primary' and 'secondary' data-collection in the context of marketing research.

12 Differentiate between qualitative and quantitative research in the context of marketing research. In your answer illustrate the most appropriate medium for data-collection in relation to a variety of marketing-research problems.

Questions relating to products (or services)

13 Suggest sources and techniques for generating new product ideas. What steps can the company take to reduce the risk of new product failure?

14 Describe the assembly of a company's product mix, giving reasons for mix optimization and ways in which this may be achieved.

15 What strategies does marketing theory recommend for each stage of the Product Life Cycle? Criticize this concept and discuss its practical limitations.

16 Packaging can be said to have two functions:

(i) Product protection
(ii) Product promotion

Discuss the function of each in relation to a product range of your choice.

Questions relating to pricing

17 What limitations are inherent in the economist's view of pricing? How might price be determined in a realistic marketing situation?

18 Discuss the practice and associated complications of pricing for a product line.

19 Write notes on FOUR of the following:
(i) Price discrimination
(ii) Mark-up pricing
(iii) Target pricing
(iv) Prestige pricing
(v) Loss leaders

LISTING OF QUESTIONS ANSWERED IN THE TEXT

Questions relating to promotion (advertising, selling and public relations)

20 For many companies the advertising budget is a notorious source of disagreement. What methods are commonly employed for the setting of advertising budgets? How can management judge the effectiveness of this expenditure?

21 Comment upon the contribution of the sales force to the marketing effort of the firm. Illustrate your answer with appropriate product examples.

22 Discuss the role of Public Relations with respect to the firm's marketing activities.

23 Explain what you understand by the term 'sales promotion' and then discuss the sales objectives that can be achieved by using these techniques. Illustrate your answer, where appropriate, by the use of examples.

24 What guidelines would you give to a sales manager wishing to recruit and train members of a sales force to achieve the results desired?

Questions relating to distribution (channels and logistics)

25 How is the application of the 'total distribution concept' or systems approach relevant to the marketing goal of 'satisfying customer requirements profitably'?

26 What considerations do you consider to be essential to the design of marketing channels? Comment as to the effects of conflict and the exercise of power within marketing channels.

27 What factors must be considered by a firm wishing to establish a level of customer service which is appropriate to its markets? Show how such a service level can be employed to gain competitive advantage.

28 Account for the rapid development of Franchising in the UK. Comment upon any factors to be considered, with regard to franchise agreements, for both the franchisor and the franchisee.

29 What factors have brought about the changes in UK retailing that have occurred since the late 1950s?

30 Direct marketing has been one of the fastest growing areas of distribution over the past 20 years. Describe what is meant by 'direct marketing' and account for its success.

Questions relating to international marketing and exporting

31 What would you describe as essential considerations for companies that wish to enter export markets? (Approach your answer from the perspective of UK companies.)

32 Write comprehensive notes on ALL of the following:
  (i)   The role of export salesmen
  (ii)   The role of the commission agent
  (iii)   The role of government aid to United Kingdom exporters
33 By treating the multi-national company as a final stage, describe how a company may develop as it becomes increasingly committed to overseas markets.

Questions relating to strategic issues

34 Comment upon the essential nature of marketing planning and strategy formulation. Illustrate your answer with appropriate industry/product analogies.
35 Marketing strategy and planning are of little value without a system of control. What control procedures can be employed by marketing management?
36 The purpose of planning is to allocate company resources in such a manner as to achieve sales anticipated from the sales forecast. Such sales forecasts are for the short, medium and long terms. Describe the purpose of each of these forecasts and state their implications for the various functional areas of a business.
37 'Segmentation is the heart of marketing strategy.' Explain the importance of market segmentation. Choose two markets (one from a consumer and one from an industrial market) and briefly show how these may be segmented.
38 Discuss the marketing objectives that a branding strategy aims to achieve.

Questions relating to more specific issues in marketing

39 Marketing has been criticized both on economic and ethical grounds. Discuss these criticisms, indicating how far you think they are justified.
40 What problems do you feel might be associated with applying the theory of marketing management to real-life situations?

THREE

Questions and answers

QUESTION 1 √

The meaning of the term 'marketing' remains an area of
confusion in the minds of many. As a marketing practitioner,
explain the implications and real meaning of marketing. Show
how this can be distinguished from 'selling'.

OBJECTIVES

This question aims to assess your basic understanding of the marketing
concept and the depth and range of matters with which it is concerned.

APPROACH

You should clearly distinguish between marketing as a business philosophy
and the role of marketing as a functional area of management, and include
some explanation of these two elements. The answer should then be developed so as to draw a distinction between 'marketing' and 'selling'. To
achieve this, some detail as to the basic tenets of each approach will be
necessary. Remember that in this context 'selling' refers to the conceptual
orientation of a firm towards its customers.

The question therefore calls for a balanced answer covering each of the
following:

- The marketing concept
- Marketing as a function
- A distinction between marketing and selling

As the question is fairly wide ranging, you will not have time to include too
much detail about any one part, say 'marketing as a function', which could in
fact form the basis of a question in its own right.

Although you must imply knowledge of how marketing has evolved, the
question *does not* require a description of the origins and development of
marketing. This information is irrelevant to the question and its inclusion
would not only waste your own time but also display to the examiner a
misunderstanding of the question.

Marks would probably be assigned on the basis of one-third for each part of
the answer. Assign therefore an equal amount of time to each part.

ANSWER

Suggested introduction

Numerous definitions exist which attempt succinctly to describe the scope and meaning of marketing. Marketing has been described as 'a human activity directed at satisfying needs and wants through exchange processes'. This is perhaps marketing at its most abstract level, and while Kotler as well as the Institute of Marketing have arrived at more comprehensive definitions, for some people the nature of marketing remains somewhat unresolved. In reality marketing as a management process is in essence a simple concept which holds that the orientation of a company should be towards the customer's point of view. As customers are the sole source of revenue for any business, it follows that attention to their needs and wants is a likely recipe for success.

The understanding of marketing is considerably aided once it is appreciated that the term implies both a business philosophy or frame of mind and a specialized functional area of management. The former implication is often referred to as the 'marketing concept'.

Explanation of the concept

1 *Customer orientation.* The first premise of the marketing concept is that the wants and needs of the customer should be the focus of all company activity. The company is therefore governed by its customers' requirements rather than purely by its production or technical facilities.

2 *An integrated management function.* Acceptance of the concept implies that a customer-orientation should be adopted by, and permeate, the company as a whole. Thus, whatever the specialized functional area (transport, finance, production, etc.), an outlook directed towards the market place should be of paramount importance. In particular it is vital that higher management ensures that this 'marketing orientation' is effectively communicated and understood throughout the company.

3 *The need for profits.* A third aspect of the marketing concept concerns the need for a company to be profit-directed. Implicit in this need is the recognition that a company's resources are finite: the aim of management is to achieve satisfactory returns whilst operating within the framework of its resource constraints. As has been suggested, the customer-oriented approach is a good basis for long-term profitability.

4 *A systematic approach.* Finally, the management role of identifying and anticipating customer requirements is axiomatic. A scientific element is therefore encompassed within the marketing concept. This means a systematic planning process, based upon marketing research, which leads to a marketing strategy with distinct objectives. The whole process must be continuously monitored and a built-in control system established. Allied to

the recognition of company constraints, the strategic nature of marketing emphasizes the need for realism in the setting of objectives. Strategic planning, by definition, also implies that marketing is directed at the long term. A formal planning system is not, however, synonymous with rigidity; the key strength of any company is its ability to adapt over time to the dynamic nature of the marketing environment.

Marketing as a function

The marketing concept identifies the strategic nature of marketing. Strategic plans are realized by the specialized functions of marketing management, i.e. the management of customer demand. These functions have been categorized as being elements of the 'Marketing Mix', often referred to as the 'Four Ps'. The major components of the four Ps are listed below:

Product   – Branding
                     Quality of performance
                     Labelling
                     Packaging
                     Attributes

Price   – Level
                     Discounts
                     Credits
                     Discrimination

Promotion   – Advertising
                     Sales promotion
                     Publicity   Price lists
                     External public relations
                     Personal selling

Place   – Physical distribution/logistics
                     Channel management

These are the tools which marketing management uses in order to translate plans into action. It is important to understand that while they are mutually interdependent, management affords varying levels of emphasis to each of these elements. In this way a company's marketing mix can be tailored to its strategy and then fine-tuned according to developing market conditions.

Marketing vs selling

It is apparent from the foregoing that marketing has far greater ramifications than a management approach which focuses merely on 'selling'. Some firms

19

still retain an approach which is centred around sales. A direct comparison between 'selling' and 'marketing' attitudes illustrates how radically the two approaches can differ.

A 'Selling' orientation assumes that:

- The company's main task is to get sales for its products.
- Customers will not, without sales pressure, buy enough of the company's products.
- Additional sales can be induced by a substantial selling and promotional effort.
- Customers can probably be induced to buy again; if they do not, other customers will take their place.

This approach to business is essentially short-sighted because it implies that customers have to be coerced into buying from the company and must, for the well-being of the firm, do so, whether or not their interests are in the process best served. It can be seen that this is a dangerously narrow view.

A 'Marketing' orientation assumes that:

- The company's main task is to satisfy the defined set of wants of a defined set of customers.
- A carefully planned approach to the market, in the form of marketing research and systematic analysis and control is necessary to learn about the customers' wants and to ensure that they are being satisfied.
- The whole company must be integrated in its approach to the market.
- The process of satisfying customer wants, if carried out efficiently, will bring about favourable customer attitudes to the company and repeat business, thus carrying company success into the long term.

From this comparison it is evident that the starting points, the means and the objectives of 'marketing' as opposed to 'selling', taken in isolation, are in serious contrast. What is needed is an integration of these ideas (since nobody doubts that a firm, to remain solvent, must dispose effectively of its output of goods and services). Levitt says that selling takes account of the needs of the seller, while marketing concerns itself with the needs of the buyer.

Possible conclusion
Once its conceptual and functional nature is understood, marketing becomes a simple and logical process. From a company perspective it is vital that the marketing concept should be understood and adopted by top management (whether this be within the highly structured cadre of large organizations or the less structured environment of small firms). This appreciation should then

be communicated throughout the whole company. The marketing practitioner has a special responsibility in this communication process; only by 'marketing' the marketing orientation within the company will results that can display the validity of the approach be achieved. The outcome should be that the company makes what it has learned customers wish to buy, and in this way succeeds in selling its output profitably.

QUESTION 2

Business activity does not take place in a vacuum. Describe a manufacturing or service company in relation to a simple marketing system and discuss the influence of wider environmental forces.

OBJECTIVE

The purpose of this question is to ensure that the student appreciates the importance of factors outside the company's control that can affect both short- and long-term planning. The student should attempt to show how the company should prepare itself, as far as possible, to deal with changing elements in the marketing environment. Finally, the question seeks to test the student's awareness of the scope of the marketing system itself.

APPROACH

Take care, before you begin your answer, to decide whether you are about to describe a *manufacturing* company or a *service* company. It is within the context of *one* of these that you are to find the examples which will illustrate your answer.

This is a straightforward question that demands a correspondingly direct answer. The answer, in the main, should be descriptive, and the use of diagrams would be appropriate, both to save time and to clarify your answer. Your answer should not neglect the examiner's request to 'discuss the influence' of the environment.

ANSWER

Suggested introduction
A manufacturing company has been chosen as the medium through which this question is to be answered.

The simplest marketing system consists of a BUYER and a SELLER. This is all that is required for a business transaction to take place, and such a transaction allows for the basic development of the marketing concept. If the buyer and seller were the only parties who were concerned in making this transaction possible, business would indeed take place in a vacuum. There are, however, a variety of other parties, as well as influences, at work which can either complicate or facilitate the basic buyer/seller relationship.

To appreciate the fuller scope of a marketing system, the marketing practitioner of a manufacturing company must be fully aware of the supply chain behind the company, together with those companies that are ahead in the chain, right up to the final end-user, whether this be another manufacturer (as in the case of a machinery maker) or the consumer (who shops in a retail store or buys from home by one means or another).

Micro environment

In order to illustrate this scope the example of a textile weaver has been chosen. The marketing system of which this company is part is shown in Figure 1, which portrays a simple system. It is important not to overlook the fact that the weaving company will have many suppliers of various goods and services, including raw material suppliers. Similarly the 'chain' also becomes a 'network' as far as customers and processors are concerned, and retailers are likely to be numerous. Thus, for the weaving company, the marketing system is in reality a rather complex structure, composed of many suppliers, middle-men and customers. The important factor to note is that although a company which is situated more or less in the middle of the system has been chosen, awareness of a firm's immediate surroundings (sometimes called the 'micro environment') is vital, whether that firm be a raw material supplier or a retailer. Any changes in the status quo, from whatever direction, can have important effects (for good or bad) on any or all members of the system.

For reasons of simplicity competitors are not shown in the figure, but they too are an important component of the marketing system. If one imagines a

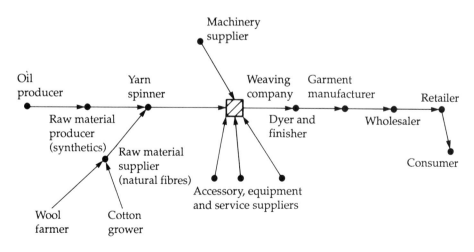

Figure 1   *Micro environment*

range of competitors placed alongside the weaver, it must be appreciated that each one of them will also have an immediate marketing environment similar to that depicted. Each one may have the same suppliers as well as the same customers and intermediaries. As these competitors become more (or less) powerful, so the fortunes of all the other companies will be affected.

Finally, within the immediate company we must consider the influences and activities of certain groups not directly part of the manufacturing chain but still important. Such groups may include, for example, the media (advertising, public relations), direct financial influences (banks, finance houses and stockbrokers), local government (planning, bye-laws and other regulations) and consumer groups (local action groups concerned with the responsibilities of a company towards its community).

Even a simply described marketing system relates therefore to a relatively complex network of interested parties that interact continually upon each other. This is made up of:

1 Suppliers.
2 Competitors.
3 Direct and indirect customers.
4 Bodies outside the company that have a direct effect upon its operations, such as the media and consumer groups.

So far we have only discussed the influences that prevail upon a company within its 'immediate' environment. We shall next consider the company's 'wider' environment.

Macro environment

This consists of influences and events that are not directly concerned with or specifically aimed at the company, but whose influence is nevertheless profound. In general they affect the company over the long term and normally they are beyond the control of the individual firm.

Whether a firm is engaged in consumer or industrial marketing, the effects of population (demographic) change will ultimately affect its opportunities. The effects of the post-war baby boom were felt in changes in consumer spending during the late 1960s and the early 1970s. As we move towards the end of the century, we know that the population of elderly people will increase to such an extent as to create new markets both in physical products and in service terms. In France, for example, the birthrate was encouraged by the government to slow down dramatically. This had an effect on both employment and consumer-goods markets. Population studies are also concerned with population types and groups, as well as merely numbers, age and sex. The influence of working women, combined with generally higher levels of disposable income in the UK since the 1950s, has meant that products and services on offer, and the methods of marketing these, have changed. This is related to the increasing amounts of leisure time that we currently enjoy in comparison to previous generations. Lifestyle changes are also related to geographical shifts in population that can create areas of under and over population. It should be noted also that an improvement in the level of education within a population is likely to influence both wealth and lifestyle.

The economic environment of a company is very relevant to its performance. Inflation is perhaps the best known of the wider environmental influences, because of its effects on consumer and manufacturer alike. The rate of growth within the economy will influence long-term planning; in the shorter term currency fluctuations and interest rates can drastically affect the plans of manufacturing companies. Such economic factors also affect the spending behaviour of consumers. A significant feature of the UK economy during the 1980s has been the rise in credit-card spending. Although the behaviour of each single household may seem insignificant, the combined behaviour of millions of consumers can be influential enough as to occasion changes in interest rates or the balance of trade through increases in imports. Economic influences are closely linked to government influence and action. The government can influence the manufacturer either by provoking economic change or by restricting it.

The government is also instrumental in bringing about new legislation that affects the ways in which firms are able to operate. The Monopolies Commission is an example of direct governmental control over business life; it has become more active since mergers and takeover bids have become commonplace. The government, usually with consumer protection in mind, is also very active in the introduction of legislation covering a wide variety of practices, ranging from anti-pollution measures to hire purchase control, fair trading in general and product safety.

A company's cultural environment changes slowly, but should be the object of constant monitoring. Fashion is an obvious example of how culture changes affect the firm. While fashions may change annually, there are long-term tendencies within what is fashionable that reflect basic changes in the cultural attitudes of society. In the UK, for example, the importance of men's lounge suits has diminished dramatically during the past 20 years; that could have serious implication for a firm like the one portrayed in Figure 1. In the food industry great changes have taken place since the early 1960s because of a basic change in consumers' attitudes towards food, with a move towards convenience and foreign food, and an increase in eating out. During the same period the confectionery industry has suffered because of greater awareness and attention being given to 'healthy eating'.

Scientific developments also affect the firm's environment. Computerization has, for example, changed our lives at work, in shops and banks, in travel, and many other walks of life. The rate of scientific change has also changed the emphasis on how we use products and what we expect from them. In the 1930s, 1940s and 1950s items were bought to 'last', whereas nowadays the tendency is to replace products as and when new refinements are added. In a relatively short space of time we can trace the development of the gramophone to the compact disc. It would be interesting to compare a list of those items considered essential to a newly married couple in the 1950s to one of today. Many people consider such products as a microwave oven 'essential', so not only do totally new products exist but many have moved from the category of 'luxury' to that of 'necessity'.

Natural environment
Finally, we should consider the 'natural' environment, which is of particular relevance to raw material supply. In the early 1970s the 'oil crisis' had catastrophic effects on western societies. Drought, famine, wars and floods constantly influence the supply and price of raw materials from all over the world. The advent of the nuclear age poses technical as well as ethical problems for individual companies and society as a whole. In more specific terms, companies are forced to pay attention to issues such as pollution, and whether or not their products are made from scarce or harmful ingredients, not only because these issues may affect their own future, but because consumers and governments are showing increasing concern as to how we use or abuse our natural environment. Thus, while an individual company has no control over the price of, say, oil or coffee, there is certainly scope for individual choice as to how products are made and from what material (more latterly evidenced in the move away from animal to synthetic skins for coats).

Conclusion
Figure 2 shows the same weaving company within the immediate marketing environment, surrounded by the influences of the wider environment. In this 'total' picture of a firm's environment many of the factors shown may appear far removed from the day-to-day life of a salesperson or factory worker, but it is the job of senior management to pay constant attention to them. Some issues, such as competitive action or raw material shortages, may 'confront' the company, but it is in the essence of marketing that they be monitored and prepared for as far as possible. Even where a firm cannot control specific aspects of its environment, the fact that it is 'aware' of them can increase the opportunities for exploiting potential opportunities or reducing the effects of adverse influences.

FURTHER READING
The issues concerned with the firm's environment affect almost every aspect of marketing. In particular, however, the student should study the subject of

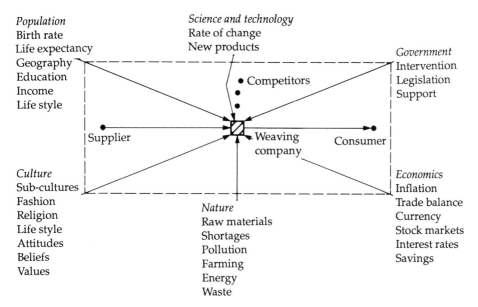

Population
Birth rate
Life expectancy
Geography
Education
Income
Life style

Science and technology
Rate of change
New products

• Competitors

Government
Intervention
Legislation
Support

Supplier

Weaving
company

Consumer

Culture
Sub-cultures
Fashion
Religion
Life style
Attitudes
Beliefs
Values

Nature
Raw materials
Shortages
Pollution
Farming
Energy
Waste

Economics
Inflation
Trade balance
Currency
Stock markets
Interest rates
Savings

Figure 2   *Influences of the total environment*

marketing channels and their management in greater detail. This will aid understanding of the chain of supply throughout the immediate environment. Additionally, further reading should include the setting up and operation of marketing intelligence or information systems. This will show how firms attempt to monitor and adapt to the influences in question.

Finally, students should choose their own industry and draw up a list or diagram of the influences that have been described. Headings for each factor specific to that industry should be inserted, and the list or diagram augmented over time simply by reading newspapers and relevant trade publications.

QUESTION 3

Explain the principal functional elements of marketing management. Illustrate your answer with reference to a product or service with which you are familiar.

OBJECTIVE

To discover how well the student is able to relate the theory of marketing functions to an actual product or service. The question does not therefore aim to test straightforward recall of information; rather, it is a test of practical application and creativity.

APPROACH

Question 1 was concerned with the meaning of marketing, whereas this question takes this knowledge as being 'understood'. Here, you are required to expand on the functional elements of marketing, and by means of a product example show how these are applied in practice.

Although there are certain basic areas which should not be omitted, there is considerable scope in this answer to use your imagination, say in the choice of media for advertising. The examples you choose must of course be sensible and appropriate, but for many of those you choose there will be no 'right' or 'wrong' answers, provided you can justify your reasoning.

As you are asked to deal with all the functional aspects of marketing, you are really concerned with the 'marketing mix'. Once you have decided upon a product, you could approach your answer from the perspective of designing a 'mix' strategy. When your illustrations and explanations are complete, you could sum up by discussing the marketing functions as a 'mix ratio', since different products require a different functional emphasis.

It would be acceptable to expand your answer to include a product line and product mix if necessary. You might want to include a deliberate 'mismatch'. Your product choice can be as restrictive or expansive as you wish, provided that you can show how it relates to the functional elements of the marketing mix.

Take care to make it quite clear from the outset what product you have chosen with which to illustrate your answer.

ANSWER

Suggested introduction

Marketing as a concept is essentially concerned with a management approach which has a customer orientation as its basis. The marketing function provides the tools and means to realize this orientation. Grouped together, they form the 'marketing mix'. Although the marketing mix embraces all the marketing functions, each element of the mix does not necessarily require the same emphasis: this depends upon the type of product and the nature of the market, which may in fact be subject to change over time.

The marketing mix is broken down into four elements:

product
price
promotion
place

Within each of these categories the various sub-functions of marketing can be identified. For example, PROMOTION is concerned with:

advertising
sales promotion
publicity
public relations (in part)

The role of marketing strategy (with reference to a specific product or a product line) is to decide which aspects of the mix should receive the most attention and how the functional elements should be employed within each mix category.

The product chosen to illustrate this answer further is a *relatively expensive, high quality camera.*

Marketing mix

1   *Product considerations.* The product has already been described as high quality. Product strategy should therefore utilize the marketing functions to reflect and consolidate this image. (For the purposes of the answer we presuppose that marketing research has identified a market segment for this product.)

Branding is considered essential, so that the product can be easily identified. The brand name may have a company connotation in keeping with an existing product line, or may seek to evoke an image of quality and technical superiority, which in turn will be supported by the promotional functions. Often when a company is well known, the two can be combined to give a 'double barrelled' effect, such as the ' ''x'' super-precision model'.

Quality. Needless to say, the camera should be constructed from high quality components so that the product image is not damaged by defective parts or adverse technical reports. Similarly the standard of workmanship should be of high quality. Both these factors should be emphasized to the potential market.

Packaging. As with any product, packaging should be a reflection of the product. For the camera (these are usually sold in boxes) the packaging should of course be attractive, but should also be designed to convey a 'high tech' image, perhaps by using metallic colours, which could infer precision and efficiency. For a camera, packaging must also perform a protective function. The labelling should match the style of the package and include enough technical data to attract the enthusiast's eye. Full technical specifications and instructions should be available within the box.

Attributes comprise either physical product features or suggested features of product image. The latter is usually concerned with promotion and sometimes pricing. The physical features refer to product design, and depend upon the market segment at which the product is aimed. The serious 'technically orientated' photographer may require the maximum number of 'extras' and may want the camera to 'appear' highly complicated in line with a certain self-image. On the other hand, the same type of user may be looking for an unobtrusive camera that combines high performance with simplicity of use. Market research should aid the product designer in deciding how physical attributes are incorporated into the product. Another market segment could be that of the wealthy, quality conscious, but non-technical user. The designer's task might be to combine ease of use with style while retaining the 'high tech' image.

2   *Pricing considerations.* The level of price is widely accepted as an indicator of quality. For this product there is a 'value added' element which should be reflected in the price level. The price function is also closely linked to the retail outlet. Highly expensive cameras are normally only to be found in specialist outlets. Although these outlets would be in competition with each other, consumers of such cameras would not expect them to appear in a supermarket or discount store. Discounting and continuous 'special offers' would tend to reduce the high quality image, and would therefore be avoided. Pricing should consequently be closely related to distribution, market segment and the stage at which the product is situated in its life cycle.

3   *Promotional considerations.* Particular care should always be taken in *sales promotion* for high value/high quality products. If too much is offered, or the product is promoted too often, there might be an adverse rather than a promotional effect on sales, because the consumer could get the impression that the product was not good enough to sell on its own merits. Price-related promotions have already been discussed, and in most cases are likely to be unsuitable.

Sales promotion for a high quality camera should therefore be of equally high quality, and ideally be related to the product. Competitions may be a suitable promotional medium (prizes could be related directly to the product (say an extra lens) or to the activity (say a holiday with photography as the main theme, such as a safari holiday). A range of films with each purchase (for a limited period) would promote sales without detracting from the product image. Although potential customers may be technically orientated and less price-sensitive, this is not to say that they are not susceptible to well planned inducements to purchase.

Advertising. The economics of advertising is concerned with 'reach', i.e. the number of people who have the opportunity to see an advertisement in relation to the cost of a campaign or individual advertisement. The market for high quality cameras is small in relation to that for detergent or coffee. Media selection is therefore vital, both for economic reasons and for effective communication. The consumer who is technically orientated will most probably subscribe to a specialist magazine, so this is an obvious medium. If the camera is targeted at the relatively wealthy (but less technically sophisticated) buyer as a prestige item, the pages of Sunday newspaper colour supplements could be considered. Material should also be available for in-store promotion. It may also be possible to enter into some form of joint advertising with a well known film manufacturer. This could assist in reducing costs, as well as using the image and obtaining the endorsement of a well known name.

Publicity. A further aspect of promotion concerns publicity. A camera manufacturer could consider the possibility of sponsorship – for a mountaineering expedition, say, or for an important yacht race. The manufacturer could also seek to have articles written about the camera in specialist publications or in the leisure pages of newspapers.

4   *Place (distribution) considerations*. To a great extent the distribution of the camera will be a function of the other elements of the marketing mix. It would be a waste of energy to concentrate on supermarkets, for example, when the whole thrust of the marketing strategy is directed at exclusivity (although it is true to say that super/hypermarkets are steadily diversifying into high quality/technical product areas). In general, however, the nature of the purchase is such as to require a high degree of personal advice and assistance, which can normally only be found in specialist outlets or perhaps in the appropriate section of large departmental stores.

Direct selling in conjunction with advertising in specialist publications could also be considered – in addition to, rather than as a replacement for, conventional retail sales. Direct selling would, however, reduce the logistical problems of distributing throughout the retail network. The logistics of service levels and physical distribution would need to be sophisticated, as the high value of the product would discourage retailers from holding high stock levels. The main problem, however, with the notion of direct selling might be consumer conservatism, which might be suspicious of such products being sold through non-traditional sales channels.

Conclusion

The marketing functions that have been described, together with suggestions for their employment, go together to form the marketing mix strategy. The two most important elements of the marketing mix are emphasis and inter-dependence. In the first case it is apparent that each product requires a different 'mix'. For the camera, PRODUCT and PROMOTION are more prominent. It is essential to recognize that, over time, markets may change and thus the emphasis given to respective marketing functions must be flexible enough to adjust to this.

Secondly, the emphasis on functions is distributed throughout the mix. All functions depend on each other to achieve success. This interdependence must be planned and tuned so that each functional strategy is not only dependent on, but must also be congruent with, another, to develop a clear theme throughout the marketing of a product.

QUESTION 4

Discuss the problems associated with a firm's transition from being sales-oriented to being marketing-oriented.

OBJECTIVE

It is to establish clearly and beyond doubt that the student has grasped the full meaning of 'marketing orientation' and is aware that a major shift in company orientation and management philosophy is not a task that can be accomplished overnight.

APPROACH

The answer to this question should be based on the assumption that you are perfectly familiar with what marketing is. There is therefore no need to 'explain' marketing in detail. The examiner's requirements will be satisfied if you are able to use this knowledge to form a comparison between marketing and sales orientation. It would still be valuable, however, to refer to the basic assumptions of the marketing concept versus those of merely 'selling', so that this comparison can be made.

Better marks will be awarded to those who pay particular attention to the word 'transition', because this is really the *key* word in the question. This discussion of transition from 'sales' to 'marketing' could be usefully introduced by making an initial comparison (perhaps in tabulated form) before going on to discuss the problems of becoming fully marketing-orientated.

ANSWER

Suggested introduction

The marketing concept holds that the core of any business is its customer base and the whole effort of the firm should be directed at the customer. Marketing also recognizes that such efforts should and must be rewarded by profit. Most managers, whatever their background, would agree that this is a sensible and logical approach to business. It is nevertheless true that many firms are not directed with a true marketing-orientation. While such firms may continue to be successful in the short term, it is more than likely that competitive activity will eventually require a 'rethink' as to how the company is responding to its customers. It is essential that senior management initiates and supervises any transition from sales to marketing orientation. Very often this transition follows the appointment of new personnel at the highest level.

Before discussing the problems of transition, it is useful to summarize the goals which a company must achieve if it is to attain a true marketing orientation.

Long-term strategic thinking

The company will need to formulate 'formal' plans and objectives about the company's future, based upon the best available marketing information as well as clear understanding of the company's own capabilities. While existing products and existing customers must be managed, they should no longer be the sole preoccupation of the company.

Over time senior management must ensure that a marketing approach is instilled into the thinking of all employees and departments.

Integration of all business functions

All departments in the company should be organized and managed so that they work in unison to the common aim of customer satisfaction. The success of a department should be judged as a function of the success of the total firm. It is no good having an ostensibly efficient and cost-effective transport department if the company is losing orders because of late deliveries. The various functions within a company must therefore be integrated and co-ordinated in order to achieve a successful marketing orientation.

New functions

Marketing necessitates the adoption of new methods and functions in the company. For example, the requirement for continuous marketing research and better information flow may necessitate the recruitment of new personnel. Sales personnel will be required to carry out new functions. If the marketing philosophy is not fully understood by all employees, these new tasks may appear to be unproductive and unnecessary.

The points outlined are all potential problem areas which the company may have to deal with once the decision to become marketing-orientated has been taken. Such problems are aggravated by fundamental differences in thinking between sales-oriented and marketing-oriented managers. These differences are concerned with the emphasis and importance placed on various functions. They are highlighted by considering and comparing how each approach is organized in Table 1.

The comparisons in Table 1 are sufficient to note that the two orientations are dramatically opposed to each other. It is also apparent that any moves towards 'marketing' are likely to cause major organizational conflict, the chief problem of the sales to marketing transition.

'Production' may provide a good example in order to consider the contrast-

Table 1

Company function	'Selling' approach	'Marketing' approach

Sales	Short-term sales + profit
	Sales most important
	
	One department
		Longer-term profit
		Customer satisfaction most
		  important
		Part of the totality of the
		  company

Purchasing	Narrow product line Standard parts	Broad product line Non-standard parts
Finance	Rigid budgets Cost-based pricing	Flexible budgets Market-oriented pricing
Accounting	Standard transactions	Special terms and discounts
Production	Long runs Few models Standard orders Long lead times	Short runs Many models Custom orders Short lead times

ing points of view. Ostensibly the production manager's concern is to organize production so as to achieve maximum efficiency from machinery and operatives. Within the confines of the production department this is achieved by maximizing output and minimizing waste. This approach makes good economic sense, but relates essentially to a sales-oriented approach. The company with such an orientation will encourage and foster this production manager's approach. Quite understandably management will wish to obtain maximum return on investment in machinery by achieving high levels of output of standard products. Management will also wish to keep labour costs to a minimum. Unfortunately the more such a policy is perpetrated, the more the company will be likely to leave its customers with a 'This is the product; take it, or leave it' attitude. Competitors may be visiting customers or conducting surveys so as to be able to say 'Tell us what you need and we will make it'. The same analysis can be applied to all the areas shown in Table 1. The manager of each functional area will be striving to achieve peak efficiency, but this may be at the expense of the effectiveness of the company as a whole.

This, then, is the essential 'organizational' problem that confronts those wishing to make the sales to marketing transition. The transition can usually only be effected by direction from the top downwards, because the principal tools which senior management can employ are seldom positively perceived by those at the receiving end. Full explanation is therefore important, together with a clear education programme. This should provide the opportunity for all members of all departments to more clearly understand their respective roles and appreciate the fact that all functions are mutually important. Managers should show, by example, that such an approach is workable; they should not 'preach' one thing and practise another. Finally, the company structure should be such that departmental managers are rewarded according to company success rather than by narrow departmental goals.

Even if the above-mentioned policies are intelligently and sensitively put into practice, a lingering problem area concerns the acceptance of marketing personnel or a marketing department within the firm – a phenomenon which may be entirely new to a previously sales-oriented organization. In particular, marketing research, advertising, promotions and product development personnel may be perceived by others as having a non-productive role, or as an 'expensive luxury'.

The problem becomes worse when these employees are grouped into a formal marketing department, which is often necessary, especially for companies selling fast-moving consumer goods (FMCGs) or consumer durables. Such a step can be construed as being one which changes the power base within a company – all the more so because marketing has been introduced as the prime function of the company. Whilst it is important that the marketing department should retain its own identity, it is essential that this identity should not be considered as the power base of the organization. Of course if marketing orientation is to be adopted, then the marketing personnel are important, but the whole company must understand that recommendations made by marketing are not acted upon because that department is more powerful than the others. The rest must realize that marketing is merely translating what the customer really requires, and, indeed, that effective marketing relies on the contribution of all the company's functions to meet the expressed needs of customers. Sensitive and skilful management is needed at senior levels for this distinction to be accepted by all the managers concerned.

In small to medium-sized consumer market companies, and for some industrial manufacturers, for the reasons discussed above, it is a question of debate as to whether a formal 'marketing department' is desirable or necessary. While there may be one employee whose whole or partial function is, say, marketing research, other personnel may be able to follow a marketing orientation without the need for formal titles. Provided that such key personnel as the managing director, financial and production managers, etc. are personally committed to marketing orientation, the policies already described can be carried out with a minimum need for formality.

The transition from a sales to a marketing orientation is thus beset by problems, but these are not insurmountable if approached correctly. For the problems to be kept to a minimum, marketing must be presented in a realistic context. It is easy to theorize about marketing and present it as an 'academic' rather than a practical business orientation. While an academic grounding in marketing techniques is desirable, the essence of successful marketing is the ability to take this knowledge and apply it in practical situations. For example, if a 'sales-oriented' manager was presented with Table 1, he or she might think that marketing was an impractical method of management. Whatever the level of 'market' price, a company could not survive in the long term if prices did not cover costs. Similarly any production unit must function on the basis of economic production runs, and large stocks of little used components cannot be held 'just in case'.

Anyone who interpreted the table in this way would, however, be misinterpreting marketing completely. A successful transition from sales to marketing orientation should concentrate strongly on what is practical and realistic. This is the whole essence of marketing orientation. It is not intended that marketing should be synonymous with the impracticality of being 'all things to all people'. On the contrary, marketing is often concerned with selecting market segments related to profit potential that are also compatible with the company's existing capabilities. Once this is understood, the problems of transition are reduced and the flexibility required to adapt to the customer's needs rather than to adhere to rigid company tradition is more freely given. This co-operation is basic to the success of any company.

A true marketing orientation can be instilled into company practice, but can never be imposed upon it without severe disruption, which can have the effect of discrediting rather than supporting the marketing concept.

QUESTION 5

Describe the principal elements of market structure for *either* an industrial market *or* a consumer market of your choice.

OBJECTIVE

To test candidates' understanding of the term 'market structure' through the medium of a practical example taken either from industrial marketing or consumer marketing.

APPROACH

Observe that candidates are required to choose an industrial marketing example or a consumer marketing example, but not both. In fact many of the elements of market structure are applicable to both, so it is really a knowledge of market structure that the examiner requires and not a tedious working through examples pertaining to each. The best approach would therefore seem to be to start with a short introduction to the chosen example and then use the example as a vehicle for demonstrating an understanding of the issues arising.

ANSWER

Suggested introduction
The example chosen is one that relates to industrial marketing and the product example chosen is that of pressure valves. The following checklist represents the likely elements in relation to this market.

Likely market structure: pressure valves
  1 Market concentration in relation to suppliers and their respective market shares.
  2 Market concentration in relation to customers' potential buying. This may mean that sales representatives will call upon larger firms more often than smaller customers, i.e. differential call frequencies will be practised.
  3 Type of industry in which pressure valves are sold: primary (raw materials), secondary (manufacturing) and tertiary (services).

4 Integration within the industry in relation to customers and competitors. Has there been horizontal integration because of acquisition or merger? Has there been vertical integration, especially forwards towards retailing?

5 Geographical concentration of customers, which is more likely in industrial markets than consumer markets, e.g. car industry concentrated in certain 'pockets' around the country, oil refining concentrated near certain ports. This will have an effect upon the company's distribution policy.

6 The degree of technological change and innovation within the pressure-valve industry.

7 Market segmentation criteria, i.e. different industries that use pressure valves. Should they be treated as separate markets in respect to product differentiation, price, credit terms, discounts and lead times?

8 The amount of 'derived' demand in markets that are served, e.g. the demand for pressure valves in the oil-refining industry depends upon the amount of oil sold, which in turn depends upon the number of cars on the road, and so on.

9 What are the 'dynamics' of the market? Is it growing, static or declining? What is the rate of change of such trends? Are there any cyclical or seasonal trends?

10 The distribution policy of competitors – the number and location of warehouses and factories together with the level of service offered, i.e. delivery period, servicing arrangements, etc.

11 The number of foreign manufacturers in the market and the degree of import penetration over a specific time period.

12 Whether or not 'reciprocal trading' exists in the market, and, if so, how many users of pressure valves are never in the market to make purchases except from the partner to the reciprocal arrangement.

13 The sector of commerce to which customers belong, e.g. to private or nationalized, to service or to manufacturing, etc. Such criteria will affect their individual purchasing strategies, so the marketing strategy of the valve producer will have to take this into consideration.

14 The price structure within the industry. For example, do competitors give volume discounts, are discounts given to certain sectors of the trade, is there a trade mark-up, etc.?

15 What volume of industry sales go to exports? What export opportunities exist in relation to joint ventures, licensing, etc.?

Conclusion

The above list is not exhaustive, but is meant to illustrate, by posing a number of statements and questions, the main areas that would need to be addressed in order to achieve an understanding of the market structure for a company engaged in the manufacture and distribution of a range of pressure valves.

QUESTION 6

One precept of economic theory holds that the consumer is an essentially rational being. What influences are at work on the consumer which would tend to contradict this?

OBJECTIVE

This is uncomplicated, in that the question is designed to assess the student's knowledge of the various influences which affect consumer behaviour. The student should, however, show a considerable awareness of the interdisciplinary nature of consumer studies.

APPROACH

The answer should begin by putting the rational consumer concept into the context of consumer behaviour. It should be explained that this is one of many contributions which have been made by various disciplines. This introductory approach will indicate to the examiner your breadth of understanding of consumer behaviour and will also serve to suggest the limitations of the economists' interpretation, thus preparing the way for your subsequent answer.

The question specifically asks you to deal with the 'influences' at work on the consumer which suggest that the consumer is not a rational being in the economic sense. Care must be taken so that your answer does not develop into an account of 'what makes consumers different from each other'. For example, to recognize that one consumer lives in a more urban area, or is older or richer than another, does not really cast any light on consumer rationality.

Following the introduction, the question should be developed by describing the 'individual' influences at work on the consumer. These, in turn, should be followed by a section which deals with 'environmental' influences.

The final section should attempt to show how these influences are integrated into a form which helps us to understand buyer behaviour. This section should also be used to put the economic precept in question into perspective.

A possible conclusion could emphasize that marketing has drawn upon various disciplines in its attempt to understand the consumer, because economic interpretation on its own has been found to be simplistic and limiting.

ANSWER

Possible introduction

Implicit within the marketing concept is the recognition that the firm must direct itself to the consumer if long-term survival is to be made possible. Understanding the consumer should therefore be critical to any strategy formulation. At its most basic level it is generally recognized that the decision to buy is a stimulus/response process. The reasons why such a process takes place are highly complex and, because of this, marketing practitioners have attempted to resolve this question by means of an interdisciplinary approach.

The rational consumer concept

The economist explains buyer behaviour through the theory of 'rational' or 'economic' man. This postulates that in order to achieve satisfaction the consumer follows the principle of utility maximization. The economist recognizes differing needs, wants and tastes, but views rational measurement of cost and value received as the governing factor of buyer behaviour. There is a degree of usefulness in such an approach, as in many situations income is known to be a critical determinant of buyer behaviour. For the purposes of market planning, however, a greater depth of knowledge is required. The behavioural sciences suggest that a whole series of influences are at work upon the consumer, and that the process is more complicated than the concept of the rational buyer searching for 'total utility' is able to offer.

Consumers' own interpretation of the various stimuli to which they are exposed will determine the buying responses or reactions. This interpretation is in turn affected by external influences. It is therefore convenient to discuss the influences on the consumer in two stages: those of individual or intra-personal influences and those of environment or inter-personal influences.

Individual or intra-personal influences

As an individual the consumer is a complex being whose buying decisions are influenced by what is taking place within his/her own mind. The buying process has been likened to a process taking place in an impenetrable 'black box'. Behavioural scientists have proposed several theories which suggest how intra-personal influences work and thus how interpretations take place and decisions are reached.

The self-concept. This theory suggests that as well as the existence of the consumer as he/she actually is (which is manifested in the real self) there are three other forms of self-concept. The self-image concerns the way in which the individual views himself/herself and may be a distortion of the real self. The consumer also has a mirror (or reference group) self-image, i.e. how a person thinks he/she is perceived by others. Again this may be quite different from the self-image, because the consumer may choose to project an image different from that of others. Finally, the ideal self is the self to which the consumer aspires.

The self-concept has therefore an important influence on buying decisions because consumers often make purchases not on the rational basis of 'utility' but in order to attempt to achieve an ideal self-image, or to reinforce the type of image which they think would be acceptable to others.

Motivation. As well as being influenced by the self, the mental transition which the consumer makes from the stage of stimulus to response in the buying process is also strongly influenced by the motives which direct him/her to the act of purchase. The motivation required for a particular purchase is derived from the consumer being either partially or wholly unsatisfied with respect to some field of products or services. Thus, the intensity and type of their needs and wants determine their buying behaviour, because it is hoped that the purchased product will solve a problem and restore the buyer to a condition of equilibrium. Psychologists have developed classification systems which ascribe varying importance to different sources of motivation. One of the best known psychologists was A.H. Maslow, who proposed a 'hierarchy of needs' and thus a hierarchy of motives. These range from the basic physiological needs to the complex influence of the need for self-actualization.

Thus, the buying decision increases in complexity as more influences on the consumer are considered. The decision to purchase a certain suite of furniture, for example, may be motivated by such needs as personal satisfaction or esteem. These, in turn, may be an expression of some form of the self-image. The decision to make this purchase at a certain store is also likely to be influenced by such considerations.

Perception. This is a further vital influence on the buying decision. A company may attempt to market its products to a predetermined set of consumers and in so doing may pay particular attention to the influences on the consumer which have been previously discussed. Although the approach of the company may be perfectly valid, and is likely to make success more likely, there is no guarantee that each consumer within the chosen group will perceive the product in the same way, since perception is a highly selective process. The consumer may not even respond to the initial stimulus, because the mind only notices what it is interested in at that time. If the stimulus is received, this selective perception process may screen out or modify the perceived information because of learned behaviour, existing attitudes or beliefs.

Perception is, therefore, the 'meaning' which the consumer attributes to a given stimulus. These two factors are now considered in more detail.

Attitudes. These are formed over a period of time and are usually resistant to change. Thus, the task of establishing product acceptance is aided, or made more difficult, according to whether favourable or unfavourable attitudes already exist in the mind of the individual. The determination of the attitudes which prevail within a consumer group is therefore of vital interest to the marketer. The subject must, however, be approached with caution, because the existence of a favourable attitude does not necessarily signify an intention to buy. We can say, however, that an attitude is an important influence on the buying decision.

Since individuals prefer their attitudes to be reinforced rather than challenged, most companies will attempt to direct their products towards positive attitudes rather than attempt the difficult and often expensive task of attitude reversal. Here an attempt by the marketer to change a negative attitude does not necessarily constitute an attempt to make the consumer buy something which is not wanted and so deny the marketing concept. Most attempts to change attitudes occur in a competitive environment of similar brands, where the objective is to increase market shares. Such a strategy may also be employed when a company (perhaps under new management) seeks to alter a corporate image which has changed over time, or which is not associated with a new strategy or product line.

Learning. The behaviour of most people is related to their past experiences. The learning process is therefore the principal influence on attitude formation. It is also a major force in attitude change. A favourable attitude may result in the purchase decision being taken, but if the purchase does not live up to expectations, this will be stored in the consumer's mind and may result in changed behaviour in the future. The opposite is also true – a buying response followed by satisfaction will reinforce the attitude and strengthen the relation between stimulus and response.

It should also be recognized that learning may result from imitation as well as from experience. Whatever form the learning process takes, the marketer must account for the powerful influence it has on behaviour. The principal marketing task here is for a company to ensure that its products are associated with satisfactory learning experiences in the mind of the consumer.

Environmental or inter-personal influences

Influences on the consumer which refer to personality have been discussed and these are largely drawn from the discipline of psychology. Marketing practitioners have also drawn on the study of anthropology and sociology in order to learn more about the influences at work on the consumer. These disciplines are concerned with the influence of others upon the individual and are therefore concerned with the social and cultural environment.

Reference groups. As the consumer moves forwards towards a buying decision, the formation of attitudes is strongly influenced by reference groups – groups of people whose values are similar to those of the consumer and with whom he/she can therefore identify. Such groups may exist at work or form part of a wider social life.

The consumer may also allow reference groups to influence decisions without necessarily belonging to them. Such 'aspirational' reference groups are important influences on standards of behaviour and personal values, a fact often used as the creative theme of advertisements. The more a purchase is likely to be seen by others, the more likely it is that the reference group will be of importance to the marketer.

Opinion-leaders. Within each reference group some people are likely to be more influential than others: these are 'opinion-leaders'. They are respected sources of information and advice within their field, since they are usually the first to try new products relevant to, say, hi-fi or gardening.

It is important to recognize that a person may be an opinion-leader in one field but not in another, and that because he/she forms part of the reference group, he/she is not necessarily otherwise different from other members of that group. Opinion-leaders are important only as they 'diffuse' new ideas and products throughout society.

The family. The family constitutes a distinctive and one of the most influential forms of reference group. Parents are the obvious opinion-leaders of young children, but this leadership tends to diminish as children grow older.

It is vital that the marketer should know who the real family decision-maker is, as well as recognizing that although one spouse may actually make the purchase, the decision process is likely to have been influenced by the other. Similarly attention should be paid to the changing nature of traditional family stereotypes.

Social class. The subject of social class is often controversial, but it is true that some structure of social division exists. Sociologists, using occupation, source of income, education and family background, and type of dwelling as the chief determinants, have identified groups of society that exhibit broadly similar behavioural characteristics. This has important implications for the study of buyer behaviour and for market segmentation.

There is a certain degree of mobility through the class structure, and those consumers who aspire to another social class can represent a market segment on their own. The class into which an individual is born remains a strong influence on his/her future behaviour. Despite their level of income, individuals tend to regard their social class as a broad form of reference group and will adopt (consciously or unconsciously) the values and attitudes of that group.

Cultural influences. This concerns the whole complex of attitudes, customs, beliefs and value systems common to a cultural grouping. These are passed down through generations. Sub-cultures (religious or ethnic minorities, for example) may exist within a culture, and may form the basis of a market segment.

It is likely that one's own culture is relatively well understood, and thus its importance as a determinant of buyer behaviour can sometimes be underestimated. When dealing with international markets, the true significance of cultural variations is revealed, and any marketing strategy must take this significance into account.

The marketing application

The consumer is subjected to a far wider range of influences than economic theory would suggest. In recognition of this marketers have developed various models which integrate this knowledge, so as to provide a ready framework which aids the understanding of buyer behaviour.

The main thing to recognize is that 'buying' is essentially a problem-solving process, one that is not necessarily completely rational and is a great deal more complicated than an attempt to maximize utility. Having identified the problem, the consumer goes through a series of mental and physical activities which, viewed in stages, are known as the 'buying process'. A typical model would show the influences to which the consumer is exposed as movement through the process takes place.

Possible conclusion

There is a consensus of opinion which would suggest that the economic interpretation of the consumer is too simplistic and limiting. The marketing interpretation (drawing as it does from a wide range of disciplines) does, however, recognize some value in economic theory.

Despite the many influences on the consumer, it is generally accepted that there is, within given limits, a relation between price and demand. Income must also be considered as a significant determinant of behaviour, as most consumers have only limited resources. Within the constraints of available income there is likely to be some element of rationality, even if this is based on factors such as quality or convenience rather than price alone.

Economics remains one of the disciplines which marketers use. But contributions also come from other disciplines, and from all these sources the marketer attempts to formulate an integrated interpretation of buyer behaviour.

QUESTION 7

Describe the theory of the diffusion of innovations and critically examine its relevance to marketing management.

OBJECTIVE

To test knowledge of the diffusion theory, but more specifically to assess how well the student can take this knowledge and relate it to marketing action. The student should also be able to draw the examiner's attention to any limitations to acceptance of this theory.

APPROACH

With reference to the examiner's objective, it is critical that your answer should be a balanced one. Avoid therefore the temptation to devote too much of your time to a *description* of the theory.

The term 'critically examine' implies consideration of both the positive and negative aspects of a subject. Your answer should include several examples of how the theory can be used in marketing planning, paying particular attention to new product launches, the product life cycle and consumer behaviour: these are positive factors. You will be able to gain extra marks if you also suggest that the theory should be applied with caution and that in some circumstances the sequence of events postulated does not necessarily follow a natural progression.

ANSWER

Suggested introduction

The theory of the diffusion of innovations postulates that new products or ideas are not simultaneously accepted *en masse* by large and differing sections of the population. This seems logical, as we should be aware that a new product has only a limited group of buyers during its early life. Diffusion theory suggests that this 'limited group' possesses certain identifiable characteristics which suggest that they will influence wider groups of the population into imitating their lead. Marketing academics and marketing management have recognized that the implications of this theory are relevant and can be applied to an understanding of how new products are accepted and by whom. Armed with this knowledge, marketing management can address these 'influencers of buyer behaviour' and can, in turn, develop strategies that can encourage and facilitate the influencing process among other, larger, groups of potential buyers.

Marketing and diffusion theory

It should be noted that marketing has adopted the diffusion theory to suit its own needs. The theory has been developed from studies in sociology, anthropology, education and psychology. Research in these disciplines has suggested that innovation is diffused throughout society in a set pattern over a period of time.

Before considering diffusion theory itself it is necessary to consider the adoption process, i.e. the decision-making activity of an individual as opposed to the gradual acceptance of a product idea by larger groups. 'Adoption' is considered to have taken place when the product has been purchased, and adoption is confirmed when repeat purchases are made. The stages of adoption are thus as follows:

1 Awareness – exposure to the product.
2 Information – interest leads to information search.
3 Evaluation – comparison is made between existing and similar alternatives.
4 Trial – limited adoption by sampling.
5 Adoption – the decision to use the product on a full-scale basis.
6 Confirmation – the search for reassurance that adoption was the correct decision.

Whatever the 'adopter category' (see below) the potential user might belong to, the development of sales through diffusion is intimately dependent upon each individual passing through all the adoption stages. Diffusion theory suggests that adoption is likely to take place earlier and more rapidly within certain groups.

Diffusion theory

Figure 3 shows that adopters, when classified according to the rate of adoption over a period of time, are distributed in a form that follows the classical 'normal' curve. Research has shown that the individuals within each adopter category possess certain identifiable characteristics, as follows.

Innovators. In comparison with later groups these are likely to be younger, more affluent and have a high social status. They are also likely to be well educated and relatively broad-minded in their social relationships. They are the 'tip of the iceberg' in terms of the ultimate target market.

Early adopters. Whereas the 'innovators' stand apart from the majority in terms of their attitudes and actions, early adopters are more easy to identify within the population as a whole. They have opinions and lifestyles which are

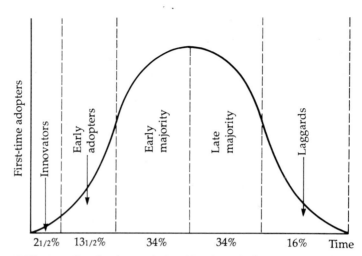

Figure 3 *Diffusion: distribution and classification of adopter categories*

more conventional but differ from the majority in the vital respect that they are very much 'opinion leaders', who, while being more cautious than the 'innovators', possess an innovative and receptive outlook upon life. Since they are relatively close to the majority, they are prime targets for marketing activity, as they can be considered agents of change. Within their local social system they are regarded with respect, and their opinions are thus more likely to be taken seriously and their actions imitated by others.

Early majority. This group accepts innovation just before the average adopter and is therefore likely to be above average in so far as social and economic factors are concerned. They are certainly more cautious than their adopter predecessors, but will be receptive to opinion leaders, advertisements and sales personnel. In industrial terms firms that make up this category are likely to be average in size, with a relatively progressive management that prefers to wait until an innovation is fairly well tried and tested before adopting it.

Late majority. This is often called the 'sceptical' group. Its decision to adopt is due almost completely to social pressure from the earlier groups rather than from any innovative instinct. In addition to the psychological and social factors that come into play, the late majority (in both consumer and industrial terms) is likely to be composed of those whose financial resources are low. This partly explains their late position amongst the adopter categories.

Laggards. This final group is more conscious of tradition than innovation. Indeed by the time it becomes a first-time adopter, the product may itself be a part of tradition and further innovations may already be available.

Marketing application of diffusion theory
In particular the diffusion of innovations theory lends itself to consideration alongside that of the product life cycle (PLC) (see Question 15), for each stage

of the PLC experience has shown that certain strategies are likely to be more successful than others. Diffusion theory can be related to the PLC so as to help in the identification of those groups to which these strategies are directed. Figure 4 shows how the two theoretical curves can be related to each other.

In the launch, or introduction and growth stages of development, marketing-mix decisions are tailored to reach those with the characteristics of 'innovators' and 'early adopters'. The same correlation can be applied to the final stages of a product's life cycle.

The relation is not mathematically based but does illustrate that in general:

1 Introduction strategy should be directed at innovators and early adopters.
2 Growth, while overlapping some of the adopter categories, is made possible by buyers who come predominantly from the early majority.
3 Buyers during maturity and decline will display characteristics associated with the late majority and laggards.

Diffusion theory also relates naturally to the study of consumer behaviour (see Questions 6 and 8). One application of the study of consumer behaviour concerns how best to direct potential buyers through the adoption process from 'interest' to 'confirmed adoption'. The self-concept is likely to be more relevant when innovators are being addressed. Knowledge of how 'peer' and 'reference' groups function can be applied when designing strategies aimed at early adopters and the early and late majorities' knowledge of 'innovative types'. These two elements of knowledge are mutually beneficial when designing an advertising campaign.

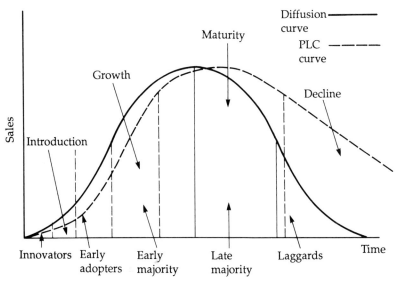

Figure 4 *Relationship between diffusion theory and the PLC*

It is not therefore suggested that diffusion theory 'shapes' marketing strategies; rather the theory can be employed in conjunction with behavioural research so that any resultant strategy is targeted more efficiently. Studies on social stratification and lifestyle research can thus be employed so that recognized features of adopter categories can be better understood and more efficiently approached.

Criticism and comment

Undoubtedly marketing practitioners can regard the theory of the diffusion of innovations as a valuable tool. Some concrete marketing applications have already been described. As is true for most theories, diffusion theory cannot be applied to actual situations in a blinkered, inflexible manner. The theory does, however, provide a basis and guideline for planning and marketing-mix design. Attention to the theory is also valuable in terms of marketing information at the higher strategic and perhaps more abstract levels, as well as at the design stage of actual research projects. At the strategic level, the Marketing Information System is concerned with trend identification. These trends can develop as a result of changes in social structure. Diffusion theory itself, as well as the wealth of research that has been published on the subject, provides one framework that the Information System can use. In the same context diffusion theory, because it is concerned with 'groups', is a good base for studies on the social structure of communication, with obvious value for advertising studies. Diffusion theory also highlights the importance of 'word of mouth' communication.

Any company that uses diffusion theory as a means to a better understanding of its customers must, however, appreciate the theory's limitations. Although the theory is widely accepted as being valid, the course and rate of diffusion will differ considerably according to the product type. Factors such as trialability, product complexity and observability will complicate the theoretical course of events.

A more serious cause for caution concerns the real difficulty of identifying adopters for particular product areas. It does not follow, for example, that a classic 'early adopter' for a product such as a compact disc player will display the same personality characteristics for, say, gardening equipment. This is a practical limitation for specific marketing situations to which marketing research must address itself.

It is also possible that some consumer groups are not receptive to influences from reference groups in certain situations. Some groups may identify more readily with peer groups. One advertising campaign for beer in the USA based its message and theme on typical 'early adopter' lifestyles, but the target group did not respond to this appeal to emulate the lifestyles of others. Many British advertising campaigns for beers and lagers seem to have benefited from this mistake.

QUESTION 8

Discuss the role and behaviour of the industrial purchaser in comparison with the domestic consumer. Would you agree that the industrial purchase is devoid of all but economic considerations?

OBJECTIVE

To ensure that the student is able to differentiate between industrial and final consumer buyer behaviour and to ensure that there is an awareness of the personal and external factors which may influence a purely rational approach on the behalf of the industrial purchaser.

APPROACH

The approach to the first part of this question is uncomplicated and you should discuss the typical assumptions that are generally made for each purchaser group. You could begin with the assertion that the industrial purchaser is essentially a 'professional consumer', and continue with a discussion of the most apparent influences at work on the purchase decision, e.g. the need for economic purchases for profit or that the industrial purchaser's decision calls for a specialist approach to problem-solving. The final consumer can then be introduced and, while acknowledging that he or she is also a 'problem-solver', you can discuss the social and psychological influences at work on this consumer, although you will not have time to discuss these in great depth.

With reference to the second part of the question, a phrase such as 'would you agree' is a cue for an argumentative approach. With this in mind you should briefly reintroduce the theme which suggests that the industrial purchaser's role is one of rational decision-making and then demonstrate (by use of appropriate examples) why this is not always the case.

How far you agree or disagree with the proposition is a matter for your own judgement. Any decision will, however, be of little value unless a reasoned argument has been previously presented. In most arguments both sides usually have equally valid contributions to make. Although it is by no means always the case, it is common to conclude such answers with qualifying statements that acknowledge this fact.

ANSWER

Suggested introduction

The main criterion that should be explained in this argument is the fact that the domestic consumer is taking a decision for self and family, while the industrial purchaser is taking decisions that depend upon his or her knowledge of the requirements of others. It can thus be clearly seen that different criteria are at work in the minds of each when arriving at the final purchase decision.

A number of models of consumer and industrial buying behaviour have been put forward by marketing theorists. Such models emphasize the effects of non-economic as well as economic factors in each type of purchasing situation. 'Emotional' considerations can include cultural norms and peer-group influences, as well as the more logical considerations, such as capacity to fulfil the task. However, it is clear to see that since the industrial purchaser is a 'professional', his or her motives are bound to be more economically based than the consumer purchaser, who is an 'amateur', whose emotions might be more inclined to cloud the issue.

Forces at work in the buying decision process

In making a purchasing decision domestic purchasers are likely to consider such criteria as:

- Family requirements.
- Style.
- Will it last?
- Is it affordable?
- If not immediately affordable, what about credit?
- When can it be delivered or collected?
- Have we 'confidence' in what we are buying? (What about after-sales service, complaints?)

An industrial purchaser is more likely to be concerned with such criteria as:

- Its ability to 'do the job' as effectively as required by the specifier.
- Will the supplier deliver the goods within the time stipulated?
- Does the price demanded represent 'value for money' alongside competitive offerings?
- Payment schedule – is credit or extended payment possible after the goods have been delivered?
- The industrial buyer's authority to make the purchase and his or her place within the decision-making unit (DMU).

Discussion

This discussion revolves around the second part of the question wherein it is contended that the industrial purchase is devoid of all but economic considerations.

When examining the motives of industrial buyers, you can show that they too respond to 'emotional' criteria. Industrial buyers have to cope with one element that in itself produces an emotional response – risk. A great part of the efforts of industrial purchasers is directed towards the minimizing of risk. Risk is a factor in consumer buying decisions as well, but there is an important distinction: the consumer is not going to lose his or her job through a bad purchase decision, whereas the industrial purchaser might well do so. For example, the purchase of a set of woodworking machinery by a consumer is unlikely to be as important as to an industrial buyer, who, in re-equipping a workshop, purchases machinery of inferior quality that subsequently is liable to breakdown and delay.

Many purchasing decisions are financially based, and they might be important both to the industrial buyer and the consumer. But the industrial buyer is not using his/her own money, and indeed the volume of purchase is likely to be higher, so that he/she is more likely to emphasize 'price' as a very important criterion.

Quite often style and colour are important when making a purchase. The domestic consumer has to make a simple, personal choice. The industrial purchaser, on the other hand, might be purchasing a range of office furniture for a suite of offices. Clearly his choice will not please everybody, but in the interests of economy a single style and colour range might have to be purchased.

It can thus be seen that there is no clear-cut, simple answer to this question, but it would be true to say that economic considerations are clearly more important in the industrial purchasing situation than in the domestic. However, this is probably a function of the fact that the industrial purchaser is more of a 'professional' purchaser than the domestic purchaser, and is thus more likely to look for 'economic' and 'value for money' considerations when making the purchase decision.

QUESTION 9

Write notes on FOUR of the following:

    (i) Latin square design
   (ii) Consumer panels
  (iii) Quota sampling
  (iv) Random (probability) sampling
   (v) Test marketing

OBJECTIVE

To assess the student's knowledge of specific matters relating to marketing research.

APPROACH

'Write notes on' means precisely that. Concise answers are essential, so make up your mind quickly which parts to answer.

With the exception of (ii) and (v), this question requires the student to show a competent understanding of the statistical techniques in market research. Although such competence is necessary, you are required to relate the answer to market research. It is not therefore necessary to be too detailed about statistical technique. The most important requirement is that you demonstrate an understanding of the relation between statistics and market research.

Most standard marketing research textbooks deal with research technique and there are also a great number of basic texts on statistics. Those students who do not consider themselves to be statisticians need not therefore be deterred from such questions.

Questions such as this one are termed 'compound questions' and the approach to answering differs from the more common 'essay' type answer. Ensure that it is absolutely clear to the examiner which section of the question is being answered. Read the question carefully and note that in this particular case you are required to answer FOUR of the topics.

Although the question asks for 'notes', some structure is required, and the following is a suggested format for such questions:

QUESTIONS 9–12, RELATING TO MARKET RESEARCH & RELATED ISSUES

1 One or two sentences of introduction like 'Test marketing is a part of marketing research that . . .' or 'It is most usually employed in markets that . . .'
2 A descriptive middle section mainly consisting of statements and facts.
3 A final section which deals with advantages and disadvantages or statements such as 'Test marketing is only appropriate when . . .' or 'Several limitations to this form of research must, however, be recognized . . .'

Where appropriate, do not hesitate to use a numbered format like:

'The following disadvantages must however be considered:
1 . . . . . .
2 . . . . etc.'

The final section serves to demonstrate your broader appreciation of the subject.

Remember that all four questions will carry equal marks (when they carry unequal marks the question paper will state this). It is therefore essential that you organize your time accordingly. A long and detailed answer to the first topic will not compensate for a few hurried lines in answer to other topics.

The following answer deals with all FIVE of the topics.

ANSWER

(i) Latin square design

This is a statistical method of data analysis which falls into that area of research known as 'experimentation'. The principal advantages of this method are economy and the facility to analyse more than one variable at a time. In order that the analysis be kept as simple as possible (and to keep time and cost to a minimum) it is normally assumed that any interaction between the variables under analysis is not significant. Like many other research and analytical techniques, the results obtained do not necessarily provide concrete recommendations, but they do provide information which suggests that a certain course of action is 'more likely' to be successful than another.

The variables under analysis are arranged into rows and columns and the object of analysis is assigned to each of the cells in the table in a random fashion. It is important, however, that each object (or effect) under test only appears once in each row and in each column of the table. For instance, a company may have become concerned that the colour of the wrapping used for one of its consumer goods is less popular than that used by competitive producers, and as a result sales of the product have been suffering. Marketing research may suggest two alternative colours, and a decision to test these two alternatives, as well as the original colours, throughout a sample of countrywide stores could form the basis of a latin square experiment. If unlimited funds and time were available, it would be possible to carry out exhaustive tests to establish, with reasonable certainty, which colour was the most popular. We know, however, that such an undertaking is not practicable. Latin square design is one method of obtaining an indication of popularity that is fast, economical and relatively uncomplicated.

Suppose that it was decided to carry out tests in three regions, and in three types of retail outlet. An appropriate Latin square might be designed as follows.

Region	Type of retail outlet		
	A	B	C
NORTH	C2	C0	C1
MIDLANDS	C1	C2	C0
SOUTH	C0	C1	C2

C0 = original colour
C1 and C2 = new colours

The design shows that each colour is tested once in each region and in each type of retail outlet. It is unnecessary to test each colour in all outlets in each region. After the test has been run, the hypothetical sales data analysis could be as shown in the next table.

	A	B	C	Total	Average
NORTH	153 (C2)	143 (C0)	175 (C1)	471	157
MIDLANDS	135 (C1)	144 (C2)	129 (C0)	408	136
SOUTH	114 (C0)	138 (C1)	144 (C2)	396	132
TOTAL	402	425	448	1275	
AVERAGE	134	142	149		142

So that actual sales by colour can be noted easily, the figures can be rearranged as shown in the next table.

	A	B	C	Total	Average
COLOUR 1	175	135	138	448	149
COLOUR 2	153	144	144	441	147
COLOUR 0	114	143	129	386	129

Variance analysis can then reveal whether or not these variances are statistically significant at various levels.

In this case, if variance analysis were to be carried out, significant differences at the area and colour level would be apparent. The analyst must take care in their interpretation. As in most areas of research analysis, the results indicate which products are less likely to be successful, while not showing conclusively which is most likely to be successful. Here the test and results would suggest that the problem about Colour 0 is justified and that further research is needed.

(ii) Consumer panels

A consumer panel is a method of continuous marketing research that is particularly useful for gathering quantitative information about trends and changes in buying behaviour over a period of time.

A group of consumers is chosen (usually by a stratified random sampling method) from persons who are representative of, and pertinent to, the market segments and products under investigation. These groups could be housewives, motorists or television viewers, etc. Some consumer panels are designed to serve many companies on a shared cost (syndicated research) basis. Here the product range under investigation is so wide that it is sufficient to be a householder in order to qualify for selection. Audits of Great Britain (AGB) runs a syndicated consumer panel serving manufacturers whose products range from lawnmowers to washing machines to kettles – in fact almost all those goods classified as 'consumer durables'. Consumer panels are also very common in the branded goods areas of FMCGs.

Panelists are chosen as respondents for a fixed period of time, say one year, and information about their purchases is collected by means of mailed questionnaires, by their keeping diaries or by personal interview. The essence of a consumer panel is that information is collected on a 'continuous' basis over a long period of time (even though individual panel members may change). The reason is that panels are designed to monitor trends in purchasing behaviour, whether these be merely in volume/value terms or whether they be concerned with changes in demographic characteristics.

A 'typical' consumer panel would provide continuous information about the following:

The product	– volume sales
	value sales
	brand penetration
	where purchase was made
	average purchase price
Promotional effort	– offer associated purchases
	the effects of offers by region
	the effects of advertising by region
The consumer	– demographic characteristics: age, sex, etc.
	psychographic (lifestyle) characteristics
	buying behaviour – heavy/medium/light users

The market
- amount bought
- brand loyalty/switching
- repeat purchasing
- seasonal patterns
  competitive action

For FMCGs it is normal (for competitive purposes) for panels to be located within ITV areas. Data is collected at varying intervals, but every 4 weeks is common.

Since the late 1940s consumer panels have developed to become an accepted and popular source of market research data.

Regular subscription to syndicated research or the commissioning of a particular panel is by no means cheap, so that a decision to subscribe should be clearly justified and not entered into lightly. Both the user and the designer of consumer panels should also be conscious of the possible drawbacks and complication associated with their use:

Recruitment. If consumers agree to become panel members, it will require a considerable level of commitment on their behalf – a commitment that many will not want to make.

Mortality. Over time it is likely that a proportion of respondents will cease to participate, distorting the original sampling frame and presenting problems in finding suitable replacements.

Conditioning. The fact that a consumer's buying habits are being monitored may result in self-conscious, untypical behaviour. It is common for new panel members' data to be ignored for the first few weeks for this reason, but it must be accepted that the risk remains throughout the duration of membership.

Random/inaccurate reporting. While diaries/questionnaires should be constructed as simply as possible, there is always the risk that response becomes inaccurate because the panelist forgets, or 'makes up' answers, since the diary was not filled in at the correct time. In short, membership becomes a 'chore'. To alleviate the problems associated with the above, the duration of panel membership should not be too long.

The following is a list of some of the better known consumer panels:

Audits of Great Britain Ltd (AGB) – syndicated research over a wide range of consumer durables drawn from UK households.

The Attwood Consumer Panel.

The Television Consumer Audit.

Television Advertising Bureau (Surveys) Ltd – the TABS 'on air' panel.

The Motorists Diary panel – based on panels of individuals rather than households.

AGB's personal purchases index.

Textile Market Studies (TMS) – designed to monitor consumer purchases of apparel throughout the UK.

(iii) Quota sampling

This method can basically be described as a 'non-random' method of stratified sampling. Any bias which may be inherent in this 'human' method of sampling is controlled as far as possible by the choice of strata and the setting of quotas within each stratum.

The choice of sub-groups is a function of the kind of information required by the survey. This is the first stage in the process; next the researcher must decide upon a quota of respondents (within the sub-group stratum) who are to be interviewed, and thus form the basis of the survey. Typical groupings are based on social class, age, sex or marital status, the incidence of which, in the community, is known, so that a representative sample based on this information can be built up.

Although quota sampling is 'non-random', this should not cause the observer to think of this method as being non-scientific or haphazard. Firstly, the sample size and organization of quotas is arrived at by the use of complex statistical techniques, as is the analysis of results. The difference between this and random sampling is that the choices to which statistical techniques are applied are arrived at by human judgement based upon knowledge of the universe in question. This leads to the second factor – any setting up of quota samples should be based on thorough pre-research of the market, so that all variables are considered, and so that sub-groups are chosen in proportion to their relative importance to the total population.

Quota sampling is mainly criticized because the choice of the participants is not based on mathematical theory and also because of the risk of bias in the actual operation of the survey. Although the quotas to be surveyed are chosen carefully, in the final analysis much of the accuracy of research findings is dependent upon the skill and experience of the interviewer.

In its defence quota sampling is cost-effective, rapid and relatively simple to organize: hence, its popularity for commercial practice.

(iv) Random (probability) sampling

The essential characteristic of a random sample is that each member of the population under study (the universe) has an equal chance of being selected as part of the sample. To achieve such a situation the researcher must have perfect knowledge of the survey population, i.e. every individual and his/her whereabouts must be known. All users of public transport would, for example, be a difficult, if not impossible, sampling 'frame' to establish. On the other hand, it would be relatively simple to ascertain all season-ticket-holders for a certain form of transport. Using this last example, the relevant transport authority could provide a list of ticket-holders, thus establishing a sampling frame.

By means of a simple lottery method, or by the use of digital tables, those individuals who are to be interviewed are selected. The 'random' element of selection enables the survey to be free from human judgement and any resultant sampling bias. This technique is known as simple random sampling.

The merit of such a technique is that it has a sound theoretical basis. In mathematical probability it is a complete and totally objective method, which is considerably aided by the increasing sophistication of computer technology. This same technology has also made it easier to identify a known group of individuals, whether they be season-ticket-holders, credit-card-holders or members of a society.

The various forms of random sampling which exist are designed

(a) to make the sampling frame more manageable in the case of very large surveys (say all telephone owners), and
(b) to identify known groups within the 'universe' with similar attributes.

This makes the resultant data more meaningful and pertinent to the researcher's aims.

When the population is divided into groups (strata), the process is known as 'stratified' random sampling. Such groups could be based on geographic area, age or social classification. Of course all the other requirements already discussed must be strictly observed. Sometimes, when there is a wide variation in the sizes of the strata in a population, the number of subjects sampled is weighted according to their relative size. This is known as disproportionate sampling (as opposed to proportionate sampling).

Although random sampling is theoretically valid, its value is often limited in practice:

1　It is not always possible to identify an entire population – any compromise in this respect would completely negate the mathematical basis of random sampling.
2　Often it is physically and economically taxing to obtain responses from the chosen sample, not only because the sample may be large but also because it may be difficult to reach because of a wide geographical spread, or because respondents are simply unavailable and repeated call-backs are

required. Such call-backs are essential because, to be valid, the list of selected respondents must be strictly adhered to.
3   In modern marketing research the results of surveys are required quickly – a random sample would not be possible in such cases.

(v) Test marketing

The essential element of any test-marketing exercise is that the chosen test area should always be representative of the proposed market. In general, test markets are confined to consumer goods markets.

While it is common to think of test markets as a final 'go–no-go' stage in new product development, this is not strictly accurate. The test market does of course serve this purpose, and products can be, and are, withdrawn subsequent to a poor test-market reception. Research should, however, have established a 'go–no-go' decision before test marketing was embarked upon. Test marketing is an expensive method of arriving at the conclusion that a product has limited potential and should really only be embarked upon after the 'go' decision has been taken: its objectives are thus to test the efficacy of the proposed marketing mix and to predict the likely penetration or brand share that the product is likely to achieve. The results of the test may recommend modifications to the planned marketing strategy if the desired market share is to be achieved. Test marketing is a recognized and popular method of reaching these goals amongst major producers of FMCGs.

In order that test marketing be performed efficiently and successfully, the following points should be noted:

● Clearly define the objectives and mix strategy. If this is not done, control of the operation cannot be carried out. Top management should always take part in this process. In addition, discussion of strategic objectives should include statements which denote 'what success is'. In this way goals can be assessed objectively, and time is not expended in the achievement of targets which may be neither feasible nor necessary at 'full-scale' level. The test market may be highly successful, but if this situation were to be reproduced at full market level, the resources of the company's distribution system might not be able to cope. However, such a situation would provide criteria to be considered for the next stage of strategic development.
● Linked to the above point is the need for the firm to behave as usual while carrying out the test market. If a normal lead time is, say, 3 weeks, the provision of a 1-week lead time (to promote sales) will only serve to distort the results of the whole operation. The test marketing effort should therefore be integrated into the 'norms' of the firm's usual capacity to serve the market.
● The need for a test market to be representative of the whole has already

been emphasized. In the UK commercial television areas are often chosen to delineate one market from another. This has clear advantages for assessing TV advertising effectiveness between regions, but the practice also provides convenient and easily identifiable test areas. Very often one area alone is insufficient to provide a true representation. It is quite common for three areas, thought to represent a scale of high, medium and low reception of the product, to be chosen. Post statistical analysis will either prove or disprove the contention. In fact Cadburys test-marketed the bar 'Wispa' in Ulster and then Tyne Tees before going 'national' on a 'rolling launch', which meant taking in ITV areas one by one as the product was gradually introduced to all regions of the country.

- Prior research should enable a firm decision on the length of test to be taken. This is always a difficult area. Too short a test may fail to supply true information. If the test is too long, however, the risk of new competitive activity, and thus distortion of the original test environment will increase.
- Finally, the company should evaluate the results of the test in the light of the set objectives. This appraisal should include a check to ensure that all departments of the company are fully prepared to participate in a full-scale launch.

Whatever the merits of test marketing are, the process is undeniably expensive and it should not be entered into lightly. Much care should be taken in evaluating possible (less expensive) alternative methods of experimentation before a product reaches a test-marketing decision stage. Test marketing remains, however, one of the most reliable methods of obtaining information. During the 1970s the idea of 'mini-marketing' emerged. Where appropriate, this can be a reliable but less expensive method than a full test market. Mini-marketing consists of launching a product into a carefully chosen form of consumer panel. This method also has the advantage of not revealing the full product strategy to the competition.

A real danger of test marketing is that of competitive activity. It is by no means uncommon for competitors to attempt to sabotage a test market by altering their marketing-mix emphasis, thus rendering the market environment unrepresentative. A competitor may, moreover, embark on a full-scale launch of a similar product while the other manufacturer is engaged in test marketing. Thus, the advantage which the test market might have obtained could then be negated and might permanently damage the full-scale launch of the test-marketed product.

In normal circumstances, however, test marketing is reliable and popular. While it may not provide all the answers and reveal all the problems, in common with other research techniques, it succeeds in its aim of risk reduction by providing more complete information for decision-making.

FURTHER READING

Consumer panels are dealt with in specialist marketing research texts. Latin square design, quota sampling and random (probability) sampling are covered in statistical rather than marketing texts, in sections that relate to sample design and analysis. The professional body in marketing research is The Market Research Society.

QUESTION 10

What do you understand by the term 'Marketing Information System'? How does it differ from Marketing Research?

OBJECTIVE

The aim of this question is simple and straightforward: to establish that the student can clearly distinguish between the two topics in question, and is able to outline their respective functions.

APPROACH

Like the motive for the question, the answer should be simple, posing no problems of interpretation or presentation. If adequately prepared for, this question could be described as a 'gift', because there is no requirement for 'discussion' and nothing is hidden within the question's phrasing.

The answer should therefore be as direct as possible. To convey this approach to the examiner and to display confidence, you should 'answer' the question in your introduction. You should then go on to describe a Marketing Information System (MkIS) and then answer the second part of the question. (NB. There is some confusion about abbreviations here, as Marketing Information System is sometimes abbreviated to MIS even in textbooks. This is incorrect, for MIS is short for Management Intelligence System.)

Your account of a MkIS should, by implication, go a long way towards answering this second part, because you will have already described the basics of Marketing Research (MR). Your concluding paragraphs should, however, be devoted to emphasizing the differences between the two.

ANSWER

Possible introduction

As is true for the subject of marketing itself, marketing research is a subject of confusion and misinterpretation among those who are not directly concerned with it. Many texts deal exclusively with marketing research, and this has led to a tendency for the practice to be regarded as the principal means that a company employs to find out about its customers and markets. MR is of course a fundamental element of marketing; its function is to discover WHAT the needs and wants of customers are, WHO the customers are, and WHERE,

WHEN and HOW they wish products to be offered to them. MR techniques can also be used to study the wider market in an attempt to predict the future wants and needs of customers and to monitor the progress of company and competitive strategies. MR's main purpose is, however, to study cause and effect in specific situations: as such, it constitutes only part of the company's requirement to understand what is going on around it and is in fact one component of the wide-ranging company activity that is the operation of a MkIS. The purpose of a MkIS is to collect, analyse and evaluate ALL the information that is of interest to ALL the firm's activities in the short and long term.

Not all companies will necessarily operate a formal MkIS. Usually the larger the company, the more sophisticated and formal a MkIS will be. In actual fact all companies assimilate marketing information. Even a sole proprietor com-pany will make decisions based upon information drawn from the immediate and wider environment – although this may not be a conscious process. As companies grow larger, and because the marketing environment is in-creasingly dynamic, there is a positive need for a formal system to be implemented so that marketing management is constantly informed and kept up-to-date about the environment in which it functions.

The management process is one of decision-making. Since decisions can only be made on the basis of information, it follows that the quality of decision-making will improve if the information on which it is based is comprehensive and as precise and up-to-date as is possible.

The component units of a MkIS comprise the following:

(a) Internal information
(b) Marketing intelligence
(c) Marketing research
(d) Marketing analysis

The first three units are responsible for the generation and collection of information drawn from the whole marketing environment. The role of marketing analysis is to sort and interpret this information and present it to the key decision-makers of the company so that action can be taken. This is a continuous process, not only because the marketing environment is dynamic but also because the results of marketing action are 'fed back' into the system so that analysis can judge its effectiveness and recommend appropriate action. Figure 5 shows the circular flow of this process and the respective roles of the information units are now described.

Internal information
The collection of internal data has traditionally been considered to be the province of accountants, who need sales and profit information, production

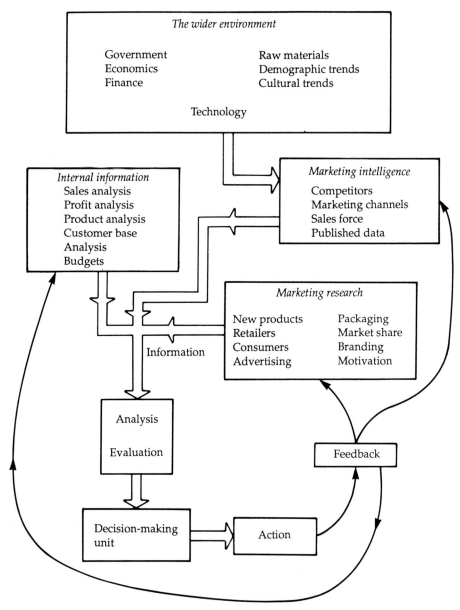

Figure 5 *MkIS – the information process*

and stock figures. The marketer requires the same basic information, but for somewhat different reasons, and looks on it from a different perspective to the accountant. Analysis of the customer base, for example, offers a wealth of information to both of them, and it can be collected and analysed within the confines of the company.

A MkIS analyst in a manufacturing company will need to know the geographic locations of customers, when and how often they require deliveries, what the most frequently ordered products are, etc. In this way he/she discovers in what ways the total marketing effort should be reduced or increased.

Knowledge of profit is insufficient, for marketing management needs to know which products generate the most profit and who are the most profitable customers – perhaps by means of 'Pareto' analysis. ('Pareto' analysis is the '80:20 rule that postulates that 80 per cent of profits are generated from 20 per cent of customers (or thereabouts). It is essential for management to know if this rule applies. Customers can be arranged along a 'curve of profitability' and then studied individually to ensure that the marketing effort is achieving maximum potential.) This information can be used to steer the marketing effort in the most effective direction. Although it should not be the case, management is often surprised at the findings of internal analysis. Lost in a mass of sales data, some customers can easily go unnoticed as being significantly more profitable than others.

With the aid of computer analysis, many managers are now able to obtain instant information on sales and profits by region, by customer and by product. Armed with such information, managers can make decisions on distribution and service, sales effort, advertising and promotion. Top management, with a MkIS in mind, should ensure that accountancy methods are designed to yield marketing information at the same time. A MkIS is not performing efficiently if information has to be generated more than once to suit respective functional areas; it is only the interpretation and information requirement that should differ.

Marketing intelligence

Using terminology borrowed from the military, marketing intelligence is concerned with gathering information from the immediate and the wider marketing environment. The basis of marketing intelligence is to ensure that the correct information is reaching the company regularly. Many companies operate a library system to monitor the wider environment. Much of the information appears in regularly published form and the following is only a selection:

(a) bank reports
(b) stock-market reports
(c) government publications
(d) academic publications
(e) trade institute published information

In time the person responsible for the 'intelligence library' can build up a picture of trends in the company's environment. This is background information in the light of which management is aided in making decisions about more specific issues. Clearly marketing intelligence is also crucial to strategic planning.

Marketing intelligence personnel should also liaise closely with the sales force, which is a valuable source of information pertaining to competitive activity. Some companies require their sales personnel to submit regular intelligence reports, but such a technique should be handled with care, because there is a risk that if this task becomes too onerous, the quality of the information gathered will diminish correspondingly. Without resort to any deviousness it is relatively simple to build substantial files of information about competitors. Such information is to be found in newspapers, trade magazines and even from competitors' own publicity material. Financial details can be obtained from public library services about publicly quoted companies. All published competitor information should be supplemented by reports from both suppliers and customers. The intelligence library should therefore consist of a section carrying files on each of the firm's competitors.

Marketing research

The units of the MkIS so far described provide direct information for the decision-making unit and provide the basis for the MR process. A market researcher embarking upon a new MR project should be able to complete much of the desk research required by referring to the MkIS library. The MkIS, including data drawn from the internal information system, should also aid research design. Once the desk research stage has been completed, MR is essentially concerned with uncovering information that is not available in published form, that is new to the company and that concerns specific situations. A MR project is undertaken so that the future can be predicted as far as is possible, either by statistical means or by gathering data that reveals attitudes and behaviour that can be used in strategy formulation. For the former, 'quantitative' analysis is used, and for the latter, attitudinal studies are carried out by 'qualitative' methods. Often qualitative methods are used in order to establish the best method of design for a questionnaire or more particularly in advertising research, where feelings, expressions and words can be discovered and tested.

Industrial MR also relies heavily on the support of the total MkIS. Although it is possible to carry out a great deal of industrial MR by the use of questionnaires and postal surveys, it is usually more feasible and more productive to conduct 'one-to-one' interviews, which should relax the interviewee and thus elicit more information of higher quality than is normally possible by impersonal methods.

In both consumer and industrial MR, 'monitoring' is equally as important as prediction. Clearly prediction comes first, otherwise no decisions could be made about strategy, e.g. the launch of a new product or an advertising campaign. Once the strategy has been implemented, it is vital that the company constantly monitors its progress. Monitoring and subsequent analysis allows management to find out if objectives are being achieved or if modifications to strategy are necessary.

Figure 5 reveals that MR, while being a discipline in its own right, is in fact only a component of a MkIS. MR differs from the other MkIS units, for the main part, by its direct contact with its subjects, i.e. potential and existing buyers. Marketing intelligence is designed with the totality of the company's activities in mind and provides an 'overview' of situations. The same is true for internal data systems. Although there is an element of overlap in the aims and goals of all MkIS units, MR can be distinguished because it is concerned with specific situations. Typical MR tasks are:

1 New product research
2 Advertising research
3 Packaging research
4 Pricing research
5 Brand penetration studies

With the exception of MR, most of the work of running a MkIS can be carried out by the company's internal staff, although they must of course be trained first. MR is characterized by the large number of MR consultants who are available to carry out work on behalf of, and as a complement to, a company's MkIS. Like advertising, MR is an industry in its own right. Except in very large companies, it is most cost-effective for a 'brief' to be prepared for a specific task and then for this to be passed to a consultant. This procedure has several advantages from the company's viewpoint: the work is undertaken by objective specialists in MR techniques as well as being specialists in certain market or product areas in many cases; and the company (because it is paying the bill) can insist on its own standards being met, so that very often (quite ethically) information company employees would be unable to discover can be provided. In industrial markets a buyer will often talk frankly to a consultant about a company's strengths and weaknesses, but would never do this directly to somebody directly employed by a competitive company.

The existence of MR consultancies has brought the practice and the industry very much to the forefront for companies and the public alike. This is perhaps the main reason why MR's place in a company structure is often confused and misunderstood by those other than marketing specialists. The company's financial and personnel resources are usually more committed to MR than to other MkIS units, merely because of the nature of their work. In addition, MR is often carried out in the public eye and tends to be regarded by company employees to be something outside routine activity.

Conclusion

For marketers the effort and expense devoted to MR as opposed to other MkIS activities is irrelevant. Whatever these may be, MR remains a component part of the total MkIS. This understanding is vital to the success of the MkIS, because the units of a MkIS are dependent upon each other. Their work should thus be co-ordinated and synchronized so as to work as one unit, whose role is to provide information for and minimize the risks of decision-making.

QUESTION 11

Describe and comment upon 'primary' and 'secondary' data-collection in the context of marketing research.

OBJECTIVE

To ensure that the student has a thorough knowledge of the various data-collection procedures and is able to display an awareness of the reasons for research, together with its limitations.

APPROACH

The distinction between 'primary' and 'secondary' data is frequently a source of confusion that leads to elementary mistakes in the examination room. Although you are not asked to do so, it would be prudent to include in your introduction a clear understanding of this distinction.

When developing your answer, remember that the word 'describe' is unambiguous, but *do not* neglect the request to 'comment'. 'Comment' would imply discussion about the aims of and logic behind each form of data-collection, and should be illustrated with examples of limitations, advantages and disadvantages. The clearest form of presentation would be to treat each form of research separately and to include your comments immediately after each descriptive section.

Although your answer will necessitate mention of data sources, you must not clutter your description with lengthy detail in this respect. But for your professional benefit, and to ensure adequate preparation for examinations, you should also be able to produce a comprehensive list of data sources with particular reference to secondary research. Such lists are to be found in most standard textbooks and can be augmented by reference to specialist marketing research texts.

The likely mark apportionment would be on the basis of half for secondary and half for primary data-collection. Within each of these, marks would probably again be split half for the explanation and half for comment.

ANSWER

Possible introduction

Primary data are data derived from a new research study; primary research is therefore concerned with data-collection for the first time. In contrast, secondary research concerns available information, derived from previously published sources.

Secondary research

Secondary research is exploratory in nature and is carried out with the aim of arriving at a set of assumptions which are used as the basis for primary research design. Aspects of the secondary data-collection process are frequently referred to as 'desk research', because the researcher can carry out most of this work without having to leave the office. The data search concerns sources both internal and external to the company.

Internal sources

Internal sources can be sub-divided into those whose origin is the firm's internal accounting system and those emanating from the firm's marketing intelligence system. The accounting system will contain information about the firm's customers and product preferences, and may, for example, show evidence of cyclical or regional purchasing behaviour. The quantity of data already available in a usable form for the researcher is frequently a measure of a company's marketing orientation.

If a marketing intelligence system exists within the company, the researcher should then be able to form a background impression of the market under scrutiny from data relating to that market's macroenvironment. Competitive information may also be available from sales force intelligence reports.

Whatever the level of marketing orientation and sophistication within the firm, internal information is often overlooked as a source of valuable data. Internal data cannot, however, discern sales potential, consumer trends, the true size of the market or the full extent of competitive activity. For such information one must turn to external secondary data sources.

External sources

The so-called 'data boom' has greatly facilitated secondary data search. Three main source areas can be distinguished: government statistics, other published data (such as that produced by trade associations and the trade press) and syndicated sources, including survey results which have been published by commercial research companies. Such sources will provide statistical data and written material which should establish the parameters of the market such that sample and survey design can be conducted in preparation for future primary research. An efficient appraisal of external secondary sources will provide information relating to the performance of competitors (thus enabling comparison with one's own company), suppliers, product sales and trends in volume/value purchases. In consumer markets it is usually possible to establish demographic characteristics, purchase frequency and what brands are bought and where.

Comment

The decision to carry the research process on to the primary stage will depend upon the nature of the marketing problem and the specific requirements of the firm. In some cases thorough secondary research will be adequate for the needs of the firm at that time. The main advantage is that a great deal of information has been gathered at a low cost, i.e. at least in comparison with the costs of primary research. The search for secondary data precedes the task of primary data-collection and should limit its cost.

The researcher must, however, be aware of the limitations of secondary data. A great deal of such data has been collected for a different purpose and may also be dated. Any inferences must be made with caution. The collection of too much data is wasteful, while too little can be misleading. As with any marketing exercise, potential benefits must be weighed against cost, and in particular the time factor must be considered. The most meticulous report is of little value if decisions it was designed to aid have already had to be taken.

Secondary data provides an essential framework for the design of future research but its ultimate limitation is that it tells us nothing about how and why products are used. This is the task of primary research.

Primary research

Primary research falls into three broad categories: observation, experimentation and various forms of survey work.

In the strictest sense data from retail audits and consumer panels are classed as observation. Observation is, however, more commonly associated with various recording devices and actually watching the behaviour of buyers. The psycho-galvanometer, cameras and various forms of counting meters are examples of recording devices. Key buying influences can be established and assessed by observation of the consumer in the real buying environment. Key factors might concern ways in which the product is handled before purchase, packaging or the degree to which the buyer requires assistance before making a choice. Store assistants themselves may be the object of observation. All observation must be carefully controlled so as to reduce the risk of bias, but in any case it is rarely sufficient on its own and does not reveal buyer motivation.

The object of experimentation is to compare the responses to several alternatives. In this way the firm is aided in deciding the most effective method of blending the marketing mix with respect to specific products. In test marketing, conclusions can be drawn before a commitment is made to a new product launch or a major alteration to the marketing mix. Advances in computer technology have contributed to the increasing sophistication of experimental techniques. The degree of external interference is a source of concern; thus, it is vital that a system of control is incorporated into any experiment.

Survey techniques rely heavily on the use of questionnaires, which can be executed by personal interviews or by post. Respondents can be chosen as representative of the population or survey universe, so the sampling method is critical to validity. Postal surveys are often used for industrial research, but suffer from poor response rates. Moreover there is no opportunity for probing, and replies must be accepted as submitted. Telephone enquiries can also form the basis of a survey, and are becoming a more commonly accepted method of contact with the increasing availability of telecommunications.

Group and depth interviews provide valuable qualitative information as to attitudes and motivation, and often form the basis of questionnaire design. In the industrial stituation personal interviewing is favoured for the gathering of informed opinion and information relating to future intentions. Some companies establish their own consumer and customer panels, so that buying behaviour can be monitored over a period of time.

Almost without exception the design of primary research is complicated and costly. The company must lay down specific marketing and research objectives before it is carried out. Such research is not necessarily a natural progression from secondary research in all cases. Apart from the cost, there is a risk of conclusions being drawn from biased information. In particular, experimentation may be carried out in atypical circumstances, while survey research is totally dependent on correct representation of the population.

Primary research cannot provide 'positive' solutions to marketing problems. It is, however, an invaluable aid to decision-making, the principal advantage being that its practice renders the company considerably less 'uncertain' than its competitors.

QUESTION 12

Differentiate between qualitative and quantitative research in the context of marketing research. In your answer illustrate the most appropriate medium for data-collection in relation to a variety of marketing-research problems.

OBJECTIVES

To ensure that the candidate is aware of the differences and uses of the research types in question, and is able to demonstrate when and why it is appropriate to use them.

APPROACH

The answer to this question should be entirely straightforward. You should 'differentiate' by presenting each research method in turn, and discuss when, why and how they are used. Do not neglect to think of examples that can illustrate the distinctions you have made.

ANSWER

Suggested introduction
The purpose of marketing research is to provide information to marketing management which 'aids' the decision-making process. It is understood that this information is never wholly complete, but is employed to reduce risk rather than to ensure certainty. If the marketing research is efficient, the level of risk is reduced in relation to the amount of time and money spent on a particular project. Marketing management must therefore optimize the relation between the deployment of resources and the required level of accuracy. This optimization is achieved by use of a mixture of both qualitative and quantitative research. Although there are some situations where one of these types of research should be employed more than the other, most marketing research requires that both should be used.

In the simplest terms the aim of quantitative research is to discover 'who' uses products and 'when', while qualitative research is designed to find out 'why' and 'how' products are used. Both research methods therefore support and are complementary to each other, but how they are used depends upon the problem in question. In particular much depends upon how much is known about a market before a research project is launched. In general it is normal to begin a project by using qualitative analysis. This provides information that is used to prepare questions for subsequent quantitative application and analysis.

Qualitative research

As has been already mentioned, qualitative analysis is concerned with 'why' and 'how', and thus with attitudes. If sufficient time and money were to be available, it would be possible to design a quantitative study that would reveal quite accurately how consumers felt about products. This study would need a large number of lengthy unstructured interviews, as well as the considerable difficulty of an analysis that would be adequate enough to draw valid statistical conclusions. A more cost-effective approach would be to use qualitative research on small selected groups of consumers, which would normally take the form of 'group discussions' and 'depth interviews'.

Group discussions are based on the careful selection of a group of consumers who are then encouraged to talk freely about their attitudes to the products and services under consideration. The fact that group discussions are relatively unstructured does not imply that they do not need to be carefully planned. The consumer selection process itself must take care to avoid respondents who are likely to intimidate others, or indeed stifle each other. For example, an articulate, confident respondent may tend to dominate a discussion whose other members may have equally valid views and feelings but are less confident about expressing them. Such a mixture would tend to introduce bias and non-response into the discussion.

The discussion leader must thus be a skilled person – often with a psychological or sociological background. His/her role is to 'guide' the discussion by means of a checklist of topics that are introduced at appropriate points in the discussion. The objective is to listen rather than to ask questions. In addition to the selection of group members by similar backgrounds of age or social class (the researcher must decide how important such criteria are), it is also important to ensure that group members have a common interest, e.g. they all favour a certain type of holiday or are 'do it yourself' enthusiasts. Normally potential discussion participants are chosen at random and are then invited to become a discussion group member after their suitability has been evaluated.

Depth interviews are employed to obtain similar information as can be gained from group discussions, but (as implied in the name) at a more personal level. This 'deeper' personal approach is required when the subject under review might prove embarrassing. Personal hygiene products or financial services might be appropriate topics for such 'depth' treatment. The skill of the interviewer is important, since a rapport must be established so that correct and truthful information can be elicited. Whereas interaction is encouraged as a stimulant in group discussions, depth interviews are used when the wish is to avoid interaction. For some topics, such as how households are run, there may be a tendency in a group situation for respondents to say what they want others to hear rather than depict their real actions and behaviour. Depth interviews are also frequently used in industrial marketing research, since busy buyers, for example, are often more amenable to spending half an hour with an interviewer on a person-to-person level than they would be to filling in a questionnaire.

Qualitative research is widely used as a source of product ideas, and in advertising research, where the 'language' of the consumer can be ascertained for use in copywriting. Feedback can also be obtained in relation to existing advertisements. Qualitative methods are also very useful when preparing the ground for segmentation studies, especially when the basis for segmentation is psychographic rather than demographic.

As a precursor to quantitative research, qualitative research establishes what is important to consumers and thereby helps to determine the content of questionnaires. It also helps to ensure that the questions use words and expressions that are familiar to the consumer. Finally, qualitative research establishes and generates attitude statements which can be subsequently quantified by means of scaling techniques.

Quantitative research

The previous section has related qualitative research to the 'exploratory' stages of marketing research. Quantitative research is concerned with describing markets by finding out 'who' buys products. The qualitative research that has been undertaken prepares the researcher to ask these questions in a more meaningful way. For example, take the proposed launch of a new holiday idea. Qualitative research must establish what are the basic attitudes to holidays in general and to the specific holiday in question. It must also establish what consumers expect 'qualitatively' from their holidays. By means of statistical sampling methods, a quantitative survey would be designed to ask specific questions. In the case of a holiday the aim would be to find out popular price brackets, preferred travel periods and desired amenities in the resort. Such studies are usually carried out by questionnaire surveys. Based on the language and prevailing attitudes that the qualitative research has unveiled, the questionnaire can include attitude scaling techniques such as 'Likert' or 'semantic differential' scales. These can be subsequently analysed quantitatively, so as to add substance to the qualitative findings.

Finally, it is necessary to describe the consumer in demographic and sociological terms, i.e. age, sex, marital status, number of children, income occupation and address. Such information, when quantified, can then be correlated with the other information from the questionnaire, so that the survey population is categorized into identifiable groups, and thus helps the researcher to decide what the bases for segmentation should be.

Once markets have been established, they must be continually monitored in order to measure success and to discover any changes in the market. While qualitative 'probes' can be made from time to time, methods such as 'consumer panels' and 'retail audits' provide continuous quantifiable information. Together with the growth and increasing sophistication of computer-aided analyses, the use of mathematical and statistical techniques to quantify information has increased dramatically in the past 20 years. Many research agencies have developed their own 'models', which are used to predict brand penetration or to perform multivariate analyses. Their aim is to provide accurate information at relatively low cost. Such techniques are generally restricted to consumer markets, where large amounts of data can be analysed by computer. It is important, however, that quantitative analysts should not lose sight of the reasons behind their research. The best research should have simple objectives, and results should be presented in a way that can be understood and acted upon easily. In other words, analysis should be practical. In real terms the limited resources of companies are liable to act as the best form of control over wasteful or over-developed research. As has already been stated, the constant task of marketing researchers is to balance costs against results.

Conclusion

The use of qualitative and quantitative research has given rise to some debate as to which method is the most efficient in terms of obtaining results. The real issue concerns what 'mix' of both types of research should be applied to a given situation, and how this can be most effectively employed within a budget. Taken out of context therefore neither method can be said to be 'better' than the other. Both qualitative and quantitative research methods are prone to bias of interpretation of results and to bias built into survey design. The fact that certain results are supported statistically does not in itself presuppose that the right questions have been asked, or that the correct interpretations have been made of the answers.

QUESTION 13

Suggest sources and techniques for generating new product ideas. What steps can the company take to reduce the risk of new product failure?

OBJECTIVES

This is an entirely straightforward question that is designed simply to test knowledge of new product development.

APPROACH

The question is really concerned with the whole process of product development, but it is still a straightforward question in that this process can be summed up in two steps: (i) idea generation, and (ii) screening (in the widest sense).

As implied in the question, you should clearly distinguish between these two stages in your answer. You should enrich your answer by putting the process into perspective in the introduction by emphasizing the importance of new products, and by linking stages (i) and (ii) with a well thought out paragraph. As usual your conclusion should 'balance' the answer.

ANSWER

Suggested introduction
The product is central to the whole being of the firm and to the whole marketing effort. Without a product the sales force has no need for customers and the production department cannot supply sales. This statement may appear so obvious as to be not worth mentioning, but it is in fact so basic that it should be continually emphasized. Once a product range has been established, there can be a tendency to take the product for granted, and for functional areas of marketing to take on an importance in their own right. There is therefore a requirement to keep the product firmly at the forefront of all activity.

The second danger associated with taking the product for granted is one of not looking to the future. Markets are dynamic, products must therefore change, and new product development is the only method that can bring about this adaptation.

In summary the product is the central element of all business activity. New products are the only means by which a company can ensure continued survival; new product development is thus the 'life blood' of all company activity.

Generating new product ideas

Any development programme must be approached with care because of the cost, the human resources needed and the consequences of launching a poorly conceived product. The initial idea for a new product must, however, come from 'somewhere', and until each idea can be carefully considered, no suggestion, from whatever source, should be ignored. The company can, however, take steps to generate a spirit of product development as well as organizing more formal systems of 'opportunity exploration'.

Research and development. This department is a clear starting point for new product ideas. The department should be run on commercial rather than 'scientific' lines – feeding in inspiration and information *from* the market place. It has been a common error for research scientists to develop a product and then ask if there is any demand for it; the process should logically be the other way around.

The production department. This department is well placed for offering suggestions and practical ways of refining and improving the product, while using existing machinery in a different way. Many UK companies and certainly Japanese companies operate formal schemes based on the 'suggestion box' idea.

The sales force. If a company is applying a true marketing orientation to its affairs, it would be normal to expect members of the sales force to provide information about market activity, which would include observations of competitive products and customer feedback. Customers can frequently provide the initial stimulus for a new product.

The Marketing Information System (including marketing research). This should be a major source of idea generation (see Question 10). The Information System should draw upon a wide variety of external sources in its capacity of monitoring the market. This process may provide ideas for imitative products as well as warnings about changes in the market which should be the stimulus for 'innovative' product development. Although many companies survive very well by marketing imitative products, it is worth remembering that market leaders are usually those that develop a truly innovative idea.

Senior management. Senior management has an important role to play in creating the correct atmosphere for new product development. This role would include the correct style of management for sales and production teams, the recruitment of forward looking employees at appropriate levels, and the promotion of an active Information System. More specifically, senior management should institute formal systems for idea generation. These may include brainstorming sessions and the organization of venture teams and planning committees.

Comment. If the correct atmosphere prevails within a company, a flow of ideas should reach management on a regular basis. It is also vital that none of these ideas, however outlandish they may seem at first, are rejected out of hand, for a seemingly 'wild' idea may have validity upon closer inspection. There is also the point that if employees begin to believe that there is a tendency to reject rather than to receive new ideas, this will eventually destroy the stimulative and creative environment that the company should be seeking to promote.

Screening

Once equipped with a series of ideas, the second stage of new product development is to begin a process of elimination which isolates potentially good ideas from those that are impractical for various reasons. As has been stated, *all* ideas, from whatever source and whatever their nature, should start the screening process with an objectively equal chance. Before any subsequent choice procedures are carried out, it should be clear at the outset that any new product must satisfy three basic requirements:

1   Is there a real consumer need?
2   Does the company have the resources and technical capacity to market and manufacture the product?
3   Is the potential market large enough to generate profit?

If these questions are asked and answered continually throughout the evaluation stage, this will provide a clear guide as to whether a new idea should be rejected or allowed to go a stage further in development. The questions can be answered by formal means, which are in fact a series of steps that aim to reduce the risk of product failure.

Initial screening. This is the first stage by which a range of new ideas can be reduced to a manageable number of possibilities. It is just as important to make sure that a good potential product is not overlooked (thereby losing an opportunity) as it is to eliminate poor ideas whose further development could result in a costly waste of time.

To develop a screening technique the company must isolate a series of factors that initial research has indicated would fit closely to the 'ideal' in terms of the answers to the three questions just mentioned. A short-list, or ranking system, can then be applied. Typical criteria under scrutiny might include raw material availability, production, distribution and product line compatibility. Marketing research techniques based upon the 'brand mapping' principle may provide a list of features that are thought desirable from the consumers' points of view.

Screening analysis is normally carried out by statistical weighting of the factors employed. A minimum rating score must be established as a 'cut-off' point. Product ideas which do not achieve this are abandoned, while the remainder proceed to the next development stage.

Business analysis

Once product ideas have passed the initial screening stage, their likely profitability must be considered. Whatever the merits of the product idea itself, it is no use proceeding with it unless it is likely to make a profit. Research and forecasting techniques are used to establish demand, then cost analyses should establish whether or not the product can be produced at a competitive price. Cost analyses should not only include estimates of actual production costs but also of such factors as capital investment and marketing costs. Statistical techniques can establish profitability, using such methods as 'break even' and 'rate of return' analyses.

Product development

When the analytical process has been completed, the company will have narrowed down the range of potential new products to a very small number. By this time the chosen product idea(s) should have passed the test in financial and market terms; and the company should also have established that it has the capacity, expertise and financial resources to launch the product. Until now, however, work has only been carried out on paper. The company needs to produce a physical prototype to test manufacturing capability and the market response.

In consumer markets reactions might be gauged by means of motivation research and concept testing. 'Hall tests' could be used to ascertain reactions about performance and packaging, with results being judged against a similar product whose level of acceptance is known. In industrial markets testing responses is a difficult task, partly because a prototype may be physically difficult to produce, and also because potential users are not massed so conveniently together. Testing in industrial markets must therefore rely upon personal approaches. Sometimes a producer will try to enlist the support of a customer to work with when putting the proposed new product on trial, and so be able to ascertain genuine user reaction.

At this 'physical product' or prototype stage of development it is important that marketing and production teams liaise closely, so that comments or problems are known to both parties. It is also vital that the prototype corresponds precisely with the proposed production product. If this is not the case, any testing could be totally misleading.

When sufficient feedback has been obtained at the end of the product development stage, the company faces the critical 'go–no-go' decision in relation to a full-scale launch. If development has been expensive (as is usually the case), the company may be reluctant to abandon the project. Whatever the rate of losses of abandonment at this stage, it is important to realize that these would represent only a fraction of the losses a failed product launch would entail. Firm decision-making is thus vital. The decision to go ahead, on the other hand, also demands courage and good judgement, because if the product fails, the company will lose some credibility as well as money. This is the reason why a carefully planned series of stages is essential. Each stage attempts to eliminate doubt, but as the product is developed further, the risks increase correspondingly.

Test marketing

If the 'go' decision is taken after all factors have been considered, the fully developed product is manufactured on a limited scale and test marketed.

In practice, and particularly in consumer markets, test marketing provides the final opportunity to withdraw the product before a full-scale launch is embarked upon. Thus, if the test market is unsuccessful, there is a final escape route. Companies who consider test markets in this way are, however, misunderstanding the reasons for test marketing. At the test market stage the decision to launch the product should have been firmly made, and the preparation leading up to the product launch such as to make failure in the test market as unlikely as possible. The real reason for test marketing is to 'fine tune' the proposed marketing strategy and to predict the level of sales that might be expected on a full-scale launch. Modifications to strategy can be made at this stage, but the company should already be sure that the product itself is acceptable in its existing form.

Sometimes more than one test market is run concurrently, so that variations to the marketing mix and marketing budgets can be tested. Test marketing is most commonly associated with consumer markets, and is increasingly carried out by marketing research agencies who specialize in such techniques as brand share prediction. IBA television areas are often used as test markets because it simplifies the monitoring of advertising effectiveness.

Full-scale commercialization

This is the natural conclusion to the various stages of product evaluation, after test marketing has run its course. The stages of evaluation and elimination of product ideas are designed to make the company as sure as possible that the chosen product is the right one for the market and for the company. Figure 6 shows the relation between the 'filtering' of product ideas and expenditure. It also emphasizes the important financial implications of product development. It is still preferable, however, to abandon an idea late in the development stages than to market an unsuitable product.

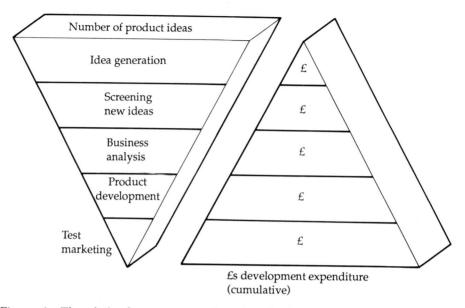

Figure 6   *The relation between cost and product development*

Conclusion

If the stages that have been described are carefully carried out, the risks of poor choice or failure are reduced, but there is still no guarantee of success. The product launch is merely 'less uncertain' than a haphazard approach would be.

The new product is essential to survival, and is the major strategic response of a company wishing to adapt to constantly changing markets. The fact that a surprising number of new products fail can only act as an incentive and a warning to companies to practise risk reduction, as described in this answer, as well as they are able.

FURTHER READING

All good marketing texts have large sections devoted to the area of new product development, so the answer should be to examine these sections closely and attain an understanding of the issues. There is, however, a now 'classic' article that those students of an investigative nature might like to refer to: 'Disastrous debuts – Despite high hope, many new products flop in the market', *Wall Street Journal*, 23 March 1976.

QUESTION 14

Describe the assembly of a company's product mix, giving reasons for mix optimization and ways in which this may be achieved.

OBJECTIVES

To ensure that the candidate understands the structure of, and interrelations within, a 'typical' product mix.

APPROACH

The answer to this question should be concise and straightforward and should include a description of how a product line forms part of the total 'mix'. As is true for all answers, any reference to actual products and real situations will add to the marks that you will be awarded.

ANSWER

Suggested introduction
In terms of both industrial and consumer markets it is unusual to find a company which markets only one product. More usually firms market a range of products. The experience and capabilities of a company (both in marketing and manufacturing) usually combine to produce products that are in some way related to each other in the physical or market sense. Of course, if a company continues to expand, there is a likelihood that any such relation between products will become more tenuous. Whatever the relation between products, their sum total constitutes the 'product mix' of a company. The idea of regarding a group of products as a 'mix' gives form to the company's activities, allows analysis to be carried out, and so permits the products to be optimized in terms of profitability, conformity to the company image and in terms of how the products relate to each other.

Product mix
The 'product mix' is the term used to describe the total number of products a company offers for sale. This mix is divided into groups of product lines. A product line is a group of products closely related to each other, either because

they have similar functions, or because they are marketed to similar customer groups. Some companies consider products to belong to the same line if they are complementary, e.g. cameras and films and other accessories could constitute the photographic line of a company.

Figure 7 portrays the total assembly of a company's products. The number of product lines denotes the 'width' of the product mix and the number of products in a particular line is described as product line 'depth'.

The hypothetical example portrays a company that has originated through manufacturing chocolate confectionery. The example traces the imaginary development of a product mix assembly which is typical of the evolution experienced in many companies.

Line 1 represents the company's original products, or at least the type of products which provided the basis for expansion, and for which the company is still probably most famous. The experience in manufacturing and marketing the company gained in this market led naturally to the development of a range of gift products in chocolate.

Line 2 shows that although the same retail outlets may be used, the customers' motives and buying behaviour would differ from those of line 1, and a completely different marketing strategy may be called for in order to promote and sustain growth in this market.

Line 3 represents another break from the original products. Here similarity in raw materials may have stimulated the development of a chocolate drink. Once the company has entered this market, it would be natural to add coffee and tea as well as other ideas to the line. If, say, coffee became particularly

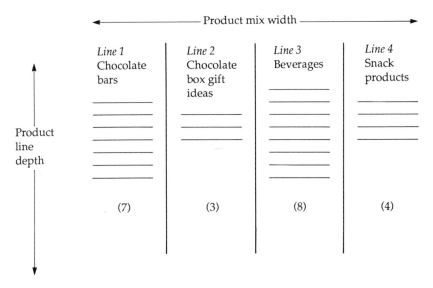

Figure 7   *Total assembly of company products*

successful, it would be logical to think of coffee products as forming a line of their own.

Line 4 is a further addition to the width of the product mix. As the company continues to expand, both the width and the depth may increase, perhaps to include increasingly dissimilar product areas.

There is considerable pressure on any company to add to the depth of product lines as well as to the total mix, since a strongly marketing-orientated company should in any case be constantly engaged in a policy of new product development. Secondly, the sales force and other company observers of the market place are continually requesting new products in order to accommodate clients' needs and match competitive action – itself a stimulus to new product development. A further reason for the expansion of the product mix is often the need to take up excess capacity in the manufacture of existing lines.

Even in the most efficient of companies it is not uncommon for the product mix to become 'less than optimum'. This can occur because of changes in the market place or because too many, or not enough, products have been added to the mix. The following rule is simple enough to relate, but considerably more difficult to carry out in practice: 'If no extra profit can be made either by adding to or subtracting from the mix, then the product mix can be said to be at an optimum level'.

General reasons for adding to the lines in the mix have been mentioned already, but there are several product strategies that can be applied to product mix management which attempt to achieve the optimum level. Taking into account the market conditions and the capabilities of the firm, the following options are open:

- A company can add lines to its mix in a way similar to that described in Figure 7. This is organized and planned expansion, but the company runs the risk of entering markets with which it is unfamiliar, and not equipped to service. On the other hand, new markets represent risk reduction when problems occur in any one of them.
- Some companies extend their lines downwards and introduce products which are cheaper than their original products. Here there is a risk that new, cheaper products can harm the image of their superior counterparts. The company can, however, enter very large, lucrative and previously untapped markets in this way. Both BMW and Mercedes have extended their product lines downwards over the years.
- Another alternative is to extend the line upwards into more prestigious product areas. This is likely to be more difficult to achieve than moving downwards, and it will be costly to establish quality and image.
- Finally, when a company has products in a line which covers a wide range of prices and qualities, it is tempting and often worthwhile to 'fill' any gaps

that may exist. A certain amount of risk comes with this strategy, because if the products are 'too close together' in the market sense, all that is achieved by introducing a new product is reduced sales for the others.

An optimum product mix can only be achieved by effective market planning and careful and constant control and analysis of performance, culminating in an annual review or 'marketing audit' of the product mix. The system of control should be such that costs and profits can be ascertained product-by-product.

The marketing ramifications of this analysis must also be considered. Although a certain product may be contributing little or nothing to profits, it may have strategic importance in terms of the image it has for the company and the line. In this case it would be unwise to remove this product from the line. Line reduction is of course an acceptable product-mix strategy, and it makes sense for any products that are expensive to market and contribute little to the well-being of the company to be removed. The possibility of developing a 'sub-optimum' product mix is reduced by following the strategies already outlined and by effective market segmentation.

Even after the market has been effectively segmented, and the company considers its product mix to be optimum, both in cost/profit and marketing strategy terms, it must be appreciated that the dynamic nature of markets makes this situation a very transitory phenomenon. Marketing control is therefore a vitally important part of 'mix' management – like 'fine tuning', with major change always under consideration. Too frequent changes are likely to detract from favourable customer perceptions of a company, but it is just as damaging to keep products for too long as it is to neglect the development of new ones.

QUESTION 15

What strategies does marketing theory recommend for each stage in the Product Life Cycle? Criticize this concept and discuss its practical limitations.

OBJECTIVES

The Product Life Cycle is a fundamental topic for the simpler levels of marketing right through to more strategic levels. The question, while not being intended to assess the latter, nevertheless requires the student to show enough maturity to recognize that the topic is a strategic issue, and to be able to see its practical limitations.

APPROACH

Your introduction should only briefly describe what the PLC concept is, as the question is so framed that such knowledge is taken for granted and will become more apparent in the main body of your answer.

To set the scene you could provide a diagram showing the typical curve and the stages of the PLC. Always remember to label the axes on such a graphical diagram. (The adage that 'a picture is worth a thousand words' is true, but in examinations do not waste time making such a diagram into a work of art. All the examiner requires is a clear, well labelled presentation which serves to show that you know the principles.)

When discussing the strategies recommended for each stage, don't bother with a formal essay format – sub-headings would be more concise. You could begin with a grid of strategies, and then go on to discuss each strategy/stage in more detail. The mode of grid/diagrammatic presentation is a matter of personal choice, but a grid presentation could serve as a useful reference or *aide-memoire* while you are writing your answer.

Do not neglect the instruction to 'criticize' in your answer, as this must show a mature understanding of the issues. This section will also allow you to reveal any reading you might have undertaken in addition to the 'set' reading. As usual, your conclusion should 'balance' the answer, showing how far you feel any criticisms are justified, and also the value of the concept.

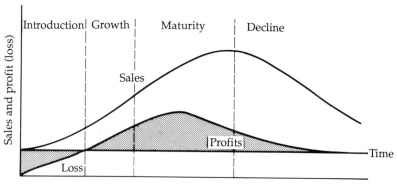

Figure 8   *The product life cycle*

ANSWER

Suggested introduction

The PLC concept theorizes that over time sales volume will follow a predict-able course, leading to the decline and eventual demise of any product. The time-scale is a function of the nature of the product itself and that of its market. Although the PLC has a theoretical base, there is much evidence to suggest that a product's life does indeed follow a predictable course. We must, however, remember that all products are not necessarily alike, and the markets in which the products are launched are themselves different and may be subject to radical changes. Time-scale is also an important variable between product types. Finally, the way the company manages its products has a great deal of bearing on whether the 'typical' curve is lengthened or shortened.

Figure 8 shows the several stages of the PLC, together with the sales/profit relation over time. Such a conceptual curve has important implications for strategy and the tactical deployment of the marketing mix. It is useful here to summarize these implications. First, however, one important factor (also an area of potential difficulty) should be considered: the marketer must be able to identify the movement of the product from one stage to another, and hence be able to decide upon the strategy to be adopted. The examination of each stage should make this task less difficult.

Introduction

At this stage expenditure on the product launch is most likely to exceed revenue in terms of profit and in some cases even that of sales, as the basic task is to create awareness among the target group of customers. If this is done efficiently, the company should be able to recoup this (seemingly excessive) expenditure as well as achieving profit at a later stage. Money spent during the introductory stage should, correctly, be regarded as an investment for the future, just as that incurred in the developmental stage.

Stimulating awareness can be achieved by means of a high level of advertising and promotional activity. This must of course be correctly targeted through the correct media to reach the chosen market segment. If the company employs a 'skimming' approach, the medium will be highly selective, perhaps even restricted to specialist or exclusive media. If the product is 'innovative', the aim will be to reach the 'early adopters'. If the aim of the company involves a 'penetration' strategy, then the task will be to reach as many potential users as possible at the most economic cost per head. Despite the high cost, in many consumer markets television is the favoured medium, because it offers sound and vision impact upon a very large section of the community.

Pricing decisions must be taken with care, as they will 'set the scene' for the future. It is likely that a price set too low in the first instance can be raised at a later stage; but if prices are set at a low level to reach a mass market, then the company must be sure that the market itself is large enough to generate sufficient demand to meet possible price reductions when competitive activity increases during subsequent stages in the life cycle. Very often new products are priced at a premium level so as to recoup as much investment as possible from consumers who are likely to be innovative and less price-sensitive. Starting from a high price, it is then possible to encourage new groups of buyers by means of a planned series of price reductions.

The product itself should be the object of constant market research, to gain feedback about its acceptability and any necessary modifications. It is not a good idea to alter the product too early or too often during introduction. After all, extensive research and trials should already have taken place, and a product modification too early in the product's life may lead to a lack of confidence and some element of confusion in the consumer's mind.

Distribution is a function of the product and the firm's strategy. The distributive outlets should reflect the promotional and advertising strategy, i.e. an exclusive message calls for exclusive outlets, whereas a penetration approach would demand a wider distribution network. While the product is not normally directed at every conceivable outlet, it is vital that distribution is organized so as to support the promotional effort adequately. It is foolish for a firm to invest heavily in promotion, only for the interested consumer to be told the product is out of stock, face indifference on the part of dealers, or, worse still, find traders unaware the line is available. Such mistakes are still made by some companies.

Growth

The company should by now have created awareness in a market consisting of existing and potential users. Among the first group promotional effort must aim to create distinct preferences, and elements of the marketing mix should encourage potential users to follow the 'example' of the innovators. Again, with reference to diffusion theory, these new consumers are described as the 'early majority'. The firm should be preparing itself (both internally and externally) to cope with the high rate of demand that should be a feature of maturity. Such preparation should also entail the formulation of strategies designed to resist the activities of competitors, who may already, or certainly will, be active in the market themselves.

Although promotional expenditure may still be high, this should be reduced in terms of its percentage ratio to sales in an effort to achieve a period of profitable returns.

Pricing should also be modified (usually reduced) in order to take account of the following:

1 Increased competitive activity
2 Wider distribution
3 An increasing usage
4 Lower unit costs of manufacture and distribution

Price is, however, always a function of market conditions, and any decision to reduce price should be made with care. It is always more difficult to increase prices than to reduce them.

Any 'fine tuning' of the product itself should take place during growth. The general aim should be to initiate improvements research has shown to be desirable in the product. The company may also have gained sufficient production experience to allow modifications in raw material usage, thus permitting cost economies. Care should be taken to ensure that such component changes do not result in a product which can be regarded in any way as being inferior to the original.

Distribution will naturally be carried out on a wider basis as sales grow. Growth is a period where market share is established (although this can be subject to changes in subsequent stages). For this reason distribution is very important: the appropriate dealerships, agents and outlets must be obtained whilst these intermediaries can still perceive a future for the product and thus view it as an attractive proposition. For consumer goods, in particular, changing patterns in retailing have tended to concentrate distributive outlets in the hands of relatively few outlets. The loss of shelf space with a large retailer can significantly affect total sales and corresponding market share.

Maturity
This would normally be the longest stage of the life cycle and therefore that in which the majority of products find themselves. Some similar producers, faced with reduced margins and strong competition, may drop out at this stage, although it is not uncommon for new market entrants who have

learned from the experience of others to appear and launch imitative products; when this happens on a sufficient scale, the 'maturity' stage merges into the 'saturation' stage.

Actual market growth has ceased at this stage, and the firm must concentrate its efforts on at least retaining, if not increasing, its market share. Whether the decision to increase market share or not is made, the chief task of the firm at this stage is to reinforce and hold the loyalty of existing users. While the firm can probably not afford to maintain continuous high expenditure on promotional activity, it is still important and must be finely tuned to achieve the objectives mentioned. Detergent commercials are typical of those employed during product maturity. More often than not they are not creative in nature, but merely designed to repeat a simple message at regular intervals. Maturity is not a stage in which a company can relax. It must begin to channel relatively more time, expense and creativity to newer products further back in the 'life cycle' curve.

In general, prices are at their competitive lowest during this period. Competitive activity is usually at its highest and price reductions are a common weapon in the battle to retain customer loyalty, though at the expense of reduced revenue and profit. A market-share-increasing strategy based on reduced prices would hope to generate sufficient sales to offset any loss in revenue per unit sold. Occasionally harmful price wars occur during this period when few, if any, companies will benefit from price reductions, some possibly being forced out of the market.

An important task of the company at this stage is to differentiate the product, since it has been on the market for some time and may be in danger of stagnation, and the greatest number of imitative products will be available. Any product differentiation is unlikely to be radical, because the resources of time and finance should be devoted in the main to new product development. In consumer markets 'new improved' or 'now with 10% extra' are often signs of product differentiation in maturity.

The role of distribution in maturity is primarily aimed at defending market share. Retail organizations will be offered a large choice of similar products by manufacturers; their reaction will be to reduce the number of brands on sale (brand rationalization), thereby reducing inventory costs and increasing turnover (and thus power) among a few suppliers. In consumer markets distribution centres heavily on keeping retail outlets and shelf space, and making sure that rationalization is restricted to competitors' lines. Distribution can play an important part in all markets at this stage by being employed as a form of non-price competition. When prices and products are very similar throughout the whole market, it is often the firm with the best delivery service that succeeds in obtaining orders.

Many distribution decisions are a function of market and product type, and here the maturity stage may prompt some firms with certain products to expand their distribution network, e.g. the increasing use of petrol stations as retail outlets. On the other hand, some outlets may be rationalized by the company itself, especially where they are considered to be too costly in terms of maintaining a commercial connection.

Decline

When industry sales fall persistently throughout the market, this is a sign of the product's entry into the decline stage of the PLC. Changes in fashion ideas among consumers or the emergence of innovatory products can both be causes of decline.

Deciding what to do with the product is a critically important marketing management decision. Very often companies experience the greatest difficulty in bringing themselves to abandon a product, especially when it may have been the backbone of the firm's original success. The company should, however, consider that an ailing product is bad for the image of the firm and it is likely to be using up resources that could be more usefully employed elsewhere. A product in decline does not stimulate or motivate those who are responsible for its management. The decision 'when' to withdraw a product or service during the decline period is critical, and must be made after taking all other market factors into consideration.

Some companies may decide quite consciously to continue to market their product right through decline as an element of strategy. By outliving their competitors, their market share should increase, although this will be relative to the rate of overall decline. It is also possible that the firm may find a speciality area to concentrate upon.

Staying in or leaving the market is a strategic decision of the highest order. Until a product is withdrawn, the management of that product should be just as critical during decline as it was in other life cycle stages. It is thus a mistake to equate the decline period with a relaxation of a company's hold over a product.

Pricing policy will depend heavily on the rate at which competitors leave the market. In general the company should try and obtain as much as possible for a product in decline. Such a pricing strategy will not necessarily hasten decline, because competition should be decreasing, and those consumers who continue to purchase are likely to be more brand-loyal and less price-sensitive than those who do not.

No changes would normally be initiated to the product at this stage, unless the company can find ways of reducing costs without substantially altering the product's nature. Nor should radical alterations to distribution strategy be contemplated. The company should take care that established (and relatively profitable) networks are not neglected. Of course, if the company decides to persevere with the product, outlets that remain with the product should be given special attention.

Comment and criticism

One of the major criticisms of the PLC refers to its use in practice by marketing managers. This may be an implied criticism of managers as much as the concept itself, but it is true that, managed without care and imagination, a product's decline can become a self-fulfilling prophecy. We know that in the very long term a product will inevitably tend to decline, or at least its management will need to change radically. There is a wealth of techniques available to find new market sectors, or new end-uses for the original product. Managers should not therefore accept decline without a thorough and imaginative attempt at prolonging the life cycle.

Another problem concerns the accurate identification of the moment when the product passes from one life cycle stage to another. In real life the various stages are not delineated as portrayed in the graphical representation. The reality is that the stages merge into each other, with varying time-scales, depending upon the nature of the product and its market. There is a danger that if the company interprets life cycle strategy too literally, it risks adopting the wrong strategy at the wrong point in time. Analysis and identification of each life cycle stage is heavily dependent upon well planned and continuous marketing research. One pointer may, however, be discerned from the foregoing PLC sketch: this is the oft noted phenomenon that profits take on a downturn appreciably before sales growth terminates, owing to the effects of competition on price and promotion outlays. Marketing accountability is a rare but substantial contributor to recognition of a change in the PLC stage.

While these criticisms should be borne in mind, it cannot be denied that the PLC concept is a valuable planning tool. It provides marketing management with a predictable pattern of product behaviour over time. The strategies which have been discussed are based on observations over a long period of

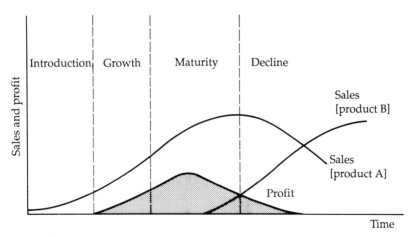

Figure 9   *Use of PLC concept*

time, and these have shown that certain phenomena occur with reasonable predictability. The recommended strategies are therefore normally appropriate, and knowledge of them allows forward planning and budgeting to take place. In particular, knowledge of the PLC aids the manager in planning for the development of products subsequent to that which is the immediate concern. Figure 9 shows how the concept can be used to do this. Products A and B overlap in their development, with the profits from A funding the launch of B.

In a less direct way the PLC is useful as a 'concept' in its own right as a framework or starting point for creative strategy. Thus, while managers acknowledge the existence of the concept, they may choose to use it more as a reference upon which alternative strategies can be based. In general such strategies will be based on the theme of product life extension by means of finding new end-uses, and thus new markets, for the original product, either with or without product modification. The marketing approach to these new markets may of course be substantially modified.

In conclusion it can be said that the PLC concept and its associated strategies have a great deal of validity for marketing management, inasmuch as the suggested course of the life cycle is relevant to most products. Indeed the increasing rate of dynamism in modern marketing is likely to accelerate rather than diminish this relevance.

The danger inherent in the use of the concept is that the manager employs a dogmatic approach to its interpretation. This is true for any marketing theory, and the point that should be made is that the PLC should be considered as a marketing tool. Treated in this way, the PLC can provide the stimulus for alternative strategies. The marketing manager should not be afraid to deviate from recommended strategies if an unpredictable occurrence renders them inappropriate or presents new opportunities.

FURTHER READING

Almost all standard marketing textbooks contain sections on the PLC, but it is worth looking at articles that expand upon these and provide a different perspective on the basic theory.

Two 'classic' articles are:

'Exploit the product life cycle', by T. Levitt, *Harvard Business Review*, Nov./Dec. 1965.

'Forget the product life cycle', by N.K. Dhalla and S. Yuspeh, *Harvard Business Review*, Jan./Feb. 1976.

Students should also look for further articles and, after reading them, build

QUESTIONS 13–16, RELATING TO PRODUCTS (OR SERVICES)

up their own list of products or services that have either followed the course of the curve or have been 'extended'. Students should also look for products that are being offered in a different way or for different end-uses from that for which they were originally intended.

QUESTION 16

Packaging can be said to have two functions:

(i) Product protection
(ii) Product promotion

Discuss the function of each in relation to a product range of your choice.

OBJECTIVE

To test that the candidate can distinguish between the two well documented roles of packaging through the medium of a practical example.

APPROACH

The obvious approach would be to take a product range and discuss each of the problems set in isolation, and there is nothing wrong in doing this. However, a more imaginative way might be to start with a philosophical overview of packaging to show that the problem has been appreciated and then go on to discuss the functions. The question does not ask for each of the functions to be discussed separately, so a more intelligent way might be to attempt to integrate them within the body of the answer.

Many textbooks tend to give a checklist approach to the above problem, so merely to reproduce this smatters of 'rote' learning. Better that your answer should, through your chosen example, attempt to show an understanding of the problem.

ANSWER

Suggested introduction
Packaging forms an inseparable part of the marketing mix, coming under the 'promotional P'. The objective of packaging, especially in today's fast-moving consumer goods society, is to increase sales of the goods inside the package. The package should thus confirm and enhance the perceived value of its contained product and impart that impression to the potential customer. Thus, part of its function is that of communication. The pack design itself

should also support and reinforce the brand name of the product or the brand image of the company.

Many industrial products are packaged in simple, plain boxes for protection during transit and storage, and clearly the context of packaging here is for product protection. Sometimes this is merely referred to as 'packing' rather than packaging: the latter has wider marketing connotations.

Practical example

The example chosen to illustrate this answer is 'baked beans', which might seem a little odd as an example, but serves to illustrate both problem areas quite well. The first facet of this example is that it is sold through retail outlets as a FMCG, and also sold through catering outlets. Clearly the marketing approach to each of these target audiences will be different.

The size of the product's package can have an effect on the total consumption of the product. When offered a larger pack, or a 'banded' pack of say four cans, consumers will often purchase and use more. The pack size, together with consumption rate, will also form a basis for market segmentation.

Another reason for attempting to persuade people to buy more at consumer level through special 'offers', such as 'buy three get one free', is an attempt to make them brand-loyal, in the expectation that they will buy the same brand next time.

To return to the earlier point of a basis for market segmentation, this type of product would be suitable for segmentation on the basis of usage, e.g. (i) heavy user, (ii) light user, (iii) occasional user. Different pack sizes would also enable the marketing firm to reach a greater amount of the potential market, e.g. small packs for single people or pensioners, etc., and larger packs for families.

Economic theory would suggest that more of a product is demanded at a lower price, but in the example of baked beans this might not be the case in that demand for the product will be relatively inelastic, i.e. there are only so many baked beans that a person can eat before needing a change of diet. On the other hand, since the price is relatively inexpensive, it is an attractive food through its economic virtues alone. The earlier points – banding packs together in, say, packs of four, and offering a financial inducement, e.g. 'buy three and get one free' – might make the best compromise. In any case who is to determine what is the cost of three on the basis of giving the fourth pack away as part of the 'deal'?

When it comes to pack sizes for the catering market, we must look at entirely different criteria. Here it will be more a matter of price related to volume purchased, and this is why catering packs tend to be much larger. On the basis that 'one baked bean is very much like another' (although this point is hotly debated) in terms of selling to caterers, pack sizes related to price will be very important. In addition, 'below the line' marketing activity will also be more important, whereas for selling to the general public the emphasis is upon 'above the line' activity.

The following checklist of points perhaps best sums up packaging in relation to the baked beans example:

1 *Protection*. Baked beans need to be hygienically packed inside their container and the container's outer (box for transporting) needs to be robust enough to withstand normal packing of cans on top and picking out by customers without providing damage to the tins. (One does of course occasionally see damaged cans for sale, but one suspects that some of this damage may well have been caused at the store materials handling stage.)

2 *Handling*. Here it is a matter of size, and clearly 'catering size' packs will be unsuitable for supermarket shelves. In so far as physically handling cans is concerned, some cans now have ridging behind the label, which presumably makes them easier to handle. (This point might seem minor, but in the case of products where brand loyalty is perhaps quite low and where it is difficult to differentiate products, any small factor, such as ridged cans, may be seen as a marketing advantage, no matter how small.)

3 *Convenience*. This again is best illustrated in the provision of a range of pack sizes. As regards opening, perhaps the manufacturer who comes up with an alternative to the 'faithful' can opener may be seen to have provided a unique selling proposition (usp).

4 *Information*. This will comprise the list of ingredients required by law, 'E' numbers and the like, in addition to some very simple instructions about heating.

5 *Outers*. The boxes in which the beans are transported must be robust enough to withstand moving by fork-lift truck and stacking on top of each other. They will contain the logo of what is inside the container, but more for information than for promotional purposes.

6 *Relationship with branding*. For many products packaging is inextricably linked with branding, e.g. 'Marmite' and 'Bovril' jars. It is, however, difficult to imagine a baked bean manufacturer being able to differentiate his brand from those of competitors from shape of the can. Consumers are used to baked beans being provided in cylindrical tubes, and it would be difficult to conceive of any other shape; plus which, other shapes would be more difficult to open with a can opener!

7 *Promotion*. The baked beans example is a good illustration of the way manufacturers have in more recent times used 'below the line' promotion via the labels on the tins. These are now far more attractive than they used to be, presenting the contents in pictures rather than simply communicating factual information. In self-service stores the package and the display arranged by the merchandiser are often the only way the manufacturer has to communicate with potential customers. Quite often the product has to

'sell itself', and the package is regarded as the 'silent salesman'.

Because of increased competition and greater consumer affluence, there are many competing brands all trying to attract the shopper's attention. Many shoppers are thus drawn to the best designed package.

Conclusion

Packaging is a valuable marketing tool, which has broadened out from playing a primarily protective role. In today's marketing environment packaging performs many functions, the most important being product differentiation, brand reinforcement, promotion and the provision of information. The reason for the increased importance of packaging is increased competition, the growth of self-service and increased consumer affluence resulting in shoppers demanding more than just a basic commodity.

QUESTION 17

What limitations are inherent in the economist's view of pricing? How might price be determined in a realistic marketing situation?

OBJECTIVES

First, to ensure that the student is able to distinguish clearly between economic price theory and the determinants of price in practice. Second, to establish that the student has a thorough understanding of pricing alternatives and the marketing goals which may affect a company's pricing strategy.

APPROACH

Students of examination technique may well tire of continual requests to 'read the question' before attempting the answer, but the point is so fundamental that it cannot be over-emphasized. This particular question provides a good example of the importance of this rule.

The first key word is 'limitations'. Although it would be useful to display *some* knowledge of economic pricing theory, you are really only being asked to discuss its limitations. This section should not therefore form the major part of your answer.

Similarly 'how might' is a vital part of the question. The word 'might' allows you the freedom to consider price-setting in its widest sense. You should, therefore, discuss actual methods of price-setting and the various marketing objectives and situations which may call for more flexible approaches to pricing.

An answer format is suggested below:

1 A brief discussion of the economist's view of pricing.
2 A discussion of how this approach can be inappropriate for marketing practitioners.
3 A paragraph that introduces pricing in the marketing situation.
4 Influences on pricing, such as competitive activity and marketing objectives.
5 Common methods of pricing.
6 Conclusion

ANSWER

Suggested introduction

The study of economics is essentially concerned with theory. The purpose of a theory is to simplify cause and effect relationships in given situations. The fact that one such situation may not be entirely realistic does not detract from the validity of the theory, because theory is necessary to provide the basis for action in more varied situations. Economics is one of the academic disciplines from which marketing gains a basis for understanding how markets work and how firms should behave in order to function efficiently. Marketing practitioners recognize, as do economists, that economic theory does not represent or explain a number of real-life situations, but it does provide certain fundamental precepts that serve as a basis for analysis.

With reference to price, the economic basis for marketing strategy is concerned with theories of supply and demand and costs. A basic assumption of economic theory is that of the downward sloping demand curve that assumes that consumers will buy more of a product as price falls. Economic theory also assumes that consumers act 'rationally' with respect to price, and that in so doing they will always attempt to maximize the 'total utility' that they can obtain from goods they purchase.

The traditional economic theory of the firm assumes that firms will always attempt to increase output to a level where profits are 'maximized', i.e. where marginal costs are equal to marginal revenue, the cost of one more unit of output being equal to the addition to total revenue that this last unit provides.

The above assumptions are basic to economic theory and provide a rather inflexible view of business activity. More detailed study will reveal that economic theory does provide considerable explanations as to variants in consumer behaviour. It provides models for diminishing utility which relate to 'inferior' and 'prestige' goods (as far as marketing practitioners are concerned), because it ignores the effects of sociological and psychological influences on the consumer, except in the most general of terms.

Pricing and marketing

Economics thus provides a valuable insight into the nature of markets, and can show how demand will change according to competitive influences. It is also invaluable in its consideration of elastic and inelastic demand. Thus, an understanding of the theoretical relations between price and quantity in various situations is a 'jumping off point' for devising marketing strategies that cannot possibly be overlooked. The fact that the sections on pricing in many marketing textbooks include a sizeable section on the economics of pricing is testimony to this. Marketing is, however, concerned with specific situations, and it is in this respect that the limitations of economics as a marketing tool begin to become apparent. For this reason some texts treat economics as an 'appendix' rather than as a part of the body of the text.

Thus far it has been established that economic theory, while being inadequate on its own for the needs of marketers, is nevertheless fundamental in providing an understanding of supply and demand. We shall now consider how, with the aid of this understanding, marketing management approaches the problem of pricing in realistic marketing situations.

All companies must pay attention to, and are influenced by, the nature of the markets in which they operate and thus by the degree of competition that prevails. Well managed marketing-orientated companies can exercise an element of control over these external factors according to how they employ the 'marketing mix', of which price is one of the component parts. Marketing management is also concerned with basic company objectives that should guide pricing, the relationship between costs and price, and how prices may require modification to suit a changing market.

Influences on pricing

Some companies are faced with a market situation that demands that their sole preoccupation is with survival. While the company is devising plans to improve the situation, its attitude to pricing may be one which merely enables it to remain solvent.

In normal circumstances, however, companies will adopt pricing strategies whose implementation will help to realize formal company objectives. They may wish to establish a certain percentage of market share or even become market leaders. Some strategists suggest that the volume production associated with market leaderships will eventually reduce costs. A low price is likely to be part of the marketing mix in order to achieve this aim, and until market leadership is obtained, profit objectives will be sacrificed. Then another pricing policy may be adopted.

Some companies deliberately set high prices because the company objective is to establish quality brand leaders. The criteria for pricing are to reflect this image. Advertisements for 'Stella Artois' lager emphasize that the product is 'expensive' rather than 'value for money' in order to promote this image.

Increasingly where smaller companies have been taken over by large groups, or holding companies, very stringent demands are made as to profit requirements and return on investment (ROI) required. It may be in such cases that longer-term strategies are inappropriate and that the company must concentrate upon a profit maximization policy. This is of course perfectly acceptable while favourable market conditions prevail. On the other hand, such short-term financial pressure may prevent the company from planning for the longer-term changes in the market place.

Whatever the objectives of the company where pricing is concerned, attention must be paid to production costs. Such costs will vary according to differing levels of production, this being an aspect of price-setting where economics is particularly useful for the marketer. An essential element of pricing is to prepare an estimate of demand in order to forecast potential sales and thus production requirements over a given period. How different companies consider costs in relation to price is a management decision which must be made by taking all market and company factors into account.

Pricing methods

A popular pricing method is 'cost plus' pricing, where the retailer or manufacturer adds a fixed percentage mark-up to the cost of each unit. The mark-up applied will vary according to the type of industry and the type of market.

Break-even pricing is another popular pricing method. Here the company must decide (by analysis) the units of production required to cover fixed costs and variable costs at different levels of production, settle on the profit required, and produce and sell accordingly. One drawback of this pricing method is that little attention is paid to market conditions and the current level of demand.

Prices can of course be set and modified on purely marketing grounds. It must be assumed that cost and demand analysis has previously taken place. Then companies can improve their margins on a consumer/psychological basis, or by reliance on non-price factors of marketing that render price 'relatively' less important to the buyer.

Conclusion

In conclusion one can say that pricing is intrinsically based upon economic theory. Marketing practitioners must therefore have a sound knowledge of economics in relation to supply and demand, so as to have a basis for their pricing/marketing strategies. Although economics recognizes that prices must be modified according to a variety of market conditions, the discipline is limited for the marketer because specific situations are not dealt with. Armed with an economic grounding, the marketer can, however, devise pricing methods according to company objectives (for example, market share acquisition) or market conditions (such as different stages in the product life cycle, or movements in the structure of competition).

FURTHER READING

Most good marketing textbooks have a reasonably comprehensive section on pricing. There are a number of specialist texts that also deal with the subject, but generally from a highly mathematical viewpoint. Students who wish to make a detailed study of the subject are advised to refer to the work of Andre Gabor, who has written, edited and co-authored numerous articles and textbooks upon the subject of pricing.

QUESTION 18

Discuss the practice and associated complications of pricing for a product line.

OBJECTIVE

To assess the student's knowledge of pricing with specific reference to product-line management.

APPROACH

Provided that you are certain that you have adequately prepared for this topic, this is a relatively uncomplicated question; it does not require a great deal of planning as to its presentation. Remember that you are required to discuss the 'complications' of pricing for a product line, and that the question is concerned with 'pricing' and not the development of a product line.

The following is a suggested guideline for the format of your answer:

1   An introduction to the reasons behind the employment and development of a product line. The question of pricing should be introduced at the end of this section.
2   An explanation of the possible relations between products in a line. (Your answer has now discussed the practice of pricing for a product line.)
3   Complications inherent in product-line pricing.

ANSWER

Suggested introduction

A product line can be defined as a broad group of products whose uses and physical characteristics are basically similar. A lawnmower manufacturer may offer a variety of mowers to the market, ranging from the cheapest and simplest manual type to a very sophisticated model designed for gardening professionals. A coffee-processing company may market several blends of instant coffee as well as offering coffee beans, ground coffee and coffee sachets. Different packaging may further differentiate products in this line. A company thus has a line of products rather than a single offering, because it needs to appeal to more than one segment of the market. The line may develop 'upwards' in terms of quality, price and image as the company becomes bigger and more sophisticated in production and marketing techniques; it may also move 'downwards' if financial pressures dictate that a wider, less prestigious market must be addressed.

Pricing decisions

Even for a single product, deciding on the price which is profitable and also attractive to the market is a difficult procedure. These difficulties are compounded when the complexities of a 'line' of products are considered. All normal pricing policies (see Questions 17 and 19) are equally applicable when dealing with a product line: the difference and complication occurs because in a product line the products are related to each other. This relation implies that the pricing of one product is likely to have some effect on the pricing of, and hence customer reaction to, other products in the line. This then is the essential difficulty of product-line pricing.

One of the chief objectives of product-line strategy is to 'position' the product. Positioning depends upon the perceived image of the product, which in turn is heavily influenced by price. The position of a product in a line is clearly related to competitive products, but it is also related to the position of other products in the line. If a company decides to reduce the price of one of its 'highly prestigious' products as a possible response to falling sales, the following effects may be seen:

- The price reduction may affect the perceived image of the product in question and thus harm the image of the whole product line, especially if the price/image relation is strong.
- Alternatively the consumer may now perceive the prices of all products in the line to be too high.
- The reduced price of the 'high image' product may appear to be a 'bargain', and have the effect of 'poaching' sales from lower priced products in the line.

It is not normal for a company to reduce all the prices in a product range, so the problem of repositioning a single product by reducing its price is a particularly difficult one. A similar 'knock-on' effect can cause problems if the company wishes to raise the price of a single product in a line. If there is a clearly established series of price levels in the minds of consumers, an ideal, but not always easy, solution would be to raise prices throughout the line. This would maintain the established price differentials.

Differentiation

For a variety of market reasons a company may decide to differentiate one or more of the products in a given line. Similarly a company may decide to pursue a segmentation strategy. Both strategies are intended to facilitate non-price competition, and if carried out effectively, would tend to reduce the problems of product-line pricing. For example, if a product in a line was accurately segmented, its price would have less effect on the others in the line. It would in this case be logical to think of a group of products which, while still consisting of a line, would be marketed and purchased independently of each other.

As the interdependence of products in a line decreases, the task of pricing should become easier. In reality any success at differentiating or segmenting a product is usually only a transitory phenomenon. The tendency will be for competitive action and pressure from within the firm to augment the product line, so that differences between products in the line become less and less apparent. At some stage analysis might reveal that a firm, in an attempt to serve the market better and fight off competition, has developed a 'deep' line of products, many of which are unprofitable. At this point the firm is faced with the problem of contracting the product line, and the pricing question becomes vital once more; it could be that the product the company is best known for is the least profitable!

If a company has one, two or even three products (hence a very 'shallow' line), the task of pricing would be considerably easier. In most companies the tendency is for lines to be augmented.

There is a great deal of pressure to develop new products. Only a few companies are able to develop products that create completely new lines. The majority of companies thus tend to have products that are similar to, and related to, each other. The main complication of pricing for a product line lies within this interrelationship. Any individual price increases or decreases may have an adverse effect on how that product is perceived by the consumer in relation to the other products in the line.

Apart from the pricing problems that occur when the consumer's point of view is considered, problems also arise in relation to profitability, i.e. when the company's internal needs are taken into consideration. The main dilemma is that even when products in a line are priced at points that are acceptable to the various customer groups, this does not necessarily mean that each product carries an equal profit margin. A firm can be faced with a situation where certain products are significantly less profitable than others – some could even be unprofitable. Such products may, however, be important as part of the total line in that they may be preventing competitors from entering areas which, in time, could affect sales in more profitable areas. While any loss-making or low-profit area is important, the company must be prepared to take a long view in relation to profitability of the entire 'line'. This can only be achieved by means of careful product-by-product sales analysis, which should reveal where profits are made or not made, and be related to the market importance of each product. This procedure can provide information for decisions to 'thin the line', and also serves as a basis for analysis of marketing expenditure for products and markets.

QUESTION 19

Write notes on FOUR of the following:

    (i) Price discrimination
   (ii) Mark-up pricing
  (iii) Target pricing
  (iv) Prestige pricing
   (v) Loss leaders

OBJECTIVES

To assess knowledge of selected components of pricing strategy.

APPROACH

This type of question is normally referred to as a 'compound' question, and Question 9 has already dealt with how to approach such questions. The following answer deals with all FIVE of the above topics, but in the real situation there usually is a choice (FOUR in this case).

ANSWER

(i) Price discrimination

This is a form of demand-oriented pricing used in conjunction with the techniques of market segmentation. Prices are based on the type of segment to be served rather than on a cost basis. Thus, although the prices for the same product may vary widely throughout respective segments, these variations do not occur in the cost structure. Similarly variations in marginal cost caused by variations to that product will not be reflected proportionately in the prices charged to each segment.

    The following are bases for price discrimination:

(a) *Product-version.* This base is concerned with pricing for products which are substantially the same but which are differentiated by small variations, thus creating a new *version* of the same product. There are therefore psychological connotations to this form of pricing.

A watch manufacturer may produce a standard product and sell at a certain price. The consumer may, however, be prepared to pay considerably more for the watch if it has, say, a different or unusual face, or if the strap is gold coloured or has a different form of fastener. For the manufacturer the highest proportion of cost is for the watch mechanism, but a considerably higher price may be charged for a slight alteration to the rest of the product. The small increase in costs required to achieve this is not therefore reflected proportionately in the selling price. The manufacturer may also modify the price increase for a product version in an attempt to generate an increase in sales revenue.

(b) *Customer basis.* This is the area of discrimination most likely to cause problems for the manufacturer, because it can lead to a loss of customer goodwill. A common source of disruption is the practice of charging less to customers who buy in large volumes. Goodwill may be lost despite the fact that such reductions may be an accurate reflection of reduced manufacturer distribution costs. 'List' prices may, in reality, amount to little more than the seller's 'first offer'. Manufacturers frequently charge less to the customer who is prepared to enquire more closely into the possibility of reductions. Customer knowledge, or expertise, thus becomes a basis for discrimination. This has expanded into the field now commonly known as 'trade marketing'.

Price reductions may also be available to readily identifiable customer groups, such as pensioners, students or members of clubs and organizations.

(c) *Time.* List prices are frequently modified to suit the level of demand at a given time. This may be on a seasonal basis, or over much shorter time spans – daily or even hourly. Such discrimination is another potential source of discontent, as prices paid may merely reflect the 'luck' of placing an order or making a purchase at a particular time. The travel trade with its 'last minute bargains' is a good example here, as well as post-Christmas store 'sales'.

(d) *Place.* The most obvious example of this base is geographic. Demand for a product may vary considerably in different regions of a country, and also in international markets, where different countries may place different values on certain products. Airlines and theatres are good examples of price discrimination in relation to the prices charged for seats. Although it is true that extra services are available in the 'better class' areas of the aeroplane or theatre, the marginal cost of providing the extra service is much the same for all passengers or theatre-goers.

The requirements for successful price discrimination are similar to those required for a successful segmentation policy. The target groups must be clearly identifiable, measurable and profitable. Care must, however, be taken to ensure that price discrimination, although profitable in the short term, does not lead to long-term protest, resentment and loss of goodwill.

(ii) Mark-up pricing

This is the simplest form of cost-plus pricing. It is most commonly practised in the retailing sector, where a predetermined mark-up to the cost of the product offered for sale is applied. It is also used in situations where it is difficult to cost in advance, e.g. large construction projects.

The reason for the popularity of this method among retailers is that costs can be calculated easily (cost is equal to the amount paid to the supplier). All that is then required is to add a mark-up sufficient to cover overhead costs and profits. The percentage of mark-up can be an expression of either cost or selling price. It is more usual for retailers to calculate mark-up as a percentage of selling price. The formula for this calculation is as follows:

$$(100\% + \text{required } \% \text{ mark-up}) \times \text{Cost} = \text{Selling price}$$

What is important to remember is that mark-up on cost price does not represent the same amount as the profit on selling price (known as the margin) which is always less than the cost-price mark-up.

Manufacturers sometimes use this technique. In their case the cost price is the sum of material, labour and overhead costs, to which they can add a fixed percentage mark-up.

A feature of mark-up pricing is that the usually accepted mark-up can vary considerably between different groups of goods. The reasons for this are not always adequately explained and may in some cases be based on tradition. As a general rule the faster the turnover of the product, the lower the mark-up will tend to be, because of the obvious relation between the rate of turnover and the cost of holding stocks. Some mark-ups may also be the result of random decisions, experimentation within the store or sensitivity to local conditions.

Although mark-up pricing is most popular in retailing, it is not uncommon in manufacturing, mainly because it is much easier to estimate cost than demand. In addition, there is no need to make constant (demand-related) adjustments to price. If such an approach to pricing is generally adopted, it is often thought to be a fair method for both competitors and customers alike. The risk of price wars is lessened, and violent fluctuations in price due to changes in demand are less likely to take place.

There is, however, some criticism of mark-up pricing, chiefly because, among all the methods of pricing, it is the least imaginative, and tends not to lead to profit maximization. A more realistic approach would be to relate the mark-up to sales turnover. Thus, a product with a high turnover would have a low percentage mark-up and vice versa. By adopting this more flexible approach, the firm is at least paying some attention to the demand for its products.

(iii) Target pricing

This is a cost-based approach to pricing which, while using total costs as the determinant of price-setting, also considers output or volume. Price is decided by the company establishing a given rate of return or 'target profit', and then calculating the output necessary to achieve this.

The determination of target price requires the company to analyse its break-even point. This is the point where a certain number of units produced at a given selling price generate exactly the revenue to equal the fixed costs plus the additional cost of producing each individual unit – the variable cost. Fixed costs must be paid, whatever the level of output. The variable cost will rise in a linear fashion as a function of the number of units produced.

Figure 10 assumes that the variable cost for the production of each unit is £10. The company requires to make £100,000 target profit. At a price of £20 per unit, the company must manufacture 10,000 units to break even thus:

$$
\begin{array}{lll}
& 20,000 \times £20 & = \quad £400,000 \\
\text{Less} & 20,000 \times £10 & = \quad £200,000 \text{ (variable cost)} \\
\text{Less} & \text{Fixed cost} & = \quad £100,000 \\
& \text{Profit} & = \quad £100,000
\end{array}
$$

The system is limited because it makes no analysis of actual demand. A more realistic approach to target pricing would be for the company (through marketing research) to assess the level of demand at various price levels, and then choose the level of price and output most appropriate to its targets. This is a modified form of break-even analysis, which is useful in that it allows the

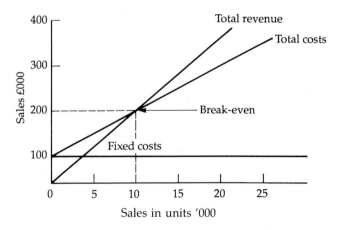

Figure 10   *Determination of target price*

marketer to evaluate what the profit consequences are over a range of price alternatives.

The degree of sophistication that a company applies to this type of analysis will be influential in the rate of success. In practice many firms use this method, but there are inherent weaknesses. Firstly, no allowance for price elasticity of demand is made and, secondly, it assumes that costs are static. Every marketer knows that in the real business situation all elements of the market can be extremely volatile. Target pricing using break-even analysis is, however, a useful tool, especially in the short run and when used with an analysis of demand.

(iv) Prestige pricing

Some products appear to defy the 'laws' of economics because more are bought at a higher than at a lower price level. Although this may seem an anomaly, it is not difficult to think of products and services whose perceived value is much higher than the true economic value. Prestige value translates therefore into a form of psychological pricing, which relies upon the consumer believing that price is an indication of quality, a quality indeed that can be related to the consumer's lifestyle.

'Designer' clothes are an example of this method of pricing. Prices far above those for similar products are achieved because of the existence of a 'label' to which the consumer attaches particular importance. The influences on the consumer which permit prestige pricing are brought to light by a study of consumer behaviour. The marketing tools used to satisfy the particular consumer needs here are advertising and promotion, choice of distributor and use of the price itself.

Prestige products are very often an expression of the consumer's 'self-concept'. The example of designer clothes is applicable here, as the consumer sees himself or herself as being highly fashionable, prepared, and able, to pay higher prices.

Advertising for such products must relate to the self-image, and the correct media must be chosen for promotion. An expensive perfume would risk having its image destroyed if it were to be advertised in the tabloid newspapers. Similarly such products would be unlikely to appear in supermarkets; rather, they would be found in an 'exclusive' retail establishment. Price itself is then a reinforcement of the image. A price reduction would only serve to reduce the perceived value of the product.

The highly priced prestige product must therefore possess an image of exclusiveness, sophistication and high quality. Changes in fashion often kill off such products, but frequently the companies who market these products can tarnish their prestige by their own actions. As soon as the number of distributors is increased, exclusivity and prestige are likely to be diminished. Furthermore, if a company launches a similar but cheaper version of the prestige product, it is likely that the image of the original will be adversely affected. In such a case, the two products would have to be very widely differentiated to prevent such an outcome.

(v) Loss leaders

These products are sold at an artificially low price, as their name implies. The purpose behind this action is to create an interest in a product line or a retail outlet.

The practice of loss-leader pricing should not be confused with pricing strategies that concern promotion at launch or penetration pricing. Loss-leader pricing is favoured by large retail outlets, because of the large number of brands and products they carry on their shelves. The practice has increased as the role of large supermarkets has gained importance in shopping patterns.

A small number of products are chosen and sold at a loss with the sole aim of encouraging shoppers into the store, where they will probably purchase other, more profitable, items as well. The chosen products for loss leaders are usually staple items like butter or sugar or well-known brands sold at low prices for a limited period.

Loss leader pricing highlights the interdependence of products in their contribution to total income. This has become more important in recent years, with the growing emphasis on 'one stop' shopping which large retailers are keen to promote.

One possible drawback to this aspect of pricing is that the consumer may come to accept a loss-leader price as normal and any attempt to move the price up could then be construed as profiteering. Manufacturers of branded goods must also take care that the use of their products as loss leaders does not affect the image of other products in their line, either in terms of price perceived as fair, or in terms of the psychological perception held by the consumer.

Question 20

For many companies the advertising budget is a notorious source of disagreement. What methods are commonly employed for the setting of advertising budgets? How can management judge the effectiveness of this expenditure?

OBJECTIVES

To ensure that the student is thoroughly aware of the complicated nature of advertising expenditure and that such expenditure is not simply a matter of 'cause and effect'.

APPROACH

The first sentence of this question is a 'statement', which is included in order to provide a basis for discussion. The two following questions can be answered in a straightforward manner – taking care that each is answered thoroughly.

The highest marks would be awarded to those students who augmented their answers with a 'summing-up' that responded to the initial statement in the question. This could form the concluding few paragraphs of your answer.

ANSWER

Suggested introduction

Advertising expenditure in the UK approaches £4000 million per annum, not including expenditure on 'below the line' media such as direct mail, sales literature and various forms of sales promotion. Total advertising expenditure is probably equal to 2 per cent of consumer spending. It is clear that spending money on advertising is not a subject that can be treated lightly. Such vast sums can be partially explained by an increasing use of television as an advertising medium, and the fact that, as the marketing concept has become more widely adopted, the realization of advertising's importance as a form of communication has increased.

Every company must organize its affairs around some form of budgeting – just as a household must balance income against expenditure. The large quantities of money spent on advertising mean that it must feature strongly in the budget. The problem of budgeting for advertising is that expenditure appears intangible – not like, say, buying a machine. Furthermore, it is often difficult to say whether or not the money has been well spent.

Although advertising can have many goals, ultimately the company will expect advertising campaigns to increase sales and correspondingly increase profits. Basically therefore advertising expenditure is worthwhile while each pound spent contributes to extra profit. Beyond this point the company will experience diminishing returns. The difficulty is in assessing precisely where this point occurs. This is a simplistic view of advertising, because very often short-term goals take precedence over long-term profit motives. Whatever the advertising objectives, how much to spend is a decision at which it is difficult to arrive. Several methods are commonly employed:

The 'affordable' approach

This is a method commonly employed by smaller companies, which only devote to advertising what they can afford after all other expenses and investments have been met. This may be a sound policy for companies with limited resources – at least it usually implies that the advertising money is not being wasted – but to be at all effective expenditure should be strictly linked to a set of objectives. If the desired objectives can be achieved by means of the resources available, then it is difficult to criticize this method. It could be, however, that opportunities are being missed, especially if it can be demonstrated that additional expenditure can generate further profits.

Percentage of sales method

This is one of the most popular means of arriving at an advertising budget, because it is simple. The amount spent on advertising is calculated as a fixed percentage of the previous year's sales.

Although this appears logical, the method does not have a sound basis, because the rationale assumes that advertising is a result of sales rather than the cause. Moreover, sales may reach a level where the fixed proportion given over to advertising is in fact showing diminishing returns, so that some of the 'fixed percentage' could in fact be better employed elsewhere. The percentage of sales method does not consider changes in the fortunes of the company or changes in the market place. If sales decline, perhaps extra advertising should be considered. Similarly expenditure additional to the fixed amount may be required to launch a new product in order to counter competitive action.

It is considerably more logical to fix the advertising budget at the level of 'anticipated' sales, because this recognizes that advertising precedes sales rather than being a result of sales. A compromise could be to use a figure which combines past and anticipated sales. This would help to ensure that expenditure was affordable (using the previous year's revenue) and would also build in flexibility to take account of market opportunities.

Competitive parity

Quite simply this method bases the advertising budget on the amount spent by the firm's competitors. Such information is relatively easily available, either by observation and estimation or by using agency data such as M.E.A.L. which is available on subscription.

Competitive parity budgeting does ensure that the firm is considering itself to be as important as its competitors, but the method has at least two major flaws. First, it assumes that the firm's objectives are the same as those of competitors and, secondly, it assumes that competitors are advertising effectively, which is of course not necessarily the case.

The method is not therefore recommended. But it should be noted that when considering the advertising budget, competitive spending should at least be one of the factors which feature in the decision-making process.

Objective (or task) method

The setting of objectives is the only real way of advertising efficiently. Not only do objectives lead logically to methods of evaluating their success, but the objectives themselves provide a guide and goal the company can work towards over a period of time.

Setting objectives also allows the company to prepare a budget specifically related to the task in hand. Typical objectives for advertising campaigns are to persuade, when faced with strong competition, for example; to inform and make aware, in the case of new products; or to reinforce preferences, when the product has reached maturity.

A company thus decides upon a specific objective, which it requires advertising to achieve, and then works out how much expenditure will be required. Of course not every company can afford this 'ideal' amount of money. In many cases the objective must be modified accordingly, and this is the reality in all forms of budgeting. The 'objective' method is particularly valuable, however, because it treats each situation as a new project that can be planned from the beginning. In practice there are usually past and future sales considerations that must be built into the objective expenditure model.

The use of sales forecasts is another method that companies can employ to arrive at a budget for advertising. Of course success for this method is entirely dependent on the proficiency of the sales-forecasting methods being used. If these are satisfactory, there is considerable validity in basing expenditure on the sales outlook rather than on past sales. The final figure is based on a combination of anticipated sales and the required earnings per product. A percentage of the sales estimate is then devoted to advertising. (This should not be confused with the percentage of sales method.) If sales are doing well, with advertising at, say, 5 per cent of the forecast figure, the company can experiment, as there is justification for increasing this percentage to ascertain whether or not sales can be correspondingly increased.

Some companies use mathematical models to arrive at advertising budgets. In one such model, the 'response and decay' technique, the company must find out the rate at which an advertisement loses its power to increase sales, and then modify the budget accordingly. In the case of new products advertising can be considered as a process which takes consumers through a series of awareness levels, e.g. awareness, interest and action. 'Communication stage' models aim to assess where consumers are in this process: advertising input is varied to pull consumers through the stages so as to arrive at the buying decisions. It must be said that such methods are a little abstract, and demand constant marketing information, which must be processed and analysed by experts. They are expensive therefore and difficult to adopt in practice.

Advertising evaluation

The chief executive of a company is quoted as saying: 'I know that half of my advertising budget is wasted. The problem is that I do not know which half!' This statement aptly illustrates the dilemma facing advertising decision-makers. Nevertheless companies must take steps to assess whether or not advertising money is being spent effectively.

The key to the whole process lies in making clear statements as to what is expected of advertising in the first place. If the aim is to increase sales, companies must ask 'By how much?', 'In which region?', 'Over what time-scale?' If the aim is to reinforce brand-loyalty, then the company must have an accurate picture of the repeat-buying situation before and after the campaign has taken place. This tends to preclude the 'percentage of sales' and 'affordable' methods of arriving at advertising budgets – unless of course the latter method specifies objectives rather than allotting a lump sum of left-over budget to advertising.

Unfortunately there is no easy way to assess the effectiveness of advertising expenditure; it depends on detailed information from within the company with reference to sales and a great deal of advertising research. (Of course advertising research also includes study of the advertisement itself. It goes without saying that the company needs to try and ensure that the copy, message and chosen medium are effective *before* these can be combined as a tool to achieve a given objective.)

The simplest preliminary gauge of effectiveness is to record how many enquiries and/or sales are generated from a campaign, and to use the figures as a starting point. Research must then take over to find out the level of recall, consumer opinion, levels of belief and disbelief and attitude changes.

Consumer panels and group interviews are popular methods of asking consumers questions about advertisements and the effect they have upon behaviour. Many research agencies specialize in carrying out recognition tests and audience measurement through television and radio media. The appropriate tests are always a function of the original intention or objective for launching a campaign. Many companies have memorably entertaining and creative television advertisements which do little to affect sales or to change attitudes.

There is much confusion and divided opinion about the best way to measure advertising effectiveness. It is certain, however, that it is a complicated and expensive procedure. A formal budget and clearly defined objectives are the essential and logical precursors to evaluation. It is also important to recognize that advertising objectives can vary according to product type and market conditions, and according to where the product is along the life cycle curve. Thus, with a new product the objective will be to build up interest and awareness. Evaluations should focus on recall, opinion and belief, linked to actual and forecasted sales. In the case of a mature product the purpose of any advertising campaign may be to fight a competitive battle by reinforcing brand-loyalty or increasing market share. Here evaluation should centre on attitudinal studies and brand-switching techniques.

Advertising evaluation should also be considered in the strategic sense. When evaluating the effectiveness of a particular campaign, the company should also attempt to isolate advertising as an influence within the marketing mix. The company should always be prepared to consider an alternative form of communication with its target audience if advertising is not achieving the desired objectives.

The advertising budget is indeed a notorious source of disagreement, and the situation is aggravated because, unlike investment in tangible items, the results of advertising are difficult to quantify. When a company prepares its corporate budget, advertising is but one of many elements of company expenditure and any propositions for advertising must be presented in a professional manner. This means that the budget proposal must show what advertising is expected to achieve, and clearly explain what steps will be taken to assess whether or not the advertising has been effective. The methods used for assessing effectiveness can also be a source of confusion, but the task is considerably aided when pre-set objectives have been made.

Whatever the specific methods used, the key to success is to regard advertising as an investment like any other investment. Then the company will tend to apply the same criteria to the advertising investment decision as would occur for, say, new machinery or extra personnel. This in turn will make objective setting and subsequent evaluation a natural part of the advertising process.

FURTHER READING

The Marketing Research Process, by Margaret Crimp (Prentice-Hall, 1981), gives good advice upon the area of advertising research, and *Spending Advertising Money*, by Simon Broadbent, is a good specialist text that covers the area of advertising budgets in a detailed professional manner.

QUESTION 21

Comment upon the contribution of the sales force to the marketing effort of the firm. Illustrate your answer with appropriate product examples.

OBJECTIVE

To assess knowledge of the wider remit which marketing management ascribes to the salesperson's role as compared with 'supply' selling.

APPROACH

It is suggested that this answer should consist of three stages:

1 A description of those elements of sales activity which overlap with, and make a contribution to, the total marketing effort of the firm. This is likely to be the largest section.
2 An appreciation of these activities, showing how the sales functions integrate with marketing.
3 This should be a concluding section, which puts the sales function into perspective. Although the importance of the marketing aspects of the salesperson's role has been fully recognized, you should mention the basic requirement which should not be lost from sight – that of making sales.

Remember to keep your answer strictly relevant; there is no requirement here to include discussion upon sales management or sales technique. Remember, too, that your answer will be improved if you can illustrate it with product examples, as the question requests.

ANSWER

Suggested introduction
Whatever the job brief of a company's sales force on the part of its individual sales personnel, it is an inescapable fact that sales activity constitutes part of the total marketing effort. Even if a company continues to adopt a traditional 'selling' approach to its markets, the salesperson is essentially a 'representative' of the firm, and thus embodies all that it stands for. This may be an unconscious act, in the sense that it has not been incorporated into the

company's strategy. Nevertheless, the sales force, in addition to promoting and selling products, is also promoting the company by its behaviour and attitudes towards customers.

This is the basic link between marketing and sales in that sales personnel convey something about the company to customers in an effort to gain long-term repeat business. Few companies, whatever their basic orientation, can hope to survive for long on 'one off' business. Companies which have established a marketing orientation also expect that sales personnel should carry out further tasks as well as promoting their company. As they are in constant touch with their customers, they are ideally placed to contribute to the 'total' marketing effort of the firm.

Tasks other than selling

A key task of the sales force is one of information-gathering, which links up directly with the firm's Intelligence and Marketing Information System. Sometimes a salesperson will face criticism about the company from buyers which marketing management would not necessarily learn about from other sources. Such criticism could relate to delivery or quality defects in comparison with competitive offerings. Competitive activity itself is a subject about which sales staff can provide information, but care should be taken to recognize when buyers 'feed' misleading information to sales personnel in order to obtain some advantage from them. The sales interview should always include some time for general discussion, related to market trends and developments. The experienced salesperson can usually judge how accurate information resulting from such discussion is by comparing a series of interviews. Ideally, sales staff should have a good working knowledge of marketing research techniques, and a thorough understanding of the need for, and uses of, the whole Marketing Information System. This will make them aware of why information is requested of them, and make them feel that carrying out this task is an important and worthwhile function.

When visits are made to retail outlets, a further sales function is that of 'merchandising'. Sales staff should therefore ensure that their products are displayed to the best advantage, and that adequate stocks are being held. The merchandising role is obviously most applicable to consumer markets and their corresponding retail outlets.

Although merchandising itself is commonly associated with fast-moving consumer goods, and has developed considerably with the growth of supermarket retailing, it has an important place in most retail situations. Supermarket merchandising will tend to concentrate upon 'product prominence' – shelf space and point of sale display. In furniture stores or clothes retailers, the emphasis is likely to be on design and presentation. Sales staff have specialist knowledge of their own markets and this can be complemented by knowledge of merchandising techniques. Most stores have their own layout designers, but it is important that sales personnel are sufficiently knowledgeable to be able to give advice and comment about product display or how promotions should be organized. Carpet manufacturers, for example, frequently supply stores with their own displays; this not only sets off their products to the best advantage, but it is also a useful sales tool to the retailer, because an attractive display enhances the store itself.

In sales 'representative' the word 'representative' is a precise term. He or she 'represents' the company as an ambassador would in national or diplomatic circles. For this reason sales staff must fulfil an important public relations role. Primarily the salesperson deals with the company's customers, and it is here that he or she should convey all that goes to make up the company's total image. A salesperson who is habitually late or untidy will form a poor impression in the customer's mind – not only of that individual salesperson but also of the whole company, because for many buyers the sales representative is the only link in the customer/supplier relationship.

The salesperson's role is, however, more for 'reaching' than for customer liaison alone. He or she, in a professional capacity, is always in the public eye and should be expected to protect and promote the company image among all people that are contacted – suppliers, customers of customers and competitors, etc. Sales personnel also meet a wide variety of people at exhibitions, training courses and business-related social functions. In such situations they are ideally placed to support the marketing effort of the organization they represent.

Sales staff can also contribute to the marketing effort by participating in planning. They are the people who have first-hand knowledge of markets and customers, and can give advice and opinions on such matters as pricing, credit, discounts and advertising. They can also provide feedback after marketing plans have been implemented. In particular, sales staff can assist in sales forecasting by providing both subjective and objective estimates of sales trends. Forecasting is a specialist procedure and salespersons should have training in its practice; this should include statistical analysis and be linked closely to the requirement of sales staff to contribute to the Marketing Information System.

Many companies provide their sales force with 'leads', or have other customer bases which are so well established that there appears little need for prospecting. But prospecting for new business should be an essential part of all sales activity, because as well as finding new customers, prospecting is also another method of exploring the market.

Finally, the sales force should make a positive contribution to new-product development and should be encouraged to do so in a formal manner. The sales force can generate new ideas by referring to customer complaints, which may show room for improvement, or by informing management of how well competitive products are being received.

Sales and marketing

The extended job description of the sales force that has just been given illustrates the importance of sales personnel, not simply in the functional role of selling but as an integrated component of the total marketing effort. As marketing becomes more accepted and adopted as a way of management, so the role of sales has naturally become more marketing-orientated. While the ability to 'make sales' remains of paramount importance, this is only one of many other demands made on the sales force. In the past there has been a tendency for management to regard sales personnel as 'loners' who work more or less independently from their colleagues in the company, and recruitment has often been based on this idea. Marketing management calls for the sales force to work as a team with the other functions of marketing, principally by providing information and feedback, and, secondly, as active contributors to marketing planning. The implication of this development is that sales personnel should have some formal training in the philosophy of marketing management and in marketing techniques – either as part of an in-house training programme or by recruiting marketing-trained personnel.

Conclusion

The integrated marketing/sales function makes many demands on the sales-person. It is not expected, however, that sales people should be specialists in the various additional roles that have been discussed; the basic requirement is that they should appreciate and understand the need for their extended job brief. This should be combined with a level of competence which reflects the nature of the product, the company and its markets.

How a company manages its sales force with marketing in mind is a matter for considerable thought and care. The first step should be to ensure that the sales force thoroughly understands why certain duties should be performed in addition to selling. Secondly, sales and marketing management should provide feedback to the sales force, showing how their contribution to the marketing effort is being used. Nothing is more likely to demoralize the efforts of sales personnel than their reports and suggestions appearing to be ignored. The third important measure is to be sure that work given to, and demands made of, the sales force are absolutely necessary. Time is precious, and unnecessary work is not only wasteful but counter-productive in the sense that the quality of all work undertaken will suffer if sales personnel are burdened with 'red tape'.

The sales/marketing liaison must therefore be planned and managed so as to optimize the efforts of everyone concerned. Sometimes an unthinking marketing department will impose too much extra work on the sales force to the exclusion of the principal task of selling. Professional sales personnel will always see their role as being one primarily of selling, and they are of course correct. While the need for additional duties must be recognized, these must be carried out in conjunction with the selling function. Any system that detracts from this will fail in its aim to integrate sales and marketing, and will also act to the detriment of the selling task itself.

QUESTION 22

Discuss the role of Public Relations with respect to the firm's marketing activities.

OBJECTIVE

Public Relations is an area of business activity that is not always included in marketing texts, since it does not fit conveniently alongside discussion of the classical marketing functions. Public relations is in reality a business function in its own right, and this explains its omission. Unlike, say, personnel management, public relations is concerned about the image of the firm as a whole, and this includes functions other than marketing. The question thus asks the student to recognize this relationship by displaying knowledge of the role of public relations in a wider context than marketing.

APPROACH

Your introduction should display to the examiner that you have a clear idea of where and how public relations (PR) fits into the totality of the firm's business activities, and how this is relevant to marketing.

From an answer-planning viewpoint it would probably be easiest to deal with the main issues of PR, step by step, and relate these to marketing in one go rather than splitting the answer into two distinct parts. Whatever your approach, it is important that your answer is not merely a discussion of PR *per se*. The essence of the answer should be to show how marketing and PR are related.

ANSWER

Suggested introduction
PR is a field of business activity that is often misunderstood, and hence misquoted. Most frequently and erroneously PR is classified alongside advertising and promotion. This error is further compounded by American tendencies to label PR loosely as 'publicity'. In reality PR is a distinct business function which complements advertising in particular and marketing in general. A second misconception, again linked to confusion with publicity, is that PR is a form of promotion whose task is to promote good news – or a

method of covering up or 'reprocessing' information that is likely to have an adverse effect on the company's image. While there is an element of promotion in PR, and while companies are not likely to seek out harmful information to communicate to the outside world, the real role of PR is to establish 'understanding' between a company and those bodies that have a potential or actual interest in it. The errors referred to have evidently arisen from the fact that, while many firms use 'publicity' as part of their marketing activity, they do not always have a Public Relations Department as such.

The firm's marketing environment

A study of the firm's marketing environment (see Question 2 for a discussion on marketing environment) will reveal that its responsibilities and its range of interested parties extend far beyond the immediate customer and supplier. Past and future customers must be considered, because they represent potential users, and because they can influence the attitudes to the company held by existing users. There is, moreover, a wide range of 'publics' whose attitudes and actions can have a direct effect upon the firm. These publics include the financial community (bankers and stockbrokers), shareholders, the media, the government and local authorities. Marketing activity cannot therefore be successful if the 'publics' are not kept informed about the firm's activities in a way that displays a sense of responsibility to its wider environment. PR's task is therefore to build up trust and understanding by honest communication, so that marketing strategies can be implemented in an atmosphere of goodwill towards the firm. It is important to recognize that it is still possible to generate goodwill (or at least a non-hostile attitude), even though the company may have unpleasant announcements to make to its publics. The trauma of lay-offs and redundancies can, for example, be alleviated if the company communicates its position honestly and effectively through its PR media, especially if it has a clear policy – in this case, of how its employees will be treated, compensated or retrained.

The first role of PR is therefore to provide corporate and long-term backing to the company, whose business activities are otherwise expressed to the informed public through its marketing functions. Typical areas where PR might provide such 'background' support to marketing might include announcements of an intention to expand, or news of actions taken to reduce pollution. A firm may wish to sponsor certain charities or simply wish to keep its publics informed of its general activities. Such communications can be made in various ways – through press releases, public meetings, company publications or open days.

Other areas of PR

PR also has an important role to play with respect to direct support to the firm's marketing activities. One task is to keep its publics informed about new-product development – an area of direct relevance to marketing. The role of advertising and promotion in this context is to appeal directly to potential customers – the first step being to create awareness. PR can support this activity by communicating through the press, TV or radio, the fact that something new exists, thereby fulfilling a corporate function as well as aiding the product launch in a tactical sense. In the industrial marketing context PR would fulfil this role more specifically through the medium of trade journals and could pass the information to interested parties through newsletters or press conferences.

PR can also 'prepare the ground' for marketing activity by explaining policy changes, such as an updating in distribution strategy or by new methods in raw material usage. Recently a large supermarket chain announced its intention to list all additives that were to be found in the products that it sold. Such a move was obviously aimed at a new group of concerned and health-conscious consumers. The announcement, with its wide implications, was issued by PR media rather than by advertising coverage, because it was aimed not only at potential consumers but also at the wider publics, in an attempt to show that a responsible and caring attitude had been engendered in the company as a whole.

If, as sometimes happens, a company makes an error of judgement or a straightforward mistake that leads to an unfavourable or hostile reaction from its publics, then PR is the only real method of offering an explanation or an apology. A single PR announcement can often be more effective than months of individual corrective action on behalf of the sales force.

PR in context

The primary role of the marketing function is one of promoting, distributing, selling and improving the company's products and services. The role of PR can be put into context if it is considered as one of promoting reputation, goodwill and image for the company as a whole. While the success or failure of PR strategy will of course depend on how well the marketing functions are carried out, marketing and PR are essentially complementary and working together should produce a 'synergistic' effect on the total company operation. The opportunities for synergy within the company are heightened because the respective roles of marketing and PR are approached in the same way – defining objectives and assessing results and the efficacy of those methods used to achieve them. Marketing strategy – say for a new product – and a PR campaign for any goal can be compared as follows:

PR	Marketing
1 Appreciation of the situation	1 Exploratory research
2 Definition of objectives	2 Definition of objectives
3 Definition of publics	3 Selection of target markets

PR	*Marketing*
4 Media selection	4 Media selection
5 Budget	5 Budget
6 Assessment of results	6 Assessment of results

Whether or not both PR and marketing programmes are aimed at the same objectives – in this case a new product launch – or at different objectives is not really important; the significance is that PR and marketing personnel understand each other's roles, and both employ similar methods to carry these out. It may well be that in some companies publicity is effected by the PR department for marketing (where that is considered most economical) but this in no way makes PR subordinate to marketing. Indeed the Public Relations Officer (PRO) will act as the 'voice' of the company and will report in this sensitive role not to marketing but to top management at board level.

Conclusion

Marketing and PR must therefore work closely together to achieve the corporate aims of the company. PR has the potential to aid marketing at a tactical level, but one cannot be substituted for the other. For example, the marketing function of advertising is essentially concerned with persuasion (although we recognize other purposes for advertising), whereas PR is concerned with communicating understanding and establishing credibility among a wider audience, but among an audience that includes that of the advertising target group. The goodwill and positive image that PR can achieve should create a receptive environment for the marketing functions to work in. Although advertising has been used as a specific example in this conclusion, the same marketing/PR relationship can be extended to all areas of marketing at both the strategic and the immediately functional levels. The essential difference is located in the fact that marketing announcements are avowedly self-interested, while PR announcements must have at least the appearance of objectivity, for without this they would not be likely to gain the necessary credibility!

FURTHER READING

Any specialist PR text, of which the major publishers almost inevitably have one in their marketing series, e.g. *All about PR*, by Roger Haywood (McGraw-Hill, 1986), or *The Practice of Public Relations*, edited by W. Howard (Heinemann, 1988).

QUESTION 23

Explain what you understand by the term 'sales promotion' and then discuss the sales objectives that can be achieved by using these techniques. Illustrate your answer, where appropriate, by the use of examples

OBJECTIVES

To ensure that the candidate understands the precise meaning of 'sales promotion' as opposed to that of 'advertising', as this can be an area of confusion. The student should also be able to show that sales promotion, like advertising, should be carried out in a carefully controlled manner, i.e. by setting specific objectives and evaluating the results of promotional action.

APPROACH

The 'explanation' of sales promotion itself should be clear and straight to the point and need not require a lengthy discussion. This will reveal to the examiner that you know exactly what you are talking about. You should then spend a little more time in explanation of the techniques of sales promotion used by marketing management. This will prepare the way for discussion of sales promotion related to objectives.

If the question is read carefully, it does in fact suggest how the answer should be structured. The following guideline is suggested:

1 Introduction – explaining the meaning of the term 'sales promotion'.
2 Description of sales-promotion techniques.
3 Discussion of the aims of sales promotion.
4 A brief appraisal of sales promotion as a conclusion.

There is a tendency for students to associate sales promotion exclusively with consumer markets, so you should not neglect to include some discussion of industrial sales promotion. Do not forget to attempt to illustrate your answer with real or hypothetical examples. One does not have to be a marketing practitioner to be able to do this, because one can witness everyday examples in supermarkets, newspaper and television advertisements, etc.

ANSWER

Suggested introduction

Sales promotion forms part of the total 'communication' mix or strategy of a company. Its role lies alongside that of advertising and public relations. Advertising agencies often have specialist sales-promotion departments, but their work, while being in harmony with advertising, can be clearly distinguished from the specific tasks that advertising itself entails. The principal distinction is due to the fact that, unlike advertising, sales-promotion campaigns are usually short-term projects. Their objectives are often those of stimulating sales during 'off-peak' periods, launching new products, or responding to competitive actions. This is not to say that sales promotion does not have strategic importance. In the first place it forms part of the strategic nature of the communications mix. Secondly, certain elements of sales promotion, such as trade fairs, exhibitions or those campaigns designed to build up brand-loyalty, have long-term effects.

Advertising agencies distinguish sales promotion from advertising by referring to 'above' and 'below the line'. 'Above the line' concerns advertising, for which the agency is paid a commission by the chosen medium. 'Below the line' concerns sales promotion, for the design of which the agent receives payment from the client without going through a third party.

Techniques

The techniques employed in sales promotion are numerous. Many are unimaginative and lack marketing orientation, in that they are linked to the 'selling' style of management rather than being integrated as a part of the marketing mix. Sales promotion is in fact an aspect of marketing that has contributed to a lack of understanding about the real goals of the marketing concept and its functions. This has led to criticisms of marketing among certain media commentators, who have confused sales-promotional 'gimmicks' and associated them with professional marketing activity. Sales-promotional techniques should have clear-cut objectives. They should be capable of being evaluated, and they should form an integral part of the marketing plan: although some sales promotions have short-term objectives, in a marketing-oriented company these should contribute to the long-term satisfaction of the customer.

In consumer markets popular sales promotional techniques include the use of the following:

(a) Free samples
(b) 'Money off' packs
(c) Two for the price of one
(d) X% more 'free'

(e) 'On pack' coupons redeemable against the next purchase

Many companies also offer free gifts on presentation of a certain number of packet tops or labels. Many such gifts are quite substantial and worthwhile. The first free gift in the United Kingdom was offered by a detergent manufacturer during the 1960s. The fact that the gift was a plastic daffodil illustrates how sophisticated sales promotion has become during the intervening period, although it is also fair to comment that society as a whole is considerably more discriminating about consumer goods in the 1980s than it was in the 1960s.

'Competitions' and 'prize draws' feature prominently in sales promotions. Like coupons, these are often attached to the product itself or are available in magazines, newspapers, or featured in advertisements. The brewing industry is particularly aggressive in its use of competitions and prize draws. The means to enter are conveniently situated around public houses, often on drip mats, and are distributed through a sophisticated network of sales personnel and merchandisers.

Sales promotion also relies heavily on point-of-sale (POS) promotion to bring the product directly to the consumer's attention. There is a limit to the amount of cards, boards and displays that a retailer can tolerate in one outlet. Some may even detract from the store ambience and thus be rejected by the retailer. On the other hand, certain displays can considerably enhance the store. Brintons, the carpet manufacturer, provides an appropriate example of this. As supermarkets/hypermarkets grow in size, it is also increasingly common to see products promoted 'in store' by professional merchandisers who are hired to give demonstrations or encourage customers to try or taste samples. Supermarket managers will, however, strictly control the number of such promotions, as too many of them being conducted at one time may distract or annoy shoppers.

As well as promoting sales directly to consumers, most manufacturers also promote to the 'trade', i.e. to the retailers themselves and to the intermediaries who make up the distribution network. Trade sales promotions should not be confused with straight discounts or special trading terms, as these are pricing and not promotional arrangements. Trade sales promotions should be aimed at specific products or product groups. A free case of goods with every order over a certain amount for a limited period is a typical trade promotion. Manufacturers may offer cash reductions in return for display prominence, visible sales or advertising effort by the wholesaler or retailer on the manufacturer's behalf. Promotional offers should normally be made in return for such extra action taken by the recipient rather than for straightforward increases in turnover, which are usually achieved by means of price incentives. A manufacturer can also direct sales-promotional attention towards the sales force of a company by offering personal incentives in return for an increase in sales.

In industrial markets promotional tools such as 'coupons' or ' "x" per cent free' are inappropriate. Sales promotion in industrial markets is, however, perfectly feasible by other means. Inducements to buy certain products during certain periods of the year are frequently offered. As for consumer markets, promotion can be aimed at the sales force of industrial customers by offering rewards for exceptional sales. Any promotion which is not aimed at the buyer in his/her professional capacity, but which is aimed personally at a group of employees should be thoroughly discussed and sanctioned by the senior management of the customer and seller before it is undertaken.

There is a 'grey' area which encircles the giving of gifts – for example, at Christmas time – in terms of business ethics. It is for individual companies to judge what is appropriate to their situations, but it is certainly a valid aspect of sales promotion to distribute diaries, calendars and desk-top articles to promote the donor company. These should always be of good quality and reflect the company image. It is better to give nothing than to distribute poor quality merchandise bearing the company's name.

Trade shows and exhibitions also provide an opportunity for sales promotion, especially in industrial markets. They are a platform for new-product launches, as well as providing, once or twice a year, a more relaxing, possibly more informal environment, than that of the buyer's office. Some firms may invite customers to 'open days' or organize a social event for their customers so as to promote a new-product or company development. Such activity, although aimed specifically at customers, may also encompass members of the press, and thus form part of a PR campaign as well as sales promotion. In the strategic sense PR activity is itself a form of sales promotion.

Aims of sales promotion

As has already been mentioned, sales-promotion activity tends to be (though by no means exclusively) short-term in nature. A fundamental objective should be that any promotional action should be part of the marketing plan. Even if a particular sales promotion is specific, short-term and thus tactical in nature, it should harmonize with the company image and should be a component part of a broader company objective. Any sales promotion which is launched to resolve a crisis is likely to be ill considered, and although crises do occur from time to time, the crisis itself may be an indication of poor management methods.

In terms of specific objectives sales promotion is of particular help to, and most often associated with, new-product launches. In conjunction with advertising the task of sales promotion here will be to encourage trial in non-users by taking the consumer through the stages of awareness, interest, desire and action (AIDA).

Sales promotion is also used to reinforce brand-loyalty and to obtain a larger market share during the maturity stage of the product's life cycle. During product maturity it is also important to keep the consumer's interest. Sales-promotional activity can help keep the product in the mind and eye of consumers. Skilful promotion can encourage the purchase of larger sized packs. In some markets this will contribute to lower unit costs of production, which in maturity is of particular value at a time when profit levels are usually under pressure.

The objectives of promotions aimed at retailers and wholesalers should be to encourage the stocking and display of the promoter's products at the expense of those of competitors. A manufacturer will clearly not want a retailer to run out of stock, but if stock levels held by retailers can be increased on a regular basis, this will reduce the manufacturer's costs as well as ensuring that an out-of-stock situation does not arise. A further objective of promotion to retailers is to obtain new outlets. Today this is increasingly difficult, as fewer, but ever more powerful, retailers constantly rationalize brands in an attempt to obtain maximum sales per square metre of sales space. Expanding the retail base is a common objective during a product's maturity phase.

An important promotional objective in seasonal markets is to encourage retailers to purchase during off-peak periods. Such promotions can be extended to include the sales force of customers, and has the effect of making cash flow more regular, as well as 'smoothing' production-planning peaks and troughs.

In industrial markets sales-promotional objectives are broadly similar to those described, although the techniques and tools of promotion are different. In addition, there is perhaps (because of the closer personal relationships that exist in industrial markets) a greater emphasis on long-term loyalty-building exercises as well as the purely sales-stimulating aspects of promotion.

Conclusion

Sales promotion should not be considered as a trivial, purely tactical or transient problem-solving function of marketing. Although there is an element of tactics and transience in sales promotion, a 'bird's eye' view of the practice should reveal that good sales promotion is integrated with, and facilitates, strategy.

While sales promotion is a valuable tool, it can also be extremely damaging to the company if not carried out with care and thought. Reference has already been made to the damage that can be done to a company's image if poor quality gifts are distributed in industrial markets. In consumer markets there is always a risk that the public will be suspicious of promotions if they are not skilfully carried out. On the one hand, advertising may be emphasizing quality, while the sales promotion may appear to be trying to 'give the product away'. If promotions are perceived in this way, such a paradox will adversely affect, rather than promote, sales. To avoid such risks, promotions should not be too frequent, and should be professionally designed.

QUESTION 24

What guidelines would you give to a sales manager wishing to recruit and train members of a sales force to achieve the results desired?

OBJECTIVES

This question is slightly ambiguous (and expect such ambiguous questions in an examination setting). It is not altogether clear whether the sales manager is setting up the sales organization from scratch, or whether he or she is conducting the above as part of his/her regular duties.

After that, the objectives are quite straightforward. Their purpose is to test guideline knowledge about recruitment and training of a sales force.

APPROACH

The introduction should begin by mentioning that the sales force mentioned may be either a new or existing one. You should then develop the body of the answer with these two points in mind (as the principles will not differ much for either situation).

In the case of a new force the problem is essentially mechanical, in that plenty of guidelines exist as to how it should be organized effectively; and recruiting and training the existing force is largely a question of attitude and approach by the sales manager. The question would therefore best be tackled on the above reasonably straightforward basis.

ANSWER

Suggested introduction

This question poses two problems: whether recruitment and training of the sales force is part of regular process, or whether (in, say, the case of a foreign company establishing a headquarters in the United Kingdom) it is a question of setting up from scratch. Clearly, in the latter case the situation will be much 'cleaner' in that one can begin with a new 'rulebook' and new organization chart in almost textbook fashion. If recruitment and training is part of a regular process, the problem will be complicated by the fact that old attitudes and rules – both official and unofficial – will exist, and there may be problems in attempting to overcome certain prejudices that might have built up over a period of time.

The following account therefore takes both situations into account.

Background to the problem

A sales department, like any other department within the organization, comprises a set of activities and duties which are required to be performed in order to meet departmental and ultimately company objectives and targets.

In setting up a sales department from scratch, an important consideration would be what activities or jobs would need to be performed in the department. For example, one would have to decide whether or not the sales force would be required to undertake market research. Similarly one would have to decide the extent to which the sales force would have the power to negotiate upon prices and conditions of contracts.

The specific tasks or jobs of a salesperson will vary from organization to organization. For example, some companies will be small, and duties usually considered to be extraneous to selling (e.g. merchandising, money taking, market research) may well have to be carried out by such personnel in addition to their principal duty of selling. The design of a new sales department must reflect these differences, as too must the detailed set of activities that are to be performed within it.

Recruitment

An organization should be prepared, if indeed one is not in existence already, to have an organization chart showing the relation between the selling function and marketing. Job titles, their respective levels and formal communication should be represented. What the chart cannot show is the detailed activities, responsibilities and methods of working of each incumbent in the various 'boxes' on it. Such details are embodied in a job description. This document, and the job analysis upon which it is based, are the cornerstones of the selection approach.

The selection approach is based on a careful and 'scientific' analysis of each position or job in the organization chart. The idea is that each job in the sales department is analysed with respect to the activities that are required to be carried out for effective performance.

On the basis of the job analysis a job description is prepared. It includes such factors as:

(a) Job title
(b) Main duties
(c) Ancillary duties
(d) Communication/liaison requirements
(e) Special working conditions/requirements

It is important to emphasize that the characteristics specified in the manpower specifications are derived from the analysis of requirements for effective performance for each job position.

The final stage in the selection process would be to recruit and select employees who match the manpower specification reasonably well.

One can thus see how in principle this approach to staffing makes sense. It constitutes a logical and ordered approach to the design of work and the selection of individuals to perform this work.

In practice the selection approach suffers from two disadvantages:

1   It may prove impossible to find and recruit an individual who matches precisely the manpower specification developed from the job analysis. This may be because no such individual exists, e.g. range of skills, abilities and experience required is simply beyond the scope of any one individual; or it may be that the 'ideal' individual simply cannot be found or attracted within the salary constraints imposed on the particular position.
2   The ordered and logical selection approach does not take sufficient account of informal factors. For example, an individual who entirely matches the formal job requirement may be selected, but he/she may be shunned by working colleagues (and quite often this is the case of the consistently good salesperson who over-achieves in terms of quotas or targets set).

This classification approach to job design and selection takes account of the individual, technical and social constraints on job design and employee selection. The essence of this approach is much more on designing the job to fit these constraints than specifying the 'ideal' way to do the job and then selecting the 'ideal' candidate to perform that job.

Training
Selling is a skill and, like any other profession, it has to be learned. Many sales people have to learn two quite separate skills: that associated with the product or service they are selling and the skill of selling as a separate training activity.

There are four generally recognized stages of learning:

(i)   Unconsciously unable
(ii)   Consciously unable
(iii)   Consciously able
(iv)   Unconsciously able

What these stages represent is self-evident. They show the process of learning from being totally unable, right up to the stage of being able to perform a task without thinking about it. A training programme should thus endeavour to take trainees to at least the third stage, the last stage largely being reached through practice in the field.

The initial sales-training course should inculcate into the individual much of what is widely known, e.g. concepts of market segmentation, organization-al buying behaviour and actual selling techniques. Empathy is important, as is commercial sense. Some sales personnel may have these characteristics in abundance, but effective training should help to bring them out. Effective selling is as much about what you do not say as what you do say. Omissions create interest.

Effective presentation is about being an actor. It is the focal point of the sales interview. That can only be learned with training; so, too, can the skill of effective negotiation and closing. The two go together, especially when financial details are being discussed. Negotiation techniques are weapons that an astute buyer can use on an inexperienced salesperson to good effect, so the salesperson should be intimately aware of the intricacies of negotiation.

Sales training should not end with the initial training course. In order to be truly effective it should be continued, and this means an active role for sales management in the field as well as in the classroom.

Conclusion

Performance in the field depends upon three criteria:

1 The ability to perform competently
2 The motivation to succeed
3 The means to carry out the task

It may also be said that the result is the product of the multiplication of these factors, not their addition. Thus, if any of them is zero, then the result will be zero!

Ability depends upon intelligence and acquired skills. Motivation depends upon the relevance and salience of the goals that the salesperson is able to set. The means to carry out the task in hand is often (at least in part) dependent upon others – in other words, correct recruitment and good training and such other forms of back-up as sales aids. More important, however, it is good sales management that must provide the ultimate back-up, and the maxim that 'a good sales force is only as good as its sales management' is a true one.

FURTHER READING

The appropriate sections in any good text on the subject of selling or sales management, but, in particular, *Sales Technique and Management*, by G.A. Lancaster and D. Jobber (Pitman), Chapters 9 and 10 (pages 163–209).

QUESTION 25

How is the application of the 'total distribution concept' or systems approach relevant to the marketing goal of 'satisfying customer requirements profitably'?

OBJECTIVE

To ensure that the student understands the 'fundamental' concept of a systems approach. This is important in that the systems approach is normally identified with physical distribution, but it is in fact valid and pertinent to a variety of management situations.

APPROACH

This question is concerned with an important aspect of physical distribution, for which your wider knowledge on the subject is taken for granted. The answer need not therefore be lengthy. Rather, you should concentrate upon explaining the 'total distribution concept' clearly and concisely, and, except for the use of examples, avoid full descriptions of how a distribution system works and what it comprises.

Remember that your answer should demonstrate that you have grasped the concept fully, by making reference to 'satisfying customer requirements profitably'.

ANSWER

Suggested introduction

Distribution is that area of the marketing mix that relates to 'the right place at the right time', to quote from a marketing definition. The need to make profits is also a feature of definitions of marketing. Companies are faced with the problem of satisfying the customer – the principal marketing goal – and at the same time making a profit. The tendency in many companies is to diminish the importance of distribution as an element of the marketing mix. Advertising and product managers formulate, and are given, specific marketing objectives, and those concerned with distribution have become conditioned to accept their role as being primarily on-cost rather than marketing-orientated.

Systems approach

The first premise of the 'systems approach' is that distribution should be considered to be a marketing tool and not merely as a means of transporting goods from 'A' to 'B' at minimum cost. Secondly, the 'systems' concept should be fully appreciated and understood. The systems approach implies that any group of functional areas that have a communal goal (in this case that of satisfying customer requirements at a profit) should recognize their inter-dependence. This does not denigrate the individual importance of a particular functional area; the systems approach merely acknowledges that the import-ance of costs in any one area should not be over-stressed to the detriment of the marketing effort. The key word in systems is 'interrelationship'.

In order to understand the 'total' distribution concept as a 'system' as defined above, it is necessary to consider three basic themes. These are a total cost approach, sub-optimization and cost trade-offs.

The total cost approach first considers the elements of distribution – transportation, warehousing, stock control, good handling, packaging and finally the standards of service as set and demanded by the customer. These areas taken together constitute the distribution system. The system objective is to minimize costs (thus increasing profits) and maximize customer satisfac-tion by integration with other elements of the marketing mix. To achieve this goal the costs of the individual parts of the distribution function are consider-ably less important than the 'total costs' incurred.

The total cost approach appears to be simple and logical in theory. In reality it is not so easy to implement. If we consider a large organization, each of the distribution functions described above may be carried out by a variety of individuals or groups who each see their role as maximizing efficiency in their respective areas. This is not at all conducive to minimizing overall costs, neither does it ensure that the customer is receiving the best and most appropriate level of service. When inter-managerial objectives are at cross-purposes, they are less than optimal. Thus, sub-optimization can occur within the distribution function or between distribution and the other sub-functions of marketing. If the production manager gives preference to long production runs in order to minimize units costs, customers may be kept waiting and stocks (including the costs of holding these) will increase. If the transport manager minimizes costs by only shipping full loads, the same conflicts will arise. Human nature, in addition to the pressures of meeting financial targets, will conspire against optimization of the distribution mix in particular and the marketing mix in general.

The systems approach is thus designed to avoid sub-optimization by the use of an 'overseer' whose function is to organize distribution as a system of 'cost trade-offs'. This assumes that some areas of distribution will experience increases in costs while others will benefit from decreases as a result of this arrangement. The objective is to ensure that the decreases are greater than the increases, and that at no time will the level of customer service be jeopardized.

A popular example of such a trade-off might comprise the use of air-freight deliveries for slow-moving items as opposed to keeping large stocks in a large number of warehouses. Analysis could show that the high costs of air freight were more than offset by reductions in stockholding costs. As a bonus, customers received their orders more rapidly than before. Stockholding costs versus transportation costs are typical trade-offs. Each company has its own possibilities as to trade-offs. The type of market that the company supplies will also help to determine 'optimal trade-offs'. In some companies analysis might reveal a weak link among the distribution functions. This might cause backlogs in the smooth flow of order receipt and despatch. Extra expenditure in the weak area could improve general efficiency and reduce total costs.

In considering the goal of 'satisfying customer requirements profitably', marketing management must view distribution from two points of view. The following viewpoints must be integrated in order to satisfy the marketing goals:

- The cost of trade-offs which the systems approach can achieve have obvious beneficial effects upon profitability. Management must take the concept a stage further by examining costs in relation to marketing objectives. While companies could not support too high a cost structure for a long period of time, there are occasions when marketing objectives require the costs of the distribution function as a whole to be raised.
- If the key to success in a certain market is distribution, then profitability could be increased in the long term by increasing market share at the expense of distribution costs.

The above are then viewed as a component of the marketing-mix costs, and thus sub-optimization of the marketing mix itself is avoided.

Conclusion

Distribution has been the most neglected of the marketing functions, but used as a 'tool' in the manner described it is no less important than the other elements of the marketing mix. The systems approach allows distribution to integrate with these other elements and provides the means for increasing profits by considering 'total costs' as opposed to individual functional area costs, which in fact are rarely mutually exclusive.

QUESTION 26

What considerations do you consider to be essential to the design of marketing channels? Comment as to the effects of conflicts and the exercise of power within marketing channels.

OBJECTIVE

To assess the candidate's basic knowledge of channel structure and to ensure that an awareness of the problems associated with the implementation of channel design is in evidence.

APPROACH

The first part of your answer that refers to channel design merely requires that you introduce the idea of a 'marketing channel'. Then by describing its basic structure you should show how the choice of channel should complement the other elements of the marketing mix. Channel design is of course one feature of distribution, sometimes referred to as 'place' in marketing textbooks.

You should then give examples of power bases within channels and show that, although the desired role of channel members is to facilitate the smooth flow of goods and services to the final consumer, the goals of individual members are sometimes in conflict with one another.

Your answer should contain examples wherever possible, and should be presented in an ordered, thoughtful manner, but this does not require detailed, discursive arguments. It would be sufficient to make an orderly presentation of basic subject knowledge gained from your reading and studies.

ANSWER

Suggested introduction

An elementary marketing system merely requires a 'seller' and a 'buyer', which represents the transfer of title of goods or services from one party to another. This is the most basic of channels. The idea and study of channel systems is concerned with, and incorporates, the final end-user, since the end-user ultimately controls the rate of flow of goods for all other parties who manufacture, convert and distribute them. The design and choice of the most appropriate channel system to perform this function is one of the main marketing decisions. All the elements of the marketing mix are vital and interdependent. Whatever 'mix' strategy is employed, it is of no value if the end-users cannot physically, and easily, obtain the product.

Intermediaries

The members of a channel who lie between the manufacturer and the consumer are by implication 'intermediaries', who physically pass on goods and title from one to another. The length of a channel depends upon the nature and structure of the market and will of course vary according to how close a given manufacturer is to the supply of a finished product. It is convenient to consider channels in relation to the manufacturer of a finished product and the final consumer.

'Cutting out the middleman' is a popular phrase, as it implies cost savings and a greater control over the marketing of a product. Middlemen are nevertheless used by the vast majority of companies; channel design is concerned with the *choice* and *number* of middlemen and the *degree of power* that the manufacturer is prepared to extend to them. In general, intermediaries are used for the following reasons:

- Logistical problems are reduced because one intermediate channel member is able to deal with many suppliers and many end-users.
- The middleman possesses specialisms, contacts and expertise that the manufacturer does not.
- The early transfer of title reduces the cost of stockholding, reduces risk and speeds up receipt of payment.
- The middleman may bear the cost of certain marketing activities, such as promotion, research and sales effort.

Channel design is therefore a function of a company's resources in these areas. Manufacturers that are capable of performing and financing all of the functions mentioned above will establish their own retailers and dispense with intermediaries altogether. Some manufacturers concentrate their efforts and resources on the production, rather than the distribution, of goods, and are thus prepared to allow others to perform this task for them.

Channel selection

Thus far channel design has been discussed in relation to how far choice is dictated by the resources and capabilities of the firm. These are considered in relation to the potentialities of prospective members. Once a framework for choice has been established, the selection of channel alternatives should be related to the marketing objectives and tasks which the company wishes to achieve. These objectives, such as target market selection and service level, should already have been decided, and a channel structure that makes these objectives realizable should now be established.

If a highly specialized market segment is chosen, the firm may wish to keep distribution as exclusive as possible. Specialist and limited retail outlets will be sought; and intermediate handlers (wholesalers, agents or distributors) should also be specialists, acquainted with the product type and possessing very good contacts with the retailers. Such a channel would be appropriate for new products where the 'innovators' and 'early adopters' form the first target segment. Exclusivity in distribution is also in harmony with marketing objectives that aim to promote a high quality 'prestige' image.

In many consumer markets companies aim to achieve the highest rate of penetration across a wide range of consumers. Here the role of the channel is to obtain correspondingly intensive distribution. The company may have to consider multiple channel systems in order to obtain the desired coverage. Petrol-filling stations provide a good example of outlets for intensive distribution strategies. In the past 10 years companies such as Esso and Shell have extended their range of products on sale in filling stations from automotive-related products only to confectionery and gift items and even a general range of groceries. Suppliers to these outlets who have relied upon supermarket outlets in the past will have had to increase their channels so as to service these new customers in an effective manner.

Sometimes, taking account of prevailing market conditions and the nature of the product, companies take the decision to control the extent of their distribution in both retail and intermediary terms. The objective of this 'selective' form of channel design is to create a core of middlemen with whom close ties can be established, thereby creating loyalty and co-operation. In return for this close selective relationship the chosen middlemen may share marketing costs, e.g. promotion.

Finally, companies can radically alter their channel systems by integrating vertically (either backwards towards suppliers or forwards towards the retailer). Vertical integration is concerned with the acquisition of, or merging with, intermediaries and should not be confused with 'cutting them out' by dealing directly with the middleman's customers. Vertical integration can provide financial savings through increases in efficiency and improvements in control. Such action also incurs the danger of drastically increasing risk. When markets change, or retail outlets decide to change suppliers, the heavily vertically integrated company must bear the full effects of stockholding, and search for new activities for companies all along the supply route.

The number of manufacturers who circumvent their channel members by dealing directly with retailers and consumers has increased significantly in recent years, as evidenced by the number of small to medium mail-order companies, 'door to door' activity, and 'party plans' that currently operate in the UK. Not all companies who deal directly are necessarily small, Avon

Cosmetics being a classic example of a highly successful direct-marketing organization. The risks, however, are similar to those run by vertically integrated companies, and, despite successes, by far the highest volumes of goods continue to be marketed through longer channel systems.

Channel design is also determined by the nature of the product itself. Perishable or short 'life cycle' products will generally be distributed through short channels. Similarly high turnover products will require shorter channels, operated by intermediaries who specialize in speed and flexibility. Spare-parts manufacturers cannot afford to operate through complicated networks, as their overriding marketing goal must be swift service.

Channel conflict

Although it is in the interests of all channel members that the channel runs smoothly and functions to their mutual benefit, it sometimes occurs that 'power play' and 'conflict' become a feature of channel management. In retailing channels the role of 'captain' has traditionally been played by manufacturers of FMCGs, or indeed larger wholesalers, since retailing establishments have tended to be small local organizations, seeing their role as providing display space for the manufacturers. However, as retail chains have become the 'norm' and retail outlets have become larger, so the power within channels has tended to switch from manufacturers to retailers, especially with the introduction of 'own label', which has tended to break down the power of the larger FMCG manufacturers (see also answer to Question 29, which catalogues the changes in UK retailing that have brought about this change).

QUESTION 27

What factors must be considered by a firm wishing to establish a level of customer service which is appropriate to its markets? Show how such a service level can be employed to gain competitive advantage.

OBJECTIVES

To ensure that the student is able to consider the major variables affecting the setting of a service level, and that the student has a sufficient depth of understanding to regard the service level as a competitive tool.

APPROACH

This answer could be presented in three basic sections. The ideas contained in each of these are discussed below:

1. The main areas of service management are concerned with costs, delivery, stock (inventory) control and warehousing. These should therefore be the primary 'factors' to be considered in relation to your answer.
2. It is *how* these factors are deployed which determines a specific level of customer service and its effectiveness. This then brings into play the notion of how 'appropriate' the service level is to the markets it seeks to serve. Factors concerning the market (size, type, location, etc.) must therefore be considered. The type of product and the nature of the competition should also be included here. To close this section it is worth mentioning that any attempt to establish a customer service level is unlikely to succeed without recognition of the 'total distribution' concept.
3. The final part of the question allows you to show that you understand not only the elements of service but also service's wider implications as a competitive tool.

   You should discuss such factors as non-price competition, the idea of service as a product in itself, the 'extended product' and the 'total product offering'. These areas are well covered in most standard textbooks.

ANSWER

Suggested introduction

The level of service that a company decides to apply to its customers is one of the most important marketing decisions it must take. It comprises detailed analysis of 'what the customer requires' and how well the company is equipped to provide this. Whatever level of service is decided upon, it must never be forgotten that this must be a level that provides *profits* (not necessarily sales). It is axiomatic that maximum service cannot be provided at minimum cost. If a market demands high service levels, the costs should be reflected in the price.

Service level considerations

In setting service levels the firm must consider the following:

- What are the market requirements with regard to service? The levels employed by competitive companies are an important consideration.
- What are the marketing objectives that have been set to accommodate this market, so as to achieve profits and ensure success in marketing strategy?
- What resources does the company have with which to implement these objectives?

It goes without saying that the firm's marketing objectives must be set realistically in the first place. The stage of resource examination is not only to 'fine-tune' these but to decide the mix of distribution resources that will be most effective in terms of profit and service objectives.

Physical distribution costs usually amount to around 15 per cent of manufacturers' sales volumes, and even more for those companies that resell products. There is therefore a vital need to examine the deployment of cost with great care. The individual cost centres within the distribution system include transport, warehousing, stock control and order-processing. These functions are interrelated: for example, an increase in delivery service through improved transport systems cannot be undertaken without an effect being felt by the other distributive functions. In such a case the company will most likely have to increase stocks and thus the cost of stockholding, which in turn will affect warehousing and order-processing. Changes and plans must therefore be made by considering the distribution system in its entirety. It could be that in a market that is not a demanding one in terms of speed of delivery, a company may decide to reduce costs in transportation. If, as a result of this, lower stocks are required, valuable space may be under-utilized and the purchasing department may lose the opportunity to buy at bulk discount prices.

The company must therefore consider all its ramifications before deciding upon a service strategy. Typical objectives may be:

1 To hold 90 per cent of all products in the portfolio.
2 To deliver to all customers in 3 days.
3 To confirm and process all orders within 48 hours.

Such ambitious goals must also be realized at an acceptable level of profit. To achieve this, the company must organize its distributive units so that they work in unison. It may be that some units, and their costs, may be reduced, while others are expanded. The marketing distribution manager must then look again at the costs to see where savings can be made, but it is vital that no aspect of the service level that has been decided upon should be sacrificed in so doing. The price charged can, however, be adjusted if the service objectives are being met. It is normal to think that good service should merit higher prices, although this view is sometimes resisted.

Establishment of a service level

This is a function of the marketing objectives the company sets. These in turn must be functions of the type of market in which the company operates. Market factors include:

- *The nature of the product.* Perishable products clearly require a sophisticated distribution system and a high level of service.
   FMCGs are distributed to a wide range of outlets with a high turnover. Additionally, large supermarket chains possess a level of power which dictates the level of service for FMCG products.
- *Competitive activity.* Unless a company has a particularly sought after product with minimal competition, the level of service is largely dictated by the 'best' of the competition.
- *Market location.* Companies engaged in markets with a wide geographical spread may have to offer a 'scale' of service levels, for which the internal distribution must be prepared. The goal of exporters should be to provide a level of service equal to that provided by competitors in the customer's domestic market.

Previous discussion on the setting of service levels has stressed the need for co-ordination between the various functional units of distribution. This is required to achieve 'total cost' optimization (see also Question 25), based upon the market requirements. If, for example, a particular export market requires a level of service that is expensive to the firm in comparison to local markets, the high costs of transportation must be considered in relation to the value that market represents to the firm.

The level of service required in a market represents a cost and a physical function. Marketing-orientated companies should, however, consider service as more than a physical function; they should use it as a tool to increase loyalty, and as a weapon to fight 'non-price' competitive battles.

Price is invariably a major determinant in the supply of goods and services, but its importance can be eroded by skilful and continuing provision of good service. Service as a feature can be built into advertising campaigns, so as to counter the physical similarities many products possess. Sales personnel can often obtain orders despite price differentials, provided they can promise an 'emergency' service from time to time. Continued good service will not escape the attention of professional buyers.

Commodity markets in particular provide enormous scope for non-price competition based upon service levels. If a company can operate successfully in the price environment of a commodity market, it has the opportunity to increase market share on the basis of good service. The company should present its products and its service as a total package. This is sometimes described as the 'total' or 'extended' product, and underlines the fact that the customer is seeking more than merely a price advantage. Of course care must be taken that all the other elements of the product – quality, design and packaging – are at least comparable with competitive offerings for such a strategy to succeed.

Conclusion

It has thus been demonstrated that service level considerations are more than merely tactical decisions. They are very much strategic considerations. In markets where delivery is very important it is often service levels rather than price that can influence customers to consider longer-term relationships with a company that is prepared to invest in a better level of service than its competitors.

QUESTION 28

Account for the rapid development of franchising in the United Kingdom. Comment upon any factors to be considered, with regard to franchise agreements, for both the franchisor and the franchisee.

OBJECTIVE

To ensure that the student knows enough to identify the positive elements of franchising, while at the same time being able to appreciate the potential drawbacks associated with franchise agreements.

APPROACH

It would be possible to produce a lengthy answer covering the technical aspects and principles of franchising. The wording of the question, however, already assumes a knowledge of these principles. The examiner will therefore expect an answer which deals with the operation and implications of franchising. *Do not* be tempted to spend half your answer time dealing with the question of what franchising is.

The answer could be introduced with brief detail as to the recent growth patterns of franchising, followed by a statement comparing the success of franchise agreements with the generally high failure rate of business ventures that are independently undertaken. This latter point is a major reason for the increasing numbers of franchises in operation.

An account of the advantages of franchising for the franchisee, contrasted with the problems other new businesses encounter, should follow. A further section should then deal with the advantages of franchising for the franchisor.

There is scope at this stage for the inclusion of any other factors, such as economic or social conditions, which you feel would help to account for the rapid development of franchising. It should also be stressed that future development of franchising is dependent upon the mutually beneficial nature of such agreements.

The section concerned with the disadvantages of franchising balances the answer and provides the opportunity to display business acumen. Your conclusion should then emphasize that you have a balanced perspective of franchise operations, and this should reaffirm the mutually beneficial nature of the franchisor/franchisee relationship.

Marks would probably be apportioned on the basis of equal marks for points relating to the franchisor and the franchisee. The suggested answer does not give them equal prominence, but the franchisee argument discusses the franchisor, so the answer is probably more balanced than it may seem at first sight. In this question most of the marks available will be for the quality of discussion, as opposed to reproducing points from memory, and the inclusion of appropriate practical product and service examples will help in this respect.

ANSWER

Possible introduction

Franchising agreements have existed in the UK for many years, particularly in the catering trade, Wimpy being one of the earliest franchise operators. Since the mid-1970s, however, the number of franchise outlets has more than doubled. Sales through these outlets in 1982 were estimated to have exceeded £300 million, and are forecast to grow substantially throughout the 1990s. The 'business format' form of franchising has accounted for most recent growth. In essence a tried and tested idea or business concept is offered to potential franchisees, who operate this idea on behalf of themselves, while providing revenue for the franchisor. Franchisees are therefore effectively starting up new businesses in an environment similar to that of self-employment. Whereas a high proportion of new independent businesses fail, new franchises enjoy a relatively high success rate.

Franchising and the franchisee

A major reason for the development of franchising is the advantages franchise agreements possess in comparison with new business ventures that are independently undertaken. In common with franchise agreements, most new ventures either seek to market an existing product idea in a new way or place, or they seek to market a completely new idea. The most significant contrast between them, however, is that business format franchises concern a business idea which has already been tried and tested and whose commercial success is already established. Much of the risk element for the franchisee is eliminated, since lessons have already been learnt from previous mistakes. Commercially and organizationally established, the franchisor is able to offer wide-ranging benefits to a potential franchisee, as follows:

1 Dependent upon the size and nature of the business, the franchisee will usually require a smaller capital outlay than if he or she were to begin trading independently.
2 The franchised business will have an established corporate identity, whether this be regional, national or international.

3   A corporate advertising and promotional service will be available.
4   Corporate functional experts, such as legal, marketing, financial or design staff, are often at the disposal of the franchisee.
5   Advice and training should always be available during the start-up period.
6   The business image will be established with respect to such matters as interior design, work clothing, service procedure and specifications.
7   The franchisee may benefit from bulk purchase discounts which have been negotiated by the franchisor.
8   Credibility with suppliers is likely to be established more quickly.

Even if an independent new business venture is based on a promising idea, that is often not enough. Although an inferior idea may be the reason for some business failures, by far the most frequent causes are to be found in the actual operating of the business. The factors presented above explain why such rapid development has been experienced by franchising as an alternative form of self-employment. Franchise agreements obviate most of the difficulties faced by the potential entrepreneur, in particular those relating to working capital and a breadth of management expertise and experience. Additionally, despite the fact that the franchisee is not promoting his/her own idea, the independence afforded by the agreement ensures a high degree of motivation, such as is found among those who are self-employed.

Franchising and the franchisor
Franchise agreements could not succeed, however, if benefits did not accrue to both parties to the agreement. A further contribution to the rapid growth of franchising is that such agreements enable the franchisor to expand his/her business at a reduced cost, since a varying proportion of the initial direct investment is provided by the franchisee. Moreover, while an outlet is operative, the franchisor receives an income without having to undertake the day-to-day running of each business. The motivation of the franchisee should ensure that this is carried out in a mutually satisfactory manner, for in some circumstances the franchisee may be more in tune with local conditions than direct employees would be – another advantage from the point of view of the franchisor.

Further factors
In broader terms development has been aided by evidence of the success of franchising in the USA and the adoption of perfected American techniques. The economic climate with respect to the employment market may also have encouraged the taking up of franchises by individuals who, in times of greater job security, might have remained in conventional employment. Most business format franchises concern services rather than physical products. On a national level any growth in commercial activity has tended to favour service

industries at the expense of manufacturing. This, too, may be another contributory factor to the development of franchising. In retrospect franchising may be seen as a natural development from the voluntary chain or symbol group operation.

Mutual dependency

The rapid growth of franchising has been shown to be largely due to the fact that it offers important advantages to both parties. This balance of benefit cannot, however, continue without constant effort and attention to the idea of fair play. In the short term it would be possible for either party to gain advantage but in the longer term this would be destructive. In order that franchising can continue to develop, it is vital that agreements are fair and that both sides honour their obligations for their mutual benefit.

Disadvantages

In some respects, however, the requirement for mutual dependence is in itself the origin of disadvantages inherent to franchising, principally because the balance is such a sensitive one. While the franchise contract is in force, the franchisor is totally reliant on the willingness and ability of the franchisee to operate the business as effectively as possible. If this is not done, the franchisor cannot break the contract, and it is likely that the poor management of one franchise will have an adverse effect on the total corporate image. If, on the other hand, the franchisor pays little attention to the outlets, the tendency for the franchisee to regard the business as 'his own' will increase. This is likely to cause resentment concerning the payment of fees, which could lead to a deterioration of the relationship. Similarly, if the entrepreneurial spirit of the franchisee is high, there is little opportunity for displays of initiative, as franchise outlets are of necessity strictly uniform in service procedure and design. This is a potential source of frustration and dissatisfaction.

The above are essentially human problems; there are, however, several technical disadvantages, in particular for the franchisee. If any disputes relate to the payment of the fees, the franchisee will usually be at a disadvantage, as his or her resources will usually be inferior to those of the franchisor in the event of litigation. The franchisee may be obliged to buy stock from the company at uncompetitive rates or pay fees that may be based on turnover rather than profit, which would clearly be to the advantage of the franchisor. Finally, if the franchisee wishes to dispose of the business, the sale may be subject to the approval of the franchisor, and in any event the goodwill would remain the property of the franchisor.

Possible conclusion

Franchising offers real advantages for both parties to the agreement. For the franchisee these are particularly apparent when considered from the perspective of an individual who wishes to exploit an idea independently. This would largely account for the increase in franchise operations over recent years. There are, however, restrictions on both parties, as well as potential areas of conflict. These must be thoroughly understood before any contracts are entered into. However innovative product ideas might be, future development will hinge on the capacity of franchise agreements to operate on a mutually beneficial basis.

QUESTION 29

What factors have brought about the changes in UK retailing that have occurred since the late 1950s?

OBJECTIVE

This is a very direct UK-specific question. Quite often this question is dressed up in less specific terms with the term 'distribution' substituted for retailing. Although distribution would tend to indicate a broader answer, it is essentially institutions within retailing that have changed most dynamically since the late 1950s. It has been stated that the question is very UK-specific, but this trend has been at work in other countries as well, so the principles upon which the following answer is based are reasonably universal. The basic objective of the question is therefore to test specific knowledge about retailing channels. This question asks not merely for a factual recitation but is designed to elicit discussion about power within retailing channels and how this power has tended to switch since the late 1950s.

APPROACH

The answer should begin with a brief overview of the various retailing institutions to put the question into perspective and to enable later discussion to take place in relation to these institutions. It should then progress into a strategic discussion as to how certain retailing institutions have been more successful than others during the period since the late 1950s. The role of wholesalers during this period should be discussed, as should the role of manufacturers of fast moving consumer goods (FMCGs). More to the point, 'power' within retailing channels should be adequately discussed in terms of where the power did lie and where it currently lies.

ANSWER

Suggested introduction

Selling methods within retailing have been revolutionized since the late 1950s. Much buying is now centralized, and it is common now for potential buyers to visit potential sellers – unlike industrial selling, where sellers normally visit buyers. Before we examine changing patterns of retailing since the late 1950s, it is appropriate to categorize the main types of distributive outlet for FMCGs, in order to provide a framework for discussion.

Chief categories of retail outlets for FMCGs

1   *Multiple chains/variety chains* (often referred to simply as the multiples) belong to large central organizations. Some specialize in particular product lines, while others sell a wider range of goods (although chiefly food-stuffs).

2   *Co-operative societies* are owned and controlled by the people who shop there, and each society is governed by a board of directors elected from its members. The movement can be traced back to the mid-nineteenth century, and its guiding principles remain in force today.

3   *Department stores* are stores with five or more departments under one roof. They tend to sell a wide range of commodities, including significant amounts of household goods and clothing.

4   *Independents* are traders who own their own retail outlets. Some belong to retail buying organizations (for bulk purchasing) and others belong to wholesaler-sponsored organizations known as voluntary chains. Participating retailers have an identifying symbol and they must agree to abide by the rules of the group, which include matters of marketing, accounting procedures, 'standard' facilities, etc.

5   *Mail order*, although not principally concerned with foodstuffs, is worthy of mention here because of its expansion since the late 1950s. Mail-order suppliers trade through a glossy mail-order catalogue held by agents who sell to their family and friends (although the recent trend is that anyone who wants to operates a catalogue as long as he/she is creditworthy). Specialist mail order has expanded in recent years. Here advertising is usually done in relation to a limited line of merchandise (often in press colour supplements).

Developments in retailing

As has been mentioned, mail order has been relatively successful, but its merchandise tends not to cover foodstuffs. In so far as the other categories of retailer are concerned, the larger departmental chains have been relatively successful, although many of them now prefer to rent out space on a profit-sharing basis to smaller franchised operations (sometimes referred to as 'shops within shops'). They thus operate the nucleus of the business themselves, and franchise out the specialist areas, e.g. clothes, perfumes, etc., to independent operators.

However, the principal success in retailing has been the multiples. In the late 1950s they had just over 20 per cent of the food trade, which was about the same as the co-operative societies. The independent sector then held over 50 per cent. Nowadays the ratios are just over 10 per cent for the co-operative societies, about 20 per cent for the independents and almost 70 per cent for the multiples.

Implications of the success of the multiples

As a result of the success already outlined, manufacturers have had to reappraise their channels of distribution. Purchasing power has become concentrated into fewer, more powerful hands.

In the 1960s and early 1970s power within retail channels tended to rest with FMCG manufacturers, which pre-sold their goods through promotional and branding activity in a 'pull' strategy of marketing. These large manufacturers were able to exercise control over distributors, which could only dismiss demand created through advertising and branding at the risk of losing business. Such control meant lower margins for retailers, and manufacturers were able to dictate the merchandising of their products at the point of sale. Such manufacturers were thus able to influence the distribution of their respective products through being able to pre-sell to prospective customers, who became 'brand-loyal'.

In the 1950s there was some resistance on the part of manufacturers to dealing directly with the multiples, as the traditional channel was via wholesalers. Manufacturers eventually found it to their advantage to deal direct, however, as the multiples dealt in bulk often for delivery to a central depot and placed large orders well in advance, enabling manufacturers to organize their production more efficiently.

Methods of selling have also changed as a result of the above developments. Goods no longer needed to be 'sold' in the old-fashioned salesmanship sense, because they were already pre-sold through advertising and branding. The selling function itself has become more a matter of negotiation with the multiples at higher levels between buyers and sales management, and the sales people servicing the actual outlets have become moved more into merchandising and after-sales service activities.

Wholesalers suffered particularly during the 1960s, and many went out of business, as a result of their traditional outlet (independents) losing market share to the multiples. For this reason a number of wholesalers established defensive voluntary chains (or groups) in order to meet the challenge of the multiples, by attempting to offer a similar type of service and 'image' to the public. The most successful of these groups is probably the Spar organization, but many of the others have failed, owing to inferior purchasing power or because wholesalers had to attempt to make independent retailing members behave in a way that would compete with the multiples, but only by using voluntary means. The wholesaler's only sanction against non-co-operating members is to expel them from the group, whereas in the case of the multiples their store managers are employees, and here the sanctions are obvious.

A more recent trend in retailing as regards the multiples is a switch in 'power' within the channel of distribution. Traditionally this power was held by manufacturers of strongly branded lines, but it is now breaking down as a result of the introduction by the larger multiple chains of 'own label' merchandise. When 'own label' was first introduced in the early 1970s, it was meant to be a cheap (and sometimes nasty) substitute. The larger manufacturers of branded merchandise tended not to process this merchandise for the multiples, as they could see that it could adversely affect sales of their own branded goods, and the multiples were obliged to use smaller manufacturers to process this merchandise for them. However, one retailer, namely Sainsburys, was the biggest retailer of 'own label' merchandise, and it ensured that 'own label' was as good as, if not better than, branded alternatives. Thus, 'own label' within Sainsburys was seen to be good quality, and this contributed to the success of Sainsburys, especially in the late 1970s. Other bigger retailers then copied Sainsburys and introduced their own good quality 'own label' lines.

The implication is that consumers now realize that 'own label' means good quality, usually at a cheaper price, and to a certain extent this has led to a diminution in the power of branded products. Most producers of FMCGs now supply 'own label', with a few notable exceptions, e.g. Nestlé and Kelloggs. The implication is that power within the channel has tended to switch in favour of the multiples, who now seek, through heavy advertising, to establish a 'house image' for themselves, based largely upon their 'own label' lines. The power of the brands has tended to diminish as consumers realize that 'own label' is very much like branded products (except for a few that cannot readily be replicated).

Conclusion

The period since the late 1950s has seen the growth of large-scale retailing, including a growth in size of individual retail establishments – from supermarkets to superstores to hypermarkets. Shopping patterns have also changed, in that consumers have been prepared to dispense with personal service, and self-selection has become fully accepted with payment at a checkout. This has meant lower overheads for retailers, but their capitalizing on this development has also meant that larger-scale operations have become the order of the day. Such savings have also been passed on to consumers in lower prices for their purchases, especially for basic foodstuffs and household commodities. However, a similar trend has more latterly been at work in relation to basic clothing and electrical goods.

'One-stop shopping' has also become popular, with consumers tending to make the bulk of their purchases at one outlet. In addition, longer periods between shopping trips has also become the 'norm', with better means of storage (e.g. refrigerators and freezers) and convenience foods becoming available. More to the point, society has changed with the roles between male and female becoming less clearly defined, with men quite often helping in the task of shopping, and one-stop shopping quite often becoming a family occasion and less of a drudge.

Increased standards of living have meant that many goods once considered luxury product have become utility items required by a greater proportion of the population, e.g. cars, televisions, telephones, 'exotic' foods. This has led to 'mass marketing', because during the period in question we have reached the situation where supply exceeds demand, and manufacturers have had to 'brand' their products in order to maintain or increase sales.

The most dynamic sector within retailing has been in relation to the marketing of FMCGs. This has witnessed the rise of the multiples, which were initially perceived as being merely efficient outlets for the moving of branded goods to consumers, with manufacturers holding real power within the channel, to one where retailers have assumed power as a result of 'own label' merchandise that has become perfectly acceptable to consumers as an alternative to branded merchandise.

FURTHER READING

A number of specialist retailing texts exist, but the problem is that these tend to 'date' quickly in the dynamic world of retailing. The best sources of material must therefore be marketing journals, management journals and the financial press, especially when they have articles or features dealing with retailing. Overseas students taking a UK-based examination should not necessarily be put off by the fact that the question looks UK-orientated. The principles are what is important.

QUESTION 30

Direct marketing has been one of the fastest growing areas of distribution over the past 20 years. Describe what is meant by 'direct marketing' and account for its success.

OBJECTIVE

To test the candidate's knowledge of direct marketing and its place within the area of retailing. Thus, a certain amount of factual and strategic discussion is required in order to fulfil the questioning objectives.

APPROACH

Direct marketing should be first put into the context of retailing in general. Then the term should be defined through the use of illustrations and examples. Finally, a conclusion could discuss the relatively recent popularity of this form of selling and its future.

ANSWER

Suggested introduction

During the past 20 years there has been a number of developments in retailing marketing channels. We have witnessed the development of supermarkets, superstores, hypermarkets, limited line discount stores, and direct marketing (or non-shop selling as it is sometimes called). Increasingly customers buy many kinds of product, ranging from clothes, books, records and tapes, electrical goods to wines and food, from non-retail outlets. Thus, the conventional retailer has been bypassed, driving many small retailers out of business.

Various forms of non-shop selling are now discussed.

Party plan

This method was mainly introduced by the 'up market' plastic houseware company Tupperware. It has since been taken on for such products as bedding, nightwear and cosmetics. The idea is that through accepting an invitation to such a 'party', upon which the hostess receives a commission from the company's local organizer, the invitee is then under a moral obligation to purchase. However, since the idea is now so widespread, it is now less of a 'confidence trick' and can be positively viewed as an excuse for a social get-together. In fact many such parties are now organized with a view to the profits being given to charity.

Door to door selling

This might be viewed as a relatively expensive method, but when one considers that wholesaler and retailer margins can be used to cover selling and distribution costs, then it begins to look more economical. Traditionally it has been used by companies employing agents to sell in a clearly defined locality, and one immediately thinks of the cosmetic company Avon, which sells from a catalogue. Kleeneze and Bettaware are two companies supplying household cleaning and other materials that have been in the business for some time. Ringtons tea merchants also use this method, taking regular orders and delivering through their van delivery network. The main facet of such a market therefore would appear to be repeat business.

More recently major 'one-off' purchases have tended to be sold by this method, although encyclopaedias were probably the first, many years ago. New products that are sold like this include double glazing, home insulation, central heating and insurance policies. Some of the less scrupulous companies sell under the guise of conducting a market research survey, and it is only well into the interview that the true nature of the survey is discovered. The process is called 'sugging'.

Mail-order catalogues

Mail-order houses rely upon an expensively produced glossy catalogue to obtain sales, but often use local agents, working among relatives and friends, to promote sales and then receive commission for goods sold. However, the business is now so competitive that virtually anybody who wants one can receive a catalogue for purely personal purchases. Payments can be spread, interest-free, over a number of weeks, which probably accounts for the fact that prices are usually higher than the same goods in a traditional shop. The main mail-order operators are very large (e.g. Littlewoods, British Mail Order Corporation, Grattan) and are thus able to achieve economies by bulk purchasing.

Non-catalogue mail order

This method of mail order has become popular relatively recently, especially with the proliferation of the Sunday 'colour supplements'. Reliance is placed upon advertising a specialist range of merchandise, and bulk purchasing is possible because of this limited range (often only one product). A company that started up in this way was Scotcade. In addition to the more prominent type of advertising in the supplements, a great deal of mail order is conducted through specialist small advertisements in national newspapers, often for home-produced craft goods such as toys, individually made clothes, knit-wear, etc.

Direct mail

Here the mailing list is the key to successful market targeting, and it is a well known fact that if one subscribes to certain magazines, then that magazine is likely to sell your name and address, along with its other subscribers, to anybody who wishes to buy the list. Banks offering charge cards have made widespread use of the names and addresses of holders for this form of merchandising.

Television direct-response advertising

Often, especially before Christmas, record collections are promoted through a series of single advertisements, with the caveat that they are not available in the shops. Many simple methods of ordering and paying are cited at the time of the advertisement, the easiest being to pick up the phone, dial a local number and quote your credit card number, name and address. Although one usually thinks of records in relation to this type of selling, other goods are now being sold in this manner.

Clubs

Book clubs, and more recently record/tape clubs, use this method to sell their respective products, normally at 'below the manufacturer's recommended price', with the rule being that one has to make a commitment to make so many purchases within a given period.

Automatic vending

This method has grown tremendously over the past 20 years, mainly through advances in slot-machine technology. The most common products sold in this manner are beverages, soft drinks, confectionery and cigarettes. Machines are located conveniently, railway and bus stations, factories, colleges, etc. Vend-ing machines also supply such services as juke-box entertainment, arcade games and computer games. In addition, they have recently become popular in a money-dispensing role through 'cash points' offered outside banks and building societies.

On-line computer via television

Although currently rather futuristic, this method of purchasing goods will probably develop and expand over the next 20 years. Through a computer, goods can be displayed on the screen and then purchases can be made immediately through an ordering procedure direct to the advertiser.

Reasons for popularity of direct marketing

Nowadays women account for about 40 per cent of the labour force and a high proportion of these are married women. Thus, women have less time to engage in leisurely shopping activity. In the past shopping was indirectly viewed as a 'leisure pursuit', which is less true nowadays because of a wider range of leisure activities available – swimming, television, videos, health clubs, etc. Nowadays most people have simply more interesting things to do in their leisure time.

A further reason for the increase in popularity of direct marketing is the fact that shopping, particularly in city centres, is a less pleasant and less secure activity than it was (although the recent establishment of 'metro centres' is attempting to change this). However, traffic congestion, parking expense, petrol costs and the sheer trouble of motoring into a city centre are causing many people to turn to direct marketing for such items as fitness machines, garden furniture and the like. In addition, non-shop purchasing, especially when the advertisement is for one particular specialist product, is often cheaper than purchasing through a retail outlet. Quite often such products have a relatively low turnover, and this has to be reflected in terms of a relatively high mark-up.

Conclusion

The popularity of non-shop selling is likely to continue to increase because of the factors already mentioned, and because methods of non-shop selling are becoming increasingly sophisticated and easy, especially when in many cases all one has to do is to make a local telephone call and read off a credit-card number.

This answer has restricted attention purely to the retailing of goods and services, but it should not be forgotten that 'direct marketing' also refers to many forms of industrial marketing. Manufacturers sell, direct to their customers, all manner of goods, including raw materials, manufacturing consumables, and many durables, such as plant and machinery.

QUESTION 31

What would you describe as essential considerations for companies that wish to enter export markets? (Approach your answer from the perspective of UK companies.)

OBJECTIVE

This question is designed to assess the student's knowledge of how a company must organize itself internally before taking any steps towards exporting – unlike Question 33, which deals with how a company might approach export markets from the strategic planning perspective. It is thus less theoretical than Question 33, and is phrased in such a way as to provoke the student's own thoughts. Many marketing texts approach the subject with the assumption that exporting already exists, and in this way neglect those factors that are of importance to small and medium-sized firms that may be new to this area.

APPROACH

As indicated above, your answer should show evidence of thought, and from the knowledge gained from revision you should be able to assemble a list of priorities very quickly. The phraseology of the question suggests 'How does one prepare for exporting?' rather than 'Describe how it is carried out'. You should therefore take care to adhere to this emphasis in your answer.

The answer format need not be complicated. A careful introduction, followed by a straightforward list of 'considerations' (headed if you think this will help) and a summing up are all that is necessary.

ANSWER

Suggested introduction

Many companies 'drift' haphazardly into exporting. Perhaps they respond to overseas enquiries, but make no real conscious effort to seek export customers. In such a situation the 'response' is likely to be structured around the firm's existing marketing procedures, and will consist of merely 'supplying' the requested goods. This may be tolerable while the firm's marketing strategy is firmly home-based, and export enquiries have been rare and irregular. If, however, these enquiries begin to increase, and the business is considered to be valuable, a more professional approach to exporting is called for. Unfortunately some companies continue with a UK-based orientation, even when export business becomes a significant part of turnover. Successful exporting in the long term requires commitment and a conscious decision to adapt business methods to the needs of overseas customers.

Overseas marketing 'mentality'

A boardroom decision to become active in exporting implies commitment on behalf of the board, but this commitment is empty unless extended and directed inside the firm itself as a first step. One of the basic requirements of exporting is that the firm (or at least its export personnel) develop and display an 'export mentality' – an intangible notion but the key to success.

To achieve this the firm should assign or recruit personnel who have a specific export role to play. To regard exporting as a subsidiary activity, carried on when home affairs are completed, is a recipe for failure. Whatever proportion of turnover exports represent, it is essential that those who carry out its functions are given clear job descriptions, responsibility and remuneration in line with their home business colleagues. This sets the scene for export affairs to be conducted in a professional manner by personnel who understand and are accredited with the importance of their roles.

The export mentality is therefore partially achieved from within the firm. Looking outwards, exporters must understand what it is they are trying to achieve. Firstly, they must realize profitable sales in markets other than those at home. Secondly, to achieve this, they must be fully aware that an export mentality is simply the application of the marketing concept, which aims to satisfy customers profitably, in foreign markets. In domestic markets the environment is familiar, but moving into foreign markets may call for lengthy documentation, quoting in foreign currencies, product and package modifications and the learning of languages.

It is a mistake, but one unfortunately common for businesses who may be good at UK marketing, to consider the marketing concept to refer only to the domestic market. Export markets are thus considered to be subject to different rules and standards. Exporting, however, is merely marketing abroad. While some products may sell because they are typically British, this does not mean that the needs and satisfactions of the customers in terms of service and approach are the same as in the UK. The essence of successful exporting is that a company should try as far as possible to offer equal or better service in a given country than the customer would receive and expect from its best national suppliers. This is especially true for industrial or consumer commodities, where the product is much the same, whatever its origin.

Commitment

The company that wishes to export must be committed to its export staff, so as to provide confidence within its markets. Often companies will enter export markets when currency rates are favourable or because of surplus capacity. Exporting in such circumstances may be expedient in the short term, but does not represent to overseas customers the commitment to develop lasting relationships. Foreign customers will soon become tired of a company that only approaches them in 'fair weather' and then withdraws from the market when the situation changes. Clearly a company cannot sustain losses over a long period, but, in general, any exporter should be fully prepared to adapt to volatile conditions of supply and demand.

The company can display long-term commitment not only by holding on during difficult periods, although this is a most basic requirement, but also by the professionalism of its total export marketing approach. The foreign customer is not necessarily able to form a first-hand impression of its supplier – as would be the case in a national context. Instead judgements can only be formed from the external impression the supplier makes – in the level of support given to agents, the quality of sales staff, the service level and the quality and smooth running of documentation and export office procedure.

Research
Before export markets can be fully developed, and before the final decision is taken to invest in them, the company should be armed with as much information as possible with respect to the real potential that exists for its products. Of course it may not be feasible for a small company to commission a full-scale international survey, but this is not the only way that research can be undertaken. The government can be most helpful to small and medium-sized companies that wish to enter new markets or begin exporting for the first time (see Question 32(iii)). It is also quite common for a firm to work with a potential agent or agents whose first task is to assess market opportunities. Then, subject to satisfactory reports, a formal arrangement can be made. If more than one agent is under consideration, this is also a method of assessing professionalism (although other criteria feature highly in agent selection).

Research in this context should also include costings for possible product modifications and for transport costs. There is no point in researching foreign markets unless the firm is reasonably sure that its products will be competitive.

The exporting research process differs in one major respect from that of home marketing research. Establishing the existence of market opportunities and then deciding on the appropriate strategy are not sufficient in exporting. Research in exporting must also address itself to cultural factors. American companies, for example, are often criticized for their failure to design export marketing strategies specifically for Europe. They may fail to take account of the wide social and cultural distinctions which exist between, say, Italy and West Germany, or even differences within national boundaries, such as the

Flemish- and French-speaking parts of Belgium. Advertising, packaging and sales approach should all be specifically designed with cultural background in mind.

Personnel

The first part of this answer discussed the need for an export mentality among the export staff. A small company may decide, however, to carry out exporting, at least initially, with existing staff, in which case some form of training should be added to the requirement for the correct mental approach to exporting. Export documentation can often be complicated and require specialist knowledge. Added to this, a small error can result in delays and extra expense, causing inconvenience, but, more important, a poor impression in the minds of customers.

In particular, sales staff should be carefully selected, and should be able to speak at least one other language. Although English remains the language of business throughout much of the world, it is essential that export salespersons are able to converse with customers in their own languages as far as possible. Even if this language knowledge is not expert, it does at least 'show willing'.

Finance/accountancy

It is a common error for exporters to expect that the terms and conditions of trade applicable in the UK are also acceptable abroad. Senior management must ensure that those responsible for financial affairs are prepared and equipped to modify their procedures, presupposing that top management is thoroughly committed to exporting. It is preferable to quote in the currency of the customer, and longer terms of credit than is common in the UK are to be expected. Financial staff should also consult their bankers and insurers before orders are obtained, to receive advice and avoid costly errors. Such errors would also display incompetence to both customers and agents.

Transport

Whether a company establishes its own shipping office or decides to work through the medium of a shipping agent or freight-forwarder, it is essential that transport methods are organized and agreed in advance of orders. It is also vital that those responsible for transport liaise closely with the production department, for production delays can have much more serious consequences in exporting than in home business. If a ship is not loaded in time, a delay of the order of weeks could result from what might seem an insignificant delay in the factory.

Budgeting

The aim of exporting is to create profitable long-term sales, but it must also be recognized that exporting should be regarded as an investment. Serious exporting cannot be conducted on funds 'left over' from other aspects of the marketing budget. Expenditure that the firm should consider includes possible recruitment of new staff, additional insurance and bank charges, foreign travel and promotional expenditure, perhaps including attendance at overseas exhibitions. The export budget is an essential consideration, as it obviously helps to establish costs but more especially it allows the company to appreciate the importance and scale of the decision to export.

Conclusion

The considerations described above are all interdependent, but while such factors as competence in documentation and transport are essential, they are of little value without the basic 'commitment' of the firm to treat exporting seriously. Of course there are many examples of firms that 'pick up' export orders erratically, and these may be profitable, although often they are not. Similarly there are firms that use export markets to offload surpluses. These actions may be acceptable in the tactical sense, and, if they are not a regular feature of the company's business, there may be no need to adopt the methods that have been discussed. If, however, the company genuinely wishes to develop export markets, then careful preparation and changes in certain procedures are essential.

As with many aspects of marketing, planning for exporting does not guarantee success; but it does encourage the application of discipline and professionalism as well as permitting a review if success is slower to arrive than anticipated. Whatever the product or service, foreign customers will expect a planned approach, and if this is carried out correctly, they should hardly be aware that their goods are arriving from a source other than their own countries. This is the test of success and the key to profitability, especially in those areas where price can be offset against quality and service.

QUESTION 32

Write comprehensive notes on ALL of the following:

(i) The role of the export salesman
(ii) The role of the commission agent
(iii) The role of government aid to United Kingdom exporters

OBJECTIVE

To examine aspects of exporting that are relevant to the small and medium-sized firm.

APPROACH

The approach to this answer is similar to that required for Question 19. There are, however, only three topics to be dealt with and this would imply that each one should be discussed in rather more depth. There is also no choice as to which topics you can attempt.

The examiner's choice of the word 'role' is quite deliberate. The implication and intention are that you should consider each subject from as wide a viewpoint as possible. You should, for example, discuss the personal qualities required of an export salesman as well as managerial factors such as training and motivation. When dealing with (iii), government aid, you should point out that although it is beneficial to individual companies in macro-economic terms, such aid is intended to encourage a healthy balance of trade.

ANSWER

(i) The role of the export salesman

The personal qualities required of the export salesman are essentially the same as those required of his domestic counterpart. Whether sales are made at home or abroad, the salesperson represents the company and must reflect the company's image and promote and achieve the objectives the company has set. The salesperson is the personal link between supplier and buyer and his/her basic role is to persuade buyers to purchase his/her company's goods in preference to those of competitors. These are basic qualities in any sales role, but it might be said that export selling requires certain additional qualities that may be desirable but are not strictly essential in the domestic market:

- *Managerial ability and potential* are needed, because visits to overseas customers are usually less frequent than those made at home. It is therefore vital that each interview achieves a positive conclusion – not necessarily a sale, but at least a definitive plan for future action. This requires that the salesman possesses the ability and authority to make decisions 'on the spot' at quite a high level. If this is not the case, the impact of costly visits is reduced, but, more seriously, the overseas buyer will feel that time has been wasted and this will engender a poor image of the company itself.
- *Managerial maturity* is also needed by the export salesman, to work closely with the company's overseas agent. Agents must be confident that they are working with someone who is competent, able to support their own efforts and to promote their integrity and respect in the eyes of customers. The export salesman must moreover motivate and encourage the agent's efforts and impart the feeling that the agency is wholeheartedly supported by the company.
- *Dependability* is closely linked to managerial competence, but the two are not necessarily to be found in the same person. Export selling means a great deal of time on one's own, without the immediate guidance of home-based colleagues; the export salesman's character should therefore include self-reliance and the ability to see things through without day-to-day encouragement and control from the home-based office. Exporting is often frustrating and progress slow, requiring the salesman to be persistent and patient.
- *Research ability* is important, for market information is not always as readily available in foreign markets as it is at home. Although it is the role of all sales personnel to gather information and provide 'feedback' to the company, this role is accentuated in exporting – not only for information gathering 'in the field' but also in terms of preparatory research before overseas visits are made.
- *Cultural adaptability and awareness* are vital. It is not sufficient that the export salesman be merely tolerant of foreign cultures. To achieve success the salesman must be able to 'identify' with foreign cultures. This identification shows the buyer that, through the medium of its chosen representative, the company is genuinely interested in establishing a close trading relationship, and is not merely seeking to offload occasional surplus capacity.
- *Linguistic ability* is linked to the above: the salesman should be able to identify with buyers in their own language. Apart from being essential in many markets, this shows a genuine intent and effort to adapt to the customer's environment.
- *Good health* is important, for foreign sales trips are frequently long and

arduous. The salesman will not only work by day but will entertain clients or agents during the evenings. Such a life requires stamina and general good health. A tired executive is unlikely to make a good impression on customers.

Some of the characteristics mentioned above require elements of humility on the salesperson's part. The nature of modern international competition requires that UK exporters empathize with their customers and be prepared to fit in with their environment.

Remuneration should be sufficient to compensate for inconveniences and frequent absences from home. The company should take care that the export salesperson does not become isolated from his/her colleagues at home. When not abroad, export personnel should be allowed to participate in the running and decision-making processes of the company as a whole, even though much of their time will, by definition, be taken up by follow-up visits and liaison with the company's overseas agents. The company should also ensure that export sales personnel are given sufficient authority and responsibility to act during their visits as the voice of the company.

(ii) The role of the commission agent

A company's overseas agent is a person who, or body which, has been appointed to act on the company's behalf in an area outside that in which the company employs its own personnel. Thus, unless a company has established its own subsidiary or offices in a foreign country, it will normally employ an agent to look after its interests – just as a company may employ an agent within its *own* country, e.g. a company located in the North of England may employ a London agent who has specialist knowledge of that area.

In general, however, 'agent' refers to an overseas activity. The agent can be a single person, a company in its own right or a major organization. It is common for companies wishing to export to Japan to work through the medium of merchant traders, some of whom are among the largest of Japanese companies, having wide-ranging international interests of their own.

The agent markets the products of a company (the principal) on an exclusive basis in a predefined area, whether this be a geographic area or a market segment. A company which manufactures agrochemicals as well as foodstuffs may have two agents in the same company, because of their respective specialist knowledge. Similarly cultural differences are such in some countries that it makes sense to appoint separate agents to work within each cultural boundary. The agent's income is derived from commission, which is usually a fixed percentage of sales. Of course the level of commission will vary according to the nature, profitability and value/volume potential of the products dealt in.

The selection process leading to the choice of an agent is of paramount importance. Agreements are more easily entered into than broken, added to which, a company that changes agency agreements too often is likely to promote insecurity among its customers. It is normal for agents to be appointed on a trial basis for a period of 6 months to a year before a more permanent exclusive agreement is entered into. During the initial appraisal period the agent should provide evidence of credentials and experience, plus a detailed market survey, which displays the agency's competence and adds a 'second opinion' to the research the principal should already have carried out. Any potential agent should possess the following qualities:

1   Sound market knowledge.
2   Knowledge of the company's product or related products. Usually an agent's existing activities will be in a field related to that of the principal's products. It does not necessarily follow, however, that an agent for, say, textile machinery is the best choice for marketing textile raw materials – even though that agent will be known to, and have connections with, the buyers of companies who purchase both of these products.
3   The agency should be known to, and respected by, potential customers, unless the agreement is concerned with an entirely new type of product.
4   It is useful to know that the potential agent has worked successfully with other principals over a period of time.
5   The agent should show willingness to visit the principal's premises, so as to become familiar with the proposed product range.

The principal has therefore the right to make demands upon the agent before a formal appointment is made. In return the agent has the right to expect certain commitments from the principal. The principal should recognize and respect the 'dual' nature of the relationship, and ensure that the agent receives the following support and consideration:

(a) *Motivation.* There is little which is more destructive to an agent/principal relationship than lack of communication. If the export market takes off quickly and successfully, regular communication will follow in any case, but if the market entry is more difficult, the relationship will quickly degenerate if contact is neglected. The onus is on the principal to stimulate and motivate the agent to ensure that all that can be done is done to support the agent's efforts.

(b) *Identification with the principal (i.e. partnership).* Although not employed by the principal, the agent has been entrusted with the representation of the company and its products. The company should make sure that the agent is genuinely treated as an associate of the company and that he/she can identify with it. This is important for motivational reasons and for illustrating to customers that the agent has the full support and trust of the principal. This can be achieved by encouraging visits to the principal's company, keeping agents up-to-date with company news and supplying material which links the agent to the principal. It is a good idea to supply agents with business cards showing both the principal's and the agent's names.

(c) *Sales support*. The agent should be fully supplied with all promotional literature, preferably in the appropriate language. It is essential that all enquiries he/she makes are dealt with quickly and efficiently. Every effort should be made to supply samples and trials as soon as possible. If the agent does not receive 'back-up', confidence will be lost among customers and the relationship will quickly deteriorate. Where appropriate, the agent's advice and opinions should be sought on advertising and promotional activity.

A good agency/principal relationship is vital if the company is to enjoy export success. The agent, though not a formal employee, is, and should be regarded as being, an extension of the company, acting in a foreign market. The relationship must embody a two-way flow, with the principal expecting certain standards of performance and behaviour from the agent, in return for which the agent should receive the fullest support. If a company is serious about exporting, such a relationship should develop naturally in the hands of a competent export manager.

(iii) The role of government aid to United Kingdom exporters

The level of government participation in exporting varies in countries throughout the world. Some countries pay large and direct subsidies to aid exports in industries which are important to the nation's economy as a whole. Other governments, while not directly aiding exports, nevertheless improve their countries' conditions of trading by creating barriers to prevent important goods from entering. The government in Britain, while not, to date, employing such measures, is concerned with the balance of trade and the success of British exporters. There is therefore a variety of services provided by the government with exporting in mind.

The largest such organization is the British Overseas Trade Board (BOTB) which operates from a central London location within the Department of Industry and through its fourteen regional offices. Its services and other schemes are described below:

1   *Market research abroad.* In many cases, especially when a company is new to exporting, the BOTB will provide financial assistance for market research undertaken by British companies. The level of support can vary, according to whether the research is carried out on a single company's behalf or for joint research projects. Of course the potential value of the proposed exports to the UK economy will feature in the decision to provide assistance or not. The government also provides an Export Intelligence Service and Library to support desk research for individual companies. The BOTB can also put the researcher in touch with British consulates and chambers

of commerce around the world so as to obtain first-hand information about a particular market. Often commercial attachés will specialize in certain industries in a particular country.

2 *Direct financial assistance.* If a firm decides to enter a new market, assistance may be available from the BOTB under the Market Entry Guarantee Scheme, which is designed to help small to medium-sized companies. Up to 50 per cent of the costs of entry (such as advertising, stockholding and legal costs of distributorships) may be paid, but in the form of a loan rather than a grant. If, however, the venture is unsuccessful, repayment losses are shared between the BOTB and the exporter. The scheme is designed for, and granted to, new ventures which can demonstrate a systematic and well planned approach to the project. Funds are not available for ad hoc projects such as a new advertising campaign in an established market

3 *The Export Credits Guarantee Department (ECGD)* is a government insurance scheme designed to cover the exporter against various risks in overseas countries. For the most part the risks refer to such items as war damage, expropriation and restriction of remittance of funds, i.e. the type that commercial insurance companies are unwilling to underwrite.

4 *Public relations.* Both the BOTB and the Central Office of Information (COI) provide detailed lists of overseas media. The COI will (free of charge) prepare professional press releases to promote British products abroad. Additionally, the BBC world service and foreign language broadcasts frequently feature British industry and new products in their programmes. They also provide a listener service which can be a useful source of sales leads to the exporter. Participation at international exhibitions is sometimes aided by government sponsorship – or at least a contribution to stand expenses. Similarly the government frequently organizes trade missions to various countries, in which individual companies can participate at subsidized rates.

5 *Agency search and selection.* Through the BOTB any company can contact consular commercial officers and chambers of commerce throughout the world. These bodies can provide lists of agents which are relevant to the company's products. They may also be able to advise upon the scope of the agents' experience and existing areas of activity.

Exporters would be imprudent to ignore the services available from the British government. As well as the services already described, the government also publishes a great deal of literature and information, such as the country by country 'Hints to Exporters' series. There is also a wealth of statistical data available for the early stages of desk research. It is probably fair to say that government bodies are most useful to the small and inexperienced exporter. As a company's export experience grows, reliance on government aid and services will probably diminish. The government has a vested interest in promoting and facilitating exports in an attempt to achieve a consistent trade surplus, and this encouragement can be exemplified by such presentations as the Queen's Award to Industry for export achievement.

QUESTION 33

By treating the multi-national as a final stage, describe how a company may develop as it becomes increasingly committed to overseas markets.

OBJECTIVE

The aim of this question is to ensure that the student is familiar with international trade in all its main forms. 'Multi-national' and international marketing in general is a topic that is well covered in most marketing (and indeed economic) texts, but it is less usual to find a text that also deals with the development of the small firm. Such discussion is normally restricted to specialist books on exporting. The question is therefore a test of wider reading.

APPROACH

The multi-national company represents the maximum possible participation in international trade. You should approach your answer by beginning with its opposite, i.e. the company just beginning to export, and suggest reasons why this 'first stage' might develop. 'Increasingly committed' implies increased overseas trade, and thus a change in sales volume, sales methods and an evolution of the company in international terms. Of course it is not suggested that every company that begins to export will eventually become a multi-national, but the question affords the opportunity and requires that you should describe the intermediate stages between the two extremes.

Once you are clear about this requirement, the answer itself should not be complicated or excessively discursive. It would be irrelevant to discuss the nature of export/international marketing: the essential requirement is one of describing increasing engagement in overseas trade stage by stage.

ANSWER

Suggested introduction
International trade is carried out by a wide variety of companies on an equally varied level. Many companies, chiefly concerned with the domestic market, may only be on the fringes of exporting. If, for whatever reason, exports increase, it is inevitable that the company structure will change so as to deal

more efficiently with its new markets. It is not suggested that a company will necessarily follow a fixed pattern of well defined stages; many companies will remain at a certain level of export sales and not develop further. Similarly some companies might continue to expand export commitment without altering their existing basic methods. It is true, however, that the more commitment to overseas marketing is increased, the more likely it is that strategy will alter.

The distinction between 'exporting' and 'international marketing' is usually made when a company begins to manufacture its products in other countries rather than send them goods made within the home market.

Exporting

Companies may begin to export for a variety of reasons:

1 A company may initially receive an isolated and unsolicited order from abroad. Although management may be pleased to supply this order, as well as others in the future, this will only apply as long as such business does not interfere with existing, home-based activities. At this stage the firm has no active plans to extend its markets and makes no particular effort to modify its approach to suit foreign customers.

2 Some companies make a conscious decision to export if, for example, their production capacity is under-utilized for a time. This may be because of seasonal activity or there may be no pattern whatsoever to it. Another reason may be to dispose of surplus stocks. The firm may become quite adept and professional in its approach to this form of exporting, or it may simply 'offload' its products abroad. Such activity may make sound business sense in tactical terms, and it may be that export customers are happy to deal in this erratic way. The core business remains in the home market and the likelihood of developing lasting relationships is not good. Price is probably the principal factor in the buying decision. Furthermore, if one company has need to export in this manner, it is likely that competing home-based firms will also be suffering under-capacity and these may also enter overseas markets on this 'hit or miss' basis.

3 The company that is considering planned growth often finds that export-ing is the best means to achieve it. The home market may be saturated, or for strategic reasons it may be inadvisable to attempt to gain too much control over that market. The conscious strategic decision is thus made to enter export markets, so that growth can be facilitated. In this situation the company must thoroughly prepare itself and tackle its new markets with the same amount of commitment that it already applies at home (see Question 31 for a fuller discussion). Exporting then becomes an intrinsic part of strategy, and some measure of control can be exercised. It is normal

for a company to aim for a certain percentage of its total turnover to come from exports.

The first two types of exporting that have been described could be called (1) PASSIVE, because no real effort is made to obtain orders and (b) TACTIC-AL. Experience of tactical exporting, combined with changes in the market place may lead to (c) PLANNED EXPORTING.

Whatever the scale of planned exporting, it obviously implies long-term commitment. Many firms operate large and highly successful export businesses without the need to employ methods other than simply shipping products direct to customers or distributors, while control of the business remains firmly in the home country. There comes a stage, however, when further growth is impractical or impossible if it is based solely on classical exporting procedures. At this point the company must look at alternative methods of marketing its products, methods perhaps better suited to in-creased volumes. Export management is likely to notice indicators of the need for strategic change, such as a requirement for an ever-increasing sales force, or for larger stocks to be held in client countries. Such indications suggest that control from the home base is becoming more difficult, and that some element of local control is now appropriate.

Branch offices

The establishment of a branch office is the first step outside straightforward exporting that a firm may take so as to handle its export affairs more efficiently. The branch office is merely an extension of the firm's export department. Export volumes will have grown to such an extent that the use of agents or middlemen will have become inappropriate.

The branch office is staffed by employees of the firm whose roles include marketing, sales and distribution. The employees may or may not be nation-als of the country concerned. Of course all major decisions are made at head office, which should receive regular reports from branch offices. For the company the advantages of branch offices are greater control and better feedback of market information. The branch office will also be concerned exclusively with the company's products, whereas an agent or distributor may be concerned with several principals. For the customer therefore the advantages should be an increased level of service, motivation and interest shown by the supplier.

The logical extension to a branch office would be for a firm to install its own manufacturing capacity in the foreign market – this decision being necessary because domestic production could no longer cope with the level of sales. Such a step is, however, not only risky but also expensive. Many firms will consider alternative methods before investing directly in an overseas market.

Contract or commission manufacturing

Alternatively, a foreign manufacturer may be selected to produce goods on behalf of the home producer. These goods can then be marketed by the branch office. The contractor must be chosen with great care to ensure that standards of quality and service are equal to those of the home company, as control of manufacture is effectively 'entrusted' to the contractor. The chief advantages are that contracting out can be effected with low investment and minimum risk, and is a relatively rapid method of increasing production and sales to export markets. If this method is chosen first, it also leaves the parent producer free to consider other alternatives after the agreed contract period has ended.

Licensing

A licensing agreement gives a foreign manufacturer, for a financial consideration, the right to manufacture and market goods whose brand name or trademark belongs to the home-based company.

Like contract manufacturing, licensing is a relatively inexpensive method of increasing turnover abroad. Unlike contract manufacturing, however, licensing brings with it a significant loss of control. The disadvantages are that the licensee may not exploit the market to its full potential or may fail to live up to the standards previously established by the licensor. Although the costs of licensing are significantly less than direct investment, the licensor has no control over profit levels and will only receive a 'licence fee', which may be much below the profits that could be obtained, say, under a contract agreement. On the positive side licensing agreements are usually encouraged by foreign governments because they create wealth and provide employment. A licence agreement may also provide a method of entry into a country which was previously closed to foreign competition because of trade barriers, quota restrictions or high import tariffs.

Joint ventures

The joint venture is not necessarily restricted to the production and marketing of the home-based company's own product. The joint-venture decision can be a method of increasing foreign commitment rather than one of increasing sales of existing products. In this sense it is a strategic 'investment' decision rather than a purely marketing/product-based strategy. Whatever the motive behind the decision, a joint venture means investment by a company in one country in a business in another country. The business may be completely new or well established. If investment is 'joint', this obviously reduces costs, but, as in any form of partnership, control is also shared. This may cause short-term conflict and hinder long-term growth. As is true for any investment decision, the key to success is careful selection and planning from the outset. The responsibilities and spheres of influence should be clearly delineated for both parties, so as to minimize the risk of conflict.

Direct investment

The major disadvantages of the stages described so far, apart from pure exporting, concern the potential and actual lack of control a company submits itself to when relying upon another party to carry out some, or all, of its production and marketing functions. When a company's export interests reach a certain level, however, there may be no other alternative than to choose a growth route such as licensing or contract manufacturing.

If sufficient funds and management expertise are available, control can be retained by the home-based company if it decides to increase its international interests by direct investment in a foreign market. This stage may result from a company acquiring one that was formerly contracted to it, or from simply installing its own manufacturing and marketing operation in another country. Of course it should be recognized that a company may be at any of the stages described, in different countries, at any one time. While market methods and product types may differ in each separate country, direct investment in as many countries as possible does allow a company to achieve greater control and establish a corporate identity throughout its markets. This identity is as important for the employees as it is for the customers, because the company is able to establish standards of quality, management style and philosophy in all its divisions.

The multi-national organization

This final stage in international trade is worldwide trading, and is sometimes referred to as 'global marketing'. To some extent it is a conceptual structure, though a simple one. To be truly multi-national the company must consider 'the world' as its market place, so that the idea of a home base from which a company controls its international affairs is no longer applicable, although the headquarters may be situated in country 'X' and operating units will report to, and be directed by it. The operating units themselves will think of themselves as independent entities in their given country. In the UK, for example, many people may think of Ford as being British. In fact Ford in Britain is simply the UK operation of the Ford multi-national operation.

Although a multi-national operating unit may appear to be, and think of itself as being, independent in the relatively short term, the headquarters-based corporate management does in reality control the strategic destiny of the operating units. This fact gives rise to one of the more serious criticisms levelled at multi-nationals – that they have an uncaring, 'profit only' orientation in their strategic plans. As a holding company will manage its portfolio of companies, a multi-national will channel investment, or withdraw it, according to the best opportunities for a return on investment. The sheer size of multi-national operations is such that if they withdraw from a country, the social consequences can be grave.

A final factor worthy of note concerns the spread of 'culture free' products throughout the world. Such products as 'Levis' jeans or 'Coca-Cola' are typical examples. Distributive methods, and sometimes advertising, may vary from country to country, but no product modifications are made – whatever the market. These are 'global' products in a global marketing system. The likelihood is that as the world gets smaller in the cultural sense, such products will increase in importance.

Conclusion

International trade is carried out by companies of all sizes in a variety of organizational and strategic ways. It is often the case that a company will not develop at the same rate in all its overseas markets. Many companies are therefore going through more than one stage of development at the same time in different overseas markets. Exporting is the simplest method of international trade, but exporting is likely (as a very general rule) to diminish in efficiency as the company moves into and develops in more and more countries at ever-increasing levels. When this occurs, intermediate stages of trade such as licensing can be considered, but these will be at the expense of an element of control over the firm's activities. Direct investment in an overseas market, despite being costly and risky, offers the best opportunity for a company to plan for growth, while exercising greater control over its own affairs. The logical extension to direct investment in many markets is to adopt a multi-national organizational structure and management approach, although few companies graduate to this stage.

QUESTION 34

Comment upon the essential nature of marketing planning and strategy formulation. Illustrate your answer with appropriate industry/product analogies.

OBJECTIVES

This is a relatively straightforward question that is designed to test the candidate's ability to recount what is known about marketing planning and strategy through the medium of practical illustrations.

APPROACH

Start by defining the purpose of a formal marketing plan, and then go on to explain different planning horizons. In addition, point out how the marketing plan fits into the company's general strategic plan.

The question calls for analogies, so 'made up' examples are not essential when answering. But you must ensure, through your answer, that you understand the practical implications.

The main body of the question should then relate to the following key marketing plan elements:

(a) Situation analysis
(b) Statement of marketing objectives
(c) Summary of strategy and action programmes

With this background the question will in fact have been answered.

ANSWER

Suggested introduction

A formal marketing planning process is intended to guide the future operations of the marketing function, and this symbolizes the principle of purposeful marketing management. The marketing plan thus sets out, usually in written form, the goals for the component elements of the marketing function, and the ways in which such goals are to be achieved. In this sense the marketing plan is a carefully prepared statement of intent.

In many companies the marketing plan forms a sub-component of a general strategic plan. Strategic plans are often financial in nature, and rather general in terms of objectives. Marketing plans tend to be operational and more specific in nature; they are in effect functional plans at the operating level, carried out in support of strategic planning.

Time horizons

The marketing planning horizon tends to be for one year ahead – usually for the forthcoming financial year. Firms engaged in multi-product marketing will usually prepare a marketing plan for each separate product line. Such individual plans are often aggregated to form the marketing plan for the organization. Many companies pay particular attention to the planning activities relating to important new products. New-product plans thus tend to be set out in considerable detail and are often separate from the general plan.

The time horizon of the marketing plan will depend to a certain extent upon the type of industry in which the firm is operating. Firms in the fashion industry, for example, will tend to prepare plans for periods shorter than 1 year ahead. Often firms will prepare detailed plans for the next 12 months, with the subsequent 12, 24 or even 36 months in broad outline only. Some firms set marketing objectives and strategies for the next 5 or 10 years, although these tend to be very general in nature, and are more like a business plan than a functional marketing plan.

Key questions in marketing planning

Because the marketing plan is intended as a detailed statement of intent, it has to cover three broad fundamental questions from a marketing perspective:

(a) Where are we now?
(b) Where do we want to go?
(c) How do we get there?

In order to answer these three fundamental questions, the marketing plan will have to cover three key elements:

1 Situation analysis
2 Statement of marketing objectives
3 Summary of strategy and action programmes

Each of these key elements is now dealt with in turn.

1 *Situation analysis.* Plans often begin with a review of the current market situation for the products or product lines covered by the plan. This review will include trend data, information on competitors' positions, relative strengths and weaknesses of products, information upon past promotion-

al expenditure, etc. Companies differ widely in what they include in this section of the plan, as well as the degree of detail given. Generally this section of the plan will be sub-divided in the following way:

(a) Product sales
(b) Previous performance, related to objectives
(c) Present market situation
(d) Details of the competitive environment
(e) Identification of possible problems and potential opportunites

2 *Statement of marketing objectives.* This section of the plan sets clear objectives for the marketing function in terms of the planning period ahead. Many firms give a statement of objectives for each element of marketing, e.g. sales, advertising, sales promotion, training, marketing research, dealer activities, distribution, etc.

3 *Summary of strategy and action programmes.* Strategy and proposed action are often considered under a single heading. The strategy statements act as a connecting link between objectives and action. An example of a strategy statement might be:

> It is the company's intention to increase its market share of roller ball pens from the current 15 per cent to 23 per cent over the next 12 months by:
> (a) Increasing the amount spent on above the line promotion.
> (b) Redesigning the packaging.
> (c) Increasing the distribution base.

Action programmes detail the action steps by which the strategy will be implemented. The steps are usually stated in terms of priorities. A time schedule for the action programme is also given, along with an indication as to which individuals will be responsible for each part of the programme.

A final part of the marketing plan is usually a contingency plan. Internal or external circumstances may alter, owing to unpredictable circumstances, or poor performance during the planning period may indicate the need for alternative courses of action.

Conclusion

In summary the marketing plan is a plan of intent. It sets out the current situation, the goals and objectives that marketing hopes to achieve during the planning period, together with a strategy for achieving these objectives. These in turn are interpreted in terms of a specific action programme. The object of the plan is thus to guide the future operations of the marketing function, and its style and content reflects its purpose.

FURTHER READING

A text in the Heinemann series by Malcolm MacDonald upon the subject of marketing planning has recently been published. It details a step-by-step approach to what is regarded as a 'mysterious' area of marketing. In addition, a simple follow-up, also published by Heinemann and entitled *A Pictorial Guide to Marketing Planning*, explains in simplistic cartoon style the elements of marketing planning and how it fits into the corporate planning process.

QUESTION 35

Marketing strategy and planning are of little value without a system of control. What control procedures can be employed by marketing management?

OBJECTIVES

Systems of control or evaluation are often omitted from marketing texts and are quite often only taught in the final stages of a marketing course. (It is our opinion that objectives and evaluation should always be considered, and taught, together.) This question is designed to ensure that the candidate has a basic knowledge of control systems. The student should also demonstrate that control systems extend across the whole spectrum of marketing activity – from the daily, essentially tactical operation to the evaluation of long-term strategic plans.

APPROACH

The basis of the answer is to give an account of the marketing control methods you have studied. The opening statement in the question does, however, imply that a basic account should be embellished by giving reasons for the importance of control, and by emphasizing the futility of making plans without any form of evaluation.

Your answer should cover the whole range of marketing control. It would seem logical to begin your account with basic elements of marketing and conclude with a discussion of 'strategic marketing' and the 'marketing audit'.

ANSWER

Suggested introduction

Marketing planning and corresponding control systems have their basic origins in budgeting. When a company (or a household) sets a budget for expenditure, it is comparatively easy to keep a continuous check on whether this is being adhered to or not. Clearly if there is difficulty in operating within the budget, an attempt will be made to find out the reason why. Either the budget has been badly set, or circumstances have changed to such an extent during a given period that the budget has become inappropriate.

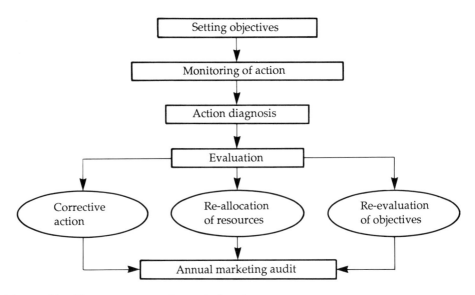

Figure 11   *The components of a control system*

Much of the planning for marketing management is similar to budgeting in that the company makes plans to spend 'x' amount on advertising and 'y' amount on sales. The idea (at least) of controlling this expenditure is relatively straightforward. Marketing planning and control become complicated, however, because marketing is concerned with more than financial considerations. A company must, of necessity, work within a set of limited financial resources (a budget), but marketing is concerned with utilizing these resources to achieve the best results for the company as a whole by meeting corporate objectives. Firstly, therefore, major objectives are set, and these are achieved by the setting of a series of tactical objectives (or sub-objectives). Control is required at both levels. In addition, the purpose of control is to evaluate whether tactical objectives are working to mutual benefit or if they are working against each other.

Marketing control is concerned therefore with finding out whether objectives are being met and with providing the mechanism for any corrective action which may be required.

Control systems
Control systems comprise an analysis of the following company objectives:

1   Sales and profit objectives
2   Financial objectives of the marketing functions
3   Marketing objectives of each of the marketing functions
4   Strategic objectives of the company

The financial and marketing aspects cannot be regarded independently of each other. While marketing objectives are formulated in order to develop the company, in reality these are only as feasible as the financial resources of the company will allow.

A control system is a relatively simple procedure as outlined in Figure 11. The control system shown in Figure 11 covers all the activities of the company. It is useful at this point to examine each area of control in more detail.

Sales and profit control. A major aspect of marketing within this context is sales forecasting. The sales forecast is the basis for a variety of decisions which must be made with reference to the marketing functions. The first task of sales control is to assess whether or not the forecast has been achieved. If the answer is 'yes', the company still needs to find out whether this could have been achieved by using less resources or whether the forecast has in fact been an underestimation. If forecasted sales have not been reached, the company must attempt to pinpoint the cause – by detailed analysis of sales by area, by customer and by product. The second element of sales control concerns analysis of sales costs. As with all other aspects of control, the objective is to assess how efficiently resources are being used.

The control of profit is achieved by analysing the expenses or costs of the marketing function. 'Costs' are often associated only with production. Marketing managers must analyse each marketing function so as to provide precise figures from within that area popularly described as selling expenses. For example, advertising may have the objective to increase brand recall by 'x' per cent, and distribution to reduce out of stock situations in retail outlets by 'y' per cent. It is obvious that the more expensive such objectives are to achieve, the less profit will be left over at the end of the year.

It is relatively easy to find out if the objectives are being achieved – that is profit control's function. One method is to treat each functional area as if it were a 'mini-company', and produce individual accounts for each one. This can be refined still further by taking this information and applying it to a single product or to a series of channels or retail outlet types. The analyst should be searching for anomalies and continually asking questions. Many of a company's methods are a reflection of tradition or even convenience – not efficiency or cost. Care should, however, be taken by senior management not to sub-optimize the marketing functions (see Question 25) when reacting to the results of such analyses.

Marketing control. In contrast to pure financial control, marketing control reduces the risks of sub-optimization because it considers the marketing objectives of the company 'in conjunction' with financial questions. Thus, it may be that expenditure on distribution in one area of marketing is disproportionate to that in another. Companies may be prepared to bear this seemingly inefficient cost in order to meet a service objective. Companies spending money on advertising when entering new markets or launching new products is one such example.

It is also the function of marketing control to consider the strategic objectives of the firm as well as being concerned with the marketing system. Strategic marketing is concerned with long-term goals which shape the future of the company. Decisions to enter and leave markets, to increase market share or to embark upon big investment programmes are described as 'strategic'. Strategic decisions can only be made on the basis of knowledge about the total marketing environment. The control process should examine the marketing strategy, or strategies, and judge whether it is still appropriate in the current environment.

Marketing audit. Strategic control is usually effected as a part of the 'marketing audit'. Although control processes are carried out on a continuous basis for both strategic and functional activities, the marketing audit is a periodic (usually once a year) exercise which examines *all* the marketing activities of the firm. It is best if the audit is undertaken by parties who are not influenced by the aims and activities of the marketing department. The audit team could come from outside the firm or consist of experienced company employees who are thoroughly familiar with the nature of marketing.

The audit should encompass the following dimensions:

1   The wider marketing environment
2   The functional or immediate marketing environment
3   The strategic objectives
4   The functional objectives
5   The marketing systems
6   The marketing organization
7   The marketing functions
8   Marketing cost and profitability analysis

The above list illustrates that the marketing audit is a periodic overhaul of many of the areas that are the subject of continuous control. The strategic element is vital in order to keep the company 'on course' – to ensure 'what business the company is in', 'why' and 'where the business expects to be in the future' is understood. The marketing audit also investigates 'how' marketing is being carried out as well as 'what' it is doing. In this respect marketing organization and marketing systems come under scrutiny.

Of all the marketing systems, it should be apparent that the control system itself relies heavily upon the Marketing Information System (see Question 10). Although each functional area should be accountable, it is only through the medium of a well developed Marketing Information System that such information can be co-ordinated and related to external influences upon the company.

Conclusion

The existence of a well developed control system provides evidence that a company is being managed according to a marketing orientation. Objectives are being set and evaluated. The company is also shown to be self-critical and prepared for change through a flexible system of planning.

FURTHER READING

As mentioned in the objectives, many marketing texts only make passing reference to this subject, but two texts in the Heinemann 'marketing' series are worthy of consideration: *Marketing Plans*, by Malcolm McDonald, and *Management Controls and Marketing Planning*, by R.M.S. Wilson.

QUESTION 36

The purpose of planning is to allocate company resources in such a manner as to achieve sales anticipated from the sales forecast. Such sales forecasts are for the short, medium and long terms. Describe the purpose of each of these forecasts and state their implications for the various functional areas of a business.

OBJECTIVE

This is a lengthy question that could easily have been asked in less than half the wordage. Do not attempt to read too much into such questions, because the idea behind the long introduction to the question is to give candidates a 'feel' for the problem. Simply put, this question is about resource planning for the short, medium and long terms.

APPROACH

The question is about forecasting horizons (short, medium and long term) and how these apply to individual aspects of business activity.

The answer could be tackled in one of two ways: first, by taking each of the aspects of forecasting and applying individual aspects of business to each of these types of forecast; or, secondly, by taking individual aspects of business and discussing each in turn in the context of short-, medium- and long-term forecasting. An alternative approach, and the one favoured in the answer given is to explain each type of forecast briefly and then go on at greater length to discuss how each might apply to each area of business.

To pass, the candidate would have to provide at least an adequate explanation of each type of forecast, with some reasoned discussion within the context of business activity. Forecasting is now becoming increasingly recognized as a sales marketing activity, so it is important that marketing students understand the place it plays within planning activity.

ANSWER

Possible introduction
Before consideration is made of individual aspects of business activity in

relation to forecasting and planning, a brief description is given of the three types of forecast in question:

1 *Short term* is for less than 1 year, with a normal range up to 3 months. It is normally made for tactical planning purposes.
2 *Medium term* is normally for one year, and it is from this forecast that the annual company budget for the year ahead is made.
3 *Long term* is for periods often well in excess of the above time-scales, though long term can mean different times for different types of industrial situation. For example, for steel-making 20 years would not be unusual, whereas for companies engaged in computer technological applications 3 years might be viewed as long term. Long-term forecasts are principally used for major strategic decision-making.

Companies prepare for change by planning and this demands that forecasts be made. An assessment should then be made of how the planning goals are to be reached. The sales forecast thus acts as the planning base upon which all internal forecasting and budgeting takes place. The effect of this is to reduce uncertainty, and allow companies to plan on a reasonably logical basis.

Forecasting and planning
At this stage it is perhaps useful to distinguish between forecasting and planning. The forecaster can predict what will happen for a set of decisions in a given set of circumstances. Planning, on the other hand, states that by taking certain actions the decision-maker can alter the subsequent events in relation to a particular situation. Consequently, if a forecast which predicts a fall in demand is made, management can prepare a plan to attempt to prevent sales from falling, e.g. increase promotional activity or cut prices.

Forecasting as it affects the functional aspects of business
Personnel needs forecasts to be able to predict future manning levels. They will assist training and recruitment. Longer term forecasts will also be useful when planning for management succession.

Production is most in need of short-term forecasting in order that production can be planned and scheduled on an orderly basis. This will lead to the more effective use of manpower and machinery. In the longer term, production will need to make decisions on levels of plant operation in order to be able to meet production levels to achieve the planned-for sales.

Purchasing requirements can be met on a more timely basis with accurate forecasts, and strategic purchasing can be entered into rather than just responding to the more immediate needs of production, e.g. longer 'lead' times may mean that purchasing can buy at a more competitive price. Stock control can also be improved with accurate forecasts, which means that stock levels can be more effectively controlled and the danger of overstocking, with resultant pressures on working capital and possible obsolescence and deterioration of stocks, can be lessened. Stock-outs can also be avoided, together with their resultant disruption to the production programme.

Research and development requires technological forecasts. From time to time products need updating or changing. A particular product line may be obsolescent, and R & D will need to plan and develop a new product or modify an existing product in order to keep it competitive in the market place. Marketing research should thus liaise with research and development, and through the medium- and long-term forecasts should co-ordinate new-product developments and new and modified product launches.

Finance is in need of forecasting in the medium term in particular in order to establish budgets that can be based on the planned-for sales. Forecasting accuracy is thus extremely important, because if the medium-term forecast upon which the business budget is based is wrong, then all company budgets will be incorrect. In the case of an over-optimistic forecast the company will overspend and will probably have to increase its overdraft, which will mean a drain on working capital. If the forecast is too pessimistic, then sales opportunities might be missed, because there will not be enough working capital to be able to capture the marketing opportunities presented by better market conditions than had been forecasted. Finance is also in need of long-term forecasts in order that it can engage in long-range profit-planning. It must make provision for long-term capital requirements in terms of plant and machinery, land and buildings, in order to meet expansion plans – based on the long-term forecast. This will be dependent upon correct estimations of cash-flow, which is itself a clear reflection of forecasting competence.

Marketing is also in need of accurate sales forecasts in order that it can plan promotional campaigns and various strategies to back up these campaigns. Remuneration plans will also need to be prepared, particularly if these are linked to sales targets or sales quotas. Such targets or quotas are of course a reflection of the sales forecast broken down among individual products and individual sales people. Long-term forecasts are also needed by marketing in order to plan such longer-term aspects as channel arrangements, e.g. if sales are predicted to increase substantially, then new channel arrangements might be called for or more dealers may need to be signed up. At a short-term level marketing needs forecasts in order to be able to plan tactically, which often means ensuring that most, if not all, customers are satisfied with regard to their immediate deliveries of goods or merchandise.

Conclusion

There is an interdependency between the plans and the operations of each of the functions described, since they are all based on the sales forecast. If indeed the original sales forecast turns out to be incorrect, then it will affect every function within the business, because each has used the forecast as its starting point. Thus the importance of timely and accurate production of sales forecasts cannot be over-emphasized because of their influence upon the effective operation of a business.

FURTHER READING

There is normally a sales forecasting section in good marketing texts, and also a number of modern specialist texts dealing with the subject in more detail. Quite often questions appear on marketing papers that ask the student to distinguish between qualitative and quantitative techniques, asking for brief descriptions of techniques under each heading. Ensure that the textbook you read has a comprehensive forecasting section or reference. For example, see *Forecasting for Sales and Material Management*, by G.A. Lancaster and R.A. Lomas (Macmillan, 1985).

QUESTION 37

'Segmentation is at the heart of marketing strategy.' Explain the importance of market segmentation. Choose two markets (one from a consumer and one from an industrial market) and briefly show how these may be segmented.

OBJECTIVE

The fact that a statement is made suggests that you should agree with it. The question is seeking to test depth of knowledge in so far as segmentation is concerned, and as such is not seeking a detailed definition, as this knowledge can be taken for granted. Application is therefore important, and it is through the examples chosen that this can be demonstrated. The question is also seeking to examine how strategy follows segmentation in terms of target marketing.

APPROACH

A brief explanation of segmentation should precede the main body of the answer, but, as mentioned in the objective, it should not cover basic detail but should discuss the contention in a positive way. The bulk of the answer should then concentrate upon the two examples – from consumer and industrial marketing perspectives.

ANSWER

Importance of market segmentation
Market segmentation analyses groups of customers in terms of their needs and wants. It is a derivative of product differentiation, which distinguishes product features that can enhance the image of the product and so command a premium in terms of price.

Markets can be segmented into groups of potential customers who possess one or more common characteristics. These are useful for explaining or predicting responses to various marketing stimuli.

Once segmentation has been considered, the company will then determine a marketing strategy in order to reach particular target markets. Basically, there are three such strategies:

1 *Undifferentiated marketing*, where the firm makes the choice not to target customers according to their individual characteristics. Instead it treats the market as homogeneous, and tries to develop a theme of mass appeal and superior imagery.

2 *Differentiated marketing*, where the company recognizes the market as being heterogeneous and targets several market segments at once. Each of these is approached by means of a different marketing mix.

3 *Concentrated marketing*, or market niching, recognizes the fact that company resources are finite and thus targets its marketing efforts on those segments which offer the best profit potential.

Requirements for evaluating market segments

Before attempting to segment a market, a company needs to be able to measure its potential success. There are three generally accepted requirements for this evaluation:

(a) The segment must be measurable and distinct, including information available that can highlight the effect of the particular buyer characteristic that makes it different.

(b) The segment must be accessible in that the company should be able to focus attention upon it.

(c) Its size should be substantial in terms of costs and potential benefits. Cultivating a separate market segment is expensive, and this expense can only be justified if the profit return is likely to outweigh it.

An example of consumer market segmentation

The example chosen is a manufacturer of hair shampoo.

Consumer markets are generally segmented on the basis of several different variables, the most frequent being as follows:

1 *Geographical* – by region, city or town.
2 *Demographical* – by age, sex, family size/structure, education, etc.
3 *Socio-economic* – by social class, occupation, etc.
4 *Psychographic* – by lifestyle, personality type, etc.
5 *Purchasing behaviour* – by number of purchasing occasions, usage rate and benefits sought.

Each of the above is now examined in more detail.

A clear leading indicator of the usage of shampoo is the population distribution throughout the country. That does not just mean the population density as such. What we really need to know is the population that can be reached by various targeting measures and also the population that the product can be profitably divided over.

Demographic segmentation follows on from the above, and here we need to look at the population in terms of its size and make-up. The number of families of child-bearing age will be a positive indication of a growing market. The number of older people is also an indication of those who will disappear from the market in coming years, and indeed their product formulation needs will tend to differ from those of younger people.

The socio-economic pattern varies from one part of the country to another and in this case it is possible to segment according to the 'benefits' required of a shampoo. Some classes will require a shampoo for functional reasons, e.g. reducing greasiness, whereas others will require a shampoo for what it will do for them, e.g. make them look better.

Following on from the above, lifestyles and personalities of consumers can be used to predict what image they most closely identify with, and to this extent shampoos are often given a brand 'image'.

Purchasing behaviour is manifest in how often consumers buy and how much they buy. They can also be segmented by the degree of their brand-loyalty and the degree to which they are prepared to switch brands.

An example of industrial market segmentation

The example chosen here is for a manufacturer of dust-extraction equipment.

The most recognized bases for segmentation are (a) macro and (b) micro. These are now looked at separately.

Macro bases for segmentation centre on the buying situation, including the organization, its type, its size and the application to which it is likely to put the products it purchases. The manufacturer will thus look at potential customers from the following viewpoints:

1 *Geographical* – by region, county or city.
2 *By size* – in terms of number of factories owned or being built by the customer.
3 *By type of purchasing influence* – e.g. architects, local authorities, factory-owners, etc.
4 *Usage rate* – frequent or infrequent purchasers.
5 *Previous purchases* – established customer or new business.

Micro bases are more concerned with the characteristics of the decision-making units (DMUs). The strategy of the purchasers is important in terms of whether they are satisficers or optimizers. The relative importance of the purchase to the organization is also significant, as are the personalities of the decision-makers. The manufacturer will thus look at purchasers from the following viewpoints:

(a) *Reason for purchase* – e.g. new plant, replacement plant.

(b) *Previous manufacturers used* – i.e. who these are, their structure, offerings, etc.
(c) *Satisfaction with previous suppliers* – i.e. low, medium or high.
(d) *Perceived risk of situation* – i.e. low, medium or high.
(e) *Attitude to risk of deciders or key influencers* – i.e. risk-takers, risk-averters or satisficers.

Conclusion

Both the above examples demonstrate the fact that firms face tight budgets for marketing their products. 'Market-niching' policies, especially in the business to business sector, enable scarce resources to be used to the best effect. Target marketing aims at the areas that offer the best short-term prospects. One important point for consumer marketers in particular is the use of below-the-line forms of promotion. These can be used to break down consumers' existing brand-loyalties.

QUESTION 38

Discuss the marketing objectives that a branding strategy aims to achieve.

OBJECTIVE

To ensure that the student has a thorough knowledge of the aims of branding strategy.

APPROACH

This question should not cause problems for the student in understanding what is required by the examiner. The objective, as stated above, bears out that the question is essentially uncomplicated. Care must be taken, however, to ensure that branding is related to marketing objectives, and that these are clearly stated.

There is obvious scope for discussing how branding can achieve a marketing objective, but detailed discussion as to 'how brand names are chosen', for example, should be avoided.

ANSWER

Suggested introduction
The importance of a brand name varies from company to company and from market to market. Brand names are most commonly associated with the marketing of consumer goods, and in particular fast-moving consumer goods (FMCGs), but they are by no means restricted only to these markets. In industrial markets branding is less prevalent, but even here a brand can still provide the means for establishing or reinforcing a corporate image, and for providing a method by which customers can identify with the company. The plethora of brand names confronting the consumer can be overwhelming, but the fact that so many brands exist does not detract from the usefulness of brands to marketing strategy. The value of exceptionally successful brand names, such as Hoover, Kleenex, Frigidaire and Nylon, cannot be calculated, as these have now become synonymous with the generic product.

For many companies the brand bears the name of the company itself, e.g. McDonald's restaurants, Kodak or Hertz car rentals. The strength of branding is underlined when one ponders how few consumers will know that Fairy liquid is made by Procter & Gamble. The brand name itself in this latter case is almost a generic term for washing-up liquid. It is the fact that consumers and industrial buyers are apt to forge extremely strong relationships with a 'name' that makes branding an integral part of strategic marketing, and this in turn facilitates the making of functional marketing plans. The perception of the brand relates directly to the perception of the corporate image.

Branding and strategic marketing

The brand must be considered as a 'strategic tool' used to implement the company's objectives. In strategic terms branding is used to promote the company image. If skilful advertising and promotional methods are used, the desired image can be projected through the branded product, in addition to the images that are created for the product itself. Branding also provides the means to build up a customer base that can be identified by the company (through marketing research), and a means by which customers can identify with the company. Marketing objectives can therefore be quantified, because customers are either 'users' or usually sufficiently acquainted with the brand to express an opinion about it.

The development of branded products aids the development of segmentation strategies. If the company objective is to segment the market by appealing to three customer groups with three products that belong to a similar category, branding provides product differentiation and thus the obvious opportunity to build a strategy for each brand.

Marketing control is also made easier by branding. In FMCG markets it is common for companies to structure themselves on a product manager basis. Each product manager may have several 'brand' managers, who give the brand their whole attention and provide detailed, up-to-date information to those responsible for control.

Since the late 1960s and early 1970s large grocery retailers have provided examples of the power of branding. These retailers have in many cases almost dispensed with suppliers' brands and have adopted an 'own brand' strategy. Marks & Spencer has always followed this course, and in the 1980s 'own branding' is the underlying thrust behind the strategy of most supermarket chains.

Like manufacturers, their objective is to create an image through the medium of the products they sell and to foster customer loyalty. Of course the supermarket chains continue to stock suppliers' brands alongside their own, since the power of suppliers' brands still illustrates the power of strong branding. Retailers realize that some brand names possess such loyalty among consumers that they could not operate successfully without them. The principal advertising slogan of a major breakfast cereal manufacturer states that the company does not make cereals for 'anyone else'. Clearly this manufacturer is fighting back at 'own labels' by the direct use of branding. The statement in the slogan also tells the consumer something about the company's attitude towards its customers, and this fosters the desired image objective. Perhaps even more significantly in this case the power of the brand is such that the cereal company is able to achieve its objectives, despite the vast buying power the major supermarket chains are normally able to exercise over their suppliers.

The phenomenon of 'own branding' is relatively new and is practised with the approval and co-operation of suppliers of such products. In different circumstances, however, a company's products can be vulnerable to imitation. The origins of branding are found in trademarks and patents. In this respect brand names provide legal protection against imitators and thus the manufacturing company's own marketing objectives. However, it is no secret that some large retailers place their own brands alongside manufacturers' brands, often in similar looking jars or packages, with the clear objective of enabling consumers to compare prices and perhaps induce them to think that the 'own label' brand is exactly the same as the manufacturer's brand, but cheaper. Quite often they are the same, but quite often they are not – a source of much irritation to manufacturers who do not produce 'own label' brands.

Conclusion

Branding enables a company to identify itself and its products. This not only aids the fulfilment of marketing strategies, but also helps customers to make the buying decision. For many FMCGs the marketing objective is to 'routinize' the buying process in the consumer's mind, so that the risk of being tempted by competitive products is minimized. The psychological objective of branding is therefore to reduce customer search as far as possible and to establish a name which, in the customer's mind, is synonymous with the desired image of the product. This could be quality, taste, prestige or some other form of non-demographic segmentation, based on lifestyle. Indeed it must be said that probably the most successful company in the world in adopting this strategy is the Coca Cola Company.

FURTHER READING

Branding in itself tends to be a specialist area, and general marketing texts, even those specifically written around the retail area, tend only to make passing reference to the subject. There is, however, a modern text that concentrates specifically upon this subject: *The Economics of the Brand: a marketing analysis*, by Trevor Watkins (McGraw-Hill, 1986). The text does, however, lean heavily upon economics for its material, but as a text that relates specifically to branding, and gives numerous references for further study, it can certainly be recommended.

QUESTION 39

Marketing has been criticized both on economic and ethical grounds. Discuss these criticisms, indicating how far you think they are justified.

OBJECTIVES

The objective of this question is to encourage the student to think. This thinking should display the results of further reading and indicate that the candidate's level of maturity is such as to reveal that marketing studies have gone further than a blind acceptance of all that is printed in standard texts.

APPROACH

Although this question offers scope for free discussion, it is important that the answer has structure and continuity. It is also necessary to include certain standard themes, e.g. marketing is wasteful, or advertising is over-persuasive. These themes and others should be outlined and discussed in turn. Remember that both 'economic' and 'ethical' criticisms should be treated, and that, rather than merely repeating sections of marketing type text, your answer should include evidence of original thought.

A possible format could be as follows:

1 An introductory section outlining what you consider to be the aims of marketing.
2 The main part of the answer, which discusses major criticisms.
3 A conclusion which appraises marketing and discusses how successful you think marketing to be in achieving the goals you have described.

ANSWER

Suggested introduction
From the various definitions of the marketing concept that exist it is possible to identify the major tenets common to all of them. These are that the aim of marketing is to satisfy the customer and that, in so doing, the company should make a profit so as to be able to continue its existence. It is probably the misuse and abuse of the word 'profit' that has called the concept of marketing into question most frequently. The profit motive of a firm is often considered as the

overriding principle of all business activity. Clearly profit must be in the forefront of business thinking. Marketing critics, however, would argue that profits are obtained at the expense and often to the detriment of the customer, marketing techniques being the tools used to carry out marketing practice.

Although it is apparent that many unscrupulous firms foster and encourage the negative image of marketing, these firms are not, however, fulfilling the marketing concept. It is highly questionable therefore that *marketing* as a practice should be condemned because certain firms use the term *marketing* to describe and practise activities which do not relate to the marketing concept. Marketing is further misunderstood by the media, which sometimes describe questionable activities as 'marketing ploys'; such language compounds any poor images that might exist, and 'feeds' the critics of marketing.

Genuinely marketing-orientated companies cannot afford to isolate their customers or the public at large. Marketing orientation calls for long-term thinking, and depends upon repeat business from satisfied customers; profit can only result from customer satisfaction and a positive image in the long term. Genuinely concerned critics of marketing have, however, raised issues which are relevant to the world of business, and to society as a whole. These issues are worthy of debate, so that the marketing concept can be better understood and more widely appreciated. Moreover, open debate allows real sources of dissatisfaction to be revealed and affords the opportunity for corrective action to be taken.

Criticisms of marketing
Typical criticisms in the 'micro' sense include:

(a) Poor product quality
(b) Poor advertising quality
(c) Deceptive packaging and labelling
(d) Unreliable delivery
(e) Poor after-sales service

Those companies who are guilty of any of the above practices are indeed deserving of criticism. Most people have at some time had cause for complaint about some aspect of their dealings with companies. This suggests that even among marketing-orientated companies there is always room for improvement. These companies should be receptive to such criticism and plan for continued improvement. They will also recognize that in the long term it is in their interests to organize their businesses so as to eliminate these complaints, because consumers always possess the ultimate sanction – to go elsewhere for their goods and services.

The more fundamental criticisms of marketing question the ways in which needs are satisfied and resources are allocated. In 'market' economies it is largely accepted that companies must make a profit so as to reinvest for greater efficiency and to develop new products. This being so, there is still debate as to the ethical and economic role marketing plays in society. The major economic criticisms are based on the premise that our system of providing goods and services is inefficient.

One aspect of this criticism is that marketing creates monopolies and thereby limits consumer choice. Critics would argue that the economic theory of 'perfect competition' is a market situation which offers the most favourable environment for consumer choice. In reality, the state of perfect competition never really exists – nor does a totally monopolistic situation.

More normally business is carried out in conditions which lie in between these two extremes. Marketing and markets are characterized more often than not by a variety of business conditions. Companies range from small to medium to large, while a few of the very large companies could be termed oligopolistic. It is true that some companies (in particular multi-national organizations) dominate certain markets, but they are, however, continually subject to competition. The existence of alternatives, allied to the notion of consumer sovereignty, will tend to reduce any feelings of complacency that companies might have towards their customers. It is also true that companies with large market shares might owe this to their financial power, but it is also true that they could not hold these shares if their products were unacceptable to their customers.

The fear that very powerful oligopolies will dictate to consumers as to what they should buy, and at what price, has been allayed to some extent in recent years by a tendency for smaller companies to offer alternative, more acceptable products. This phenomenon is well illustrated by the resurgence of such products as traditional beer and bread, which have challenged the imposition of 'standard' products on consumers. Large companies who standardize their products to gain profit at the expense of consumer choice have summarily neglected the marketing concept.

A further economic criticism is that marketing systems are wasteful. It is a common claim that if less money was spent on advertising, for example, companies could then afford to sell products more cheaply. Moreover, if we must have advertising, then its main role should be informative rather than competitive. Why, critics ask, should vast amounts be spent on advertising a variety of products which are essentially the same?

In the 1980s advertising does appear to be a pervasive influence on our lives. The subject is a topic of a great deal of intellectual debate, in particular the advertising of such products as credit services, which gives rise to an ethical as well as an economic challenge. Two points in defence of marketing expenditure can be offered:

● Companies have financial limitations, and cannot continue to promote

products which are not well received by consumers.
- This leads to the second point, that when consumers buy a product they purchase more than the physical object or service. They are also purchasing a product image which corresponds to their self-image, and, in so doing, fulfil needs which go beyond those of mere utility. This fact diminishes the relative importance of price, which implies that in many cases the consumer is prepared to pay a price whose cost includes an element of marketing expenditure in addition to the basic production cost.

The fact that consumers seem to be prepared to pay such costs leads to the socially based criticism that marketing has promoted materialism and has created artificial needs and values. In other words, marketing is not satisfying inherent needs, but has in fact invented a series of needs which are based on an appeal to status consciousness, envy and indulgence. Advertising aimed at children bears the brunt of such criticism and much of this is questioned by far wider groups than recognized intellectual critics. In economies where the 'wealth gap' is large the same critical rationale can be applied, although marketing is not responsible for such situations of inequality. The psychological needs of consumers are so complex that it is difficult to distinguish between a real need and one that has been created. It is also true that general rises in living standards and disposable income permit consumers to buy products which are not practically necessary.

Large organizations in particular are frequently criticized for unethical approaches in their business activities. Such criticism goes much further than attacks on dubious practices at the 'tactical' level. They concern issues such as pollution, conservation, waste, health and safety. Without doubt the post-war decades have witnessed a great deal of negligence in these areas. Policies pursued have not always taken into account the long-term ramifications of ecological pollution or the harmful effects of food additives or lead in petrol – two very topical issues.

Marketing ethics and the marketing concept become a little blurred at this stage. Marketing practitioners might argue that they are satisfying consumer needs, that they could modify their actions, but only at a price that the consumer would *not* be willing to pay. It is becoming more and more acceptable, however, that marketing has social responsibilities as well as responsibility to immediate customers. Such thinking adds considerably to the scope of the marketing concept, and recognizes that, like other social structures, marketing must evolve. Companies must recognize that while serving one sector of society, they could be alienating another.

It cannot be denied that there are substantial areas of business activity that deserve criticism. Unfortunately for genuinely marketing-oriented companies, the actions of others who are less scrupulous and short-term-oriented have tended to besmirch the image of marketing as a whole. For marketing-orientated companies the emphasis on the long-term satisfaction of the customer means that actions that provoke criticism are counter-productive – this in itself is a defence for marketing activity. The existence of continual competition is a further check against malpractice, reducing further the likelihood that companies can act against the interests of their customers.

Consumer choice is also the major argument in defence of marketing expenditure. Attempts by some large retailers to sell unbranded goods with a minimum of packaging at lower prices have only met with limited success (e.g. white label and yellow label lines that were in vogue in the late 1970s). This would suggest that price is only one element of the product and that when consumers make a purchase, part of the satisfaction process is concerned with image and presentation.

Conclusion

The concept of socially oriented marketing augments the original marketing concept. Many firms still fall short of a totally responsible attitude towards their marketing activities, but there is evidence to suggest that social marketing is being adopted throughout industry. Examples include the changes in attitudes towards waste and recycling, choice of packaging material, food additives and lead in petrol – the latter being helped by the Chancellor of the Exchequer, who has deliberately kept down duty in order that lead free fuel can sell at comparable prices to leaded fuel.

The goal of social marketing is thus to fulfil the marketing concept, while at the same time ensuring that society as a whole does not suffer from the process of satisfying a particular privileged consumer group.

QUESTION 40

What problems do you feel might be associated with applying the theory of marketing management to real-life situations?

OBJECTIVE

To enable the examiner to judge the level of maturity in the student's approach to marketing. Although marks will be awarded according to the breadth of knowledge of marketing, the objective of the question requires that the emphasis in mark allocation should be placed on the student's clarity of thought and reasoning ability.

APPROACH

Your answer should rely less on the recall of fact and information, which is common to the 'describe' and 'account for' type of question, and more upon the presentation of a few situations you think are relevant. As well as drawing upon your studies to provide examples/discussion points, your answer will be improved and made more original by the inclusion of material drawn from your own professional experience (or if this is not possible, material that you have gleaned 'second hand' from cases, press items, etc.). Care must be taken not to be too specific, but there is certainly no doubt that original ideas, if relevant and well presented, will add to your marks.

As stated above in the objective, the question should allow you to demonstrate that you have a mature perspective of marketing management. The following guideline may prove useful:

Discussion point example

It would be constructive to discuss say, *personnel* as a discussion topic. You would probably cover problems such as:

1 Conflicting personal objectives within the company.
2 Differing levels of marketing awareness amongst employees.
3 Problems of morale and motivation.

If this happens to be a problem which you had experienced, you should not cite detail of specific personnel, names, dates, etc. Rather, treat your paragraph with a format such as: 'One problem area concerns personnel. In my own experience, differing levels of marketing awareness can cause difficulties when setting the advertising budget.'

You could then go on to discuss the problem of funding when a short-term, purely financial view is taken of an expensive, long-term, image-building campaign which research had shown the company badly needed. Your own opinion could be expressed and you could suggest possible solutions to the problem.

The situation described above is an example only, and you must of course use your own examples. A similar approach format is useful in many of the situations where there is scope for your personal observations.

As usual your introduction should 'set the scene' for the answer to follow.

In conclusion, an important theme which should be emphasized is that, while recognizing the absolute importance of the marketing concept and its functions, successful marketing should be versatile enough to be adapted to individual situations. The answer required is thus essentially creative: it draws upon one's knowledge, but is more concerned with perceptions and interpretations. For this reason the answer given should not be regarded as a definitive 'model' but rather as an example of the author's ideas, which are intended to stimulate the reader's own thoughts, opinions and perhaps recall of experiences.

ANSWER

Suggested introduction

The theory of marketing management can be introduced in a variety of ways to those who practise marketing in reality. Some will have attended full-time courses and others will have worked for some time before embarking upon evening classes or day-release courses which lead to formal qualifications. Other inquiring minds, perhaps older than those just described, but recognizing the need for continued learning, may educate themselves simply by reading or by attending the occasional short course or seminar. All have something in common – sooner or later they will encounter situations difficult or impossible to reconcile with a textbook solution.

As is true for any practical working system, difficulties in applying the theory of marketing in real life are caused by internal and external influences. It is useful to consider the 'functional' and 'conceptual' aspects of marketing (see answer to Question 1) separately in order to understand how and why problems can occur. The marketing functions cannot be exercised efficiently unless the concept is clearly understood. This is fundamental to the practice of marketing – many firms that still possess a selling or a production orientation carry out advertising campaigns. They must be concerned with packaging and physical distribution, but unless these functions are performed against the background of the marketing concept, the results are likely to be less effective in the long term. Even with a sound marketing orientation, the functional areas can provide their own problems, but basic problems are a result of the marketing concept not being thoroughly understood throughout the firm.

Acceptance/understanding of the marketing concept in the firm is a problem area for the marketing practitioner

What is marketing? Ideally all employees should be able to answer this question. In practice this is not always the case. A cost accountant, or a member of production management may not view the world with the same eyes as a marketing-oriented employee. This statement is not meant to denigrate or even criticize 'non-marketers' (all employees are valuable members of a team). It merely means to say that the marketer's plans could be misunderstood by those who have not had the same training. In real life this is one area of difficulty for the application of theory. Such communication breakdowns manifest themselves in a variety of functional aspects of marketing. For example:

1 *Marketing research* could be regarded as expensive, time-consuming, non-productive, not cost-effective. The setting up of an integrated information system could be regarded as disruptive – putting an unnecessary burden of extra paperwork on already busy staff. In such an environment the marketing researcher will find that putting theory into practice leads to conflict and a lack of co-operation.
2 *Distribution.* The marketing-orientated sales person may find that the company's transport and distribution system is designed around 'cost' rather than 'customer' orientation. A small amount of money saved on delivery while reducing short-term costs may lose customers in the longer term.
3 *Production flexibility.* The longer the production run, the more the production team will be able to increase output and efficiency. This, however, is not necessarily what the customer requires. Thus, a product-line manager may experience difficulty in maintaining supplies of the full line if his or her objectives are in conflict with the production team.

The reader should note that other examples can be added showing how marketing goals are sometimes in conflict with other areas of management.

Even taking into account the frustrations the marketer may experience when endeavouring to put theory into practice, it is vital, if success is ultimately to be achieved, that he/she always maintain a mature and professional approach. If not, existing problems will only be compounded. Each section of the company will attempt to perform its role with maximum effect and efficiency – as it sees it. The marketer should respect this, using tact and discretion rather than conflict as the means to co-ordination.

All the efforts of the firm should be brought together with one person in mind – the customer. When different departments are pulling in different directions, this is known as 'sub-optimization'. While efficiency seems apparent 'on paper', the real requirements of the firm, i.e. satisfied customers, are often overlooked.

Understanding the marketing concept and promoting this throughout the company is a top management responsibility

Given that some element of conflict and sub-optimization can be a fact of working life, the major task of management is to keep this to an absolute minimum. Only the highest levels of management have the authority to engender a marketing orientation throughout the workforce. Top managers should head a 'top down' filter process by example, and, by designing systems, ensure that the whole company is pulling in the same direction. Some companies organize formal educational programmes to explain their objectives and to ensure that each department understands the nature of the others' roles. If long-term goals are explained, there is less likelihood of opposition to what may appear to be ill founded or extravagant expenditures in the short term.

Marketing functions themselves — theory to reality

Sometimes we read in the press of 'textbook' operations or of the performance of a 'classical marketing strategy'. Such achievements are worthy of mention, because behind them lies a great deal of hard work, careful planning, discipline and, more than likely, an element of luck.

Most students and managers will at some time have played management games or answered problems relating to a case study. Whatever the constraints built into these hypothetical situations, they are rarely as unpredictable as real life. Here marketing personnel may be subjected to the human, internal difficulties just described. Secondly, they must be prepared for external factors which can disrupt the best made plans. These should not be confused with practical problems at work. A market researcher may experience difficulty in obtaining an adequate sample size, or an advertising executive may run into problems with media selection. These are problems of the job itself, and are not issues with which this answer is concerned. Some examples of external influences are discussed later.

The 'textbook' strategy already described may well have been the result of a combination of circumstances where all factors were on the side of the firm. More likely, however, various limiting constraints and influences are against the firm. The 'trick' is that the company should succeed despite the problems with which it is confronted.

Finance. All companies which remain profitable work closely to financial budgets. Whether such companies be Procter & Gamble, IBM or a small firm with only a handful of employees, the amount of money available to them is always finite. The best theoretical course of action, say, in advertising strategy may wildly exceed the company's available resources. A modified strategy must therefore be conceived, and it is here that the creativity of the marketer is put to the test. Whatever the resources of a company, marketing management should always be mindful of the need for allocation of resources with long-term results in mind. In this way seemingly excessive expenditure at the time should form part of long-term strategy, and lead to the achievement of strategic objectives.

Environmental factors. These are thoroughly discussed in the answer to Question 2. In general these are long-term changes which good marketing should be in tune with at a 'macro' level. Long-term strategy should be geared to gradual demographic, economic or cultural changes. In the short term several environmental factors may cause problems in the appliance of a theoretical approach to any of the marketing functions:

1 Unpredictable competitive action. This could include the sudden entry of a competitor into a previously well ordered market. A competitor may adopt a particularly aggressive pricing policy which disrupts the existing status quo. It is not unknown for competitors to alter their existing marketing tactics with the sole aim of disrupting a new-product launch or test market of another company.
2 A carefully planned export strategy may have to be modified owing to dramatic changes in currency rates. Although the 'watchword' of exporting is continued commitment, the company may have to rethink its expansion strategy.
3 An existing or proposed channel may be the subject of sudden change. A chosen middleman could be taken over by a competitor or go into liquidation.

Conclusion and comment

Faced with any of the problems which have been the subject of this answer, the marketer experiences a situation where theory does not 'fit' with reality. Cynics may then say what is the use of theory? The answer to such a challenge is in 'how' the theory is related to practice. Taking the product life cycle concept as an example, textbooks will advise on the best strategy to adopt at each given stage in the cycle. Marketing is not chemistry or physics, however, and we cannot say with certainty that a particular action will result in a predictable outcome. Textbook theory is the result of logic and experience drawn from observation made over a long period. Other things being equal, we know the likely results of certain actions. When other things are not equal, this does not totally negate the theory, because the theory has acted as a framework or guideline in a set of reasonably familiar circumstances.

Success in marketing depends, therefore, upon a sound knowledge of theory before the 'real life' practice can properly begin. Of course this cannot take the place of natural talent and business acumen, but at the very least it provides a starting point and a disciplined approach to business problems – such knowledge should stimulate imaginative reactions to given situations. Successful marketing also depends upon the marketer's ability to 'adapt' his or her knowledge of theory to a given situation. One of the hallmarks of a successful company is a flexible approach to marketing. At times the rigid marketing theorist can be as harmful to the well-being of a company as one who does not accept the marketing concept at all.

FURTHER READING

This question and answer are not designed to suggest answers to problems; rather they are meant to alert the reader to the fact that they exist. To help find answers, the following areas of reading are recommended: case studies of actual business/marketing situations; textbooks and articles on organizational behaviour (how to deal with growth within the company and the management of innovation); sub-optimization, usually dealt with in sections of texts covering logistics and physical distribution management.

FOUR

Mini case studies

This text has selected three mini case studies which correspond to the three key areas of the Institute of Marketing Diploma examination:

1 International aspects of marketing
2 Planning and control
3 Marketing communications

All three cases are based upon live situations in companies and are designed to enable students of marketing to respond to the situations presented and to answer the questions posed.

Mini cases such as these are intended as relatively brief scenarios which should not be treated in depth with sophisticated analysis techniques. A mini case study sets the scene and questions are designed to elicit an answer realistically tailored to the practical background of the stated situation.

Under examination conditions these mini case studies are presented at the time of the examination. Therefore candidates must respond under examination conditions. There is not the time to analyse the situation before the examination day.

Mini cases, used in this way, are aimed to test the candidate's ability to select from acquired knowledge, attitudes and skills those appropriate to the questions asked, and equally to reject that which is inappropriate. Such an examination aims to avoid the totally academic or knowledge-by-rote-learning type of answer.

A concise format is expected, and essays largely are considered inappropriate. A structured report style format is favoured. Being more efficient in the use of words, it encourages a succinct approach and aids the development of the real skill needed by all practitioners of marketing.

Again, candidates would not be expected to replicate the standard of answer posed after each mini case, and indeed this would not be physically possible within the space of about 1½ hours. The answers represent acceptable solutions; students should present their examination answers, taking into consideration the time-constraints imposed.

International marketing : Exotic Siam Ltd

Just 4 years ago John Redwood resigned as International Operations Director of A.C. Reed, a UK-based multinational corporation, to form a partnership with Alan Rees-Jones, a Thai naturalized UK expatriate, to import cane and rattan furniture from South East Asia into the United Kingdom. Two companies were formed – Thai Arts & Crafts (TAC) in Bangkok to source, procure and consign cane products to the United Kingdom, and Exotic Siam Ltd in London, to import and retail furniture throughout retail concessions in one major host departmental-store group, Windsor Stores, and one major host high-street soft-furnishings retailer, Andersons.

Progress to date has resulted in forty-five retail outlets for Exotic Siam throughout the UK, which employ the promotional theme 'Exotic Siam: a showcase of oriental treasures'. Product range extension through TAC multi-sourcing offers to the general public:

- cane and rattan lounge, dining-room and conservatory furniture
- authentic handcrafts
- silk and cotton soft furnishings
- pottery and ceramics
- oriental fashion jewellery
- bronzeware and fine silverware
- solid wood carvings and original art

all attractively merchandised and displaying an Exotic Siam statement of authenticity on each product label.

Countries of origin include China, Hong Kong, Indonesia, Malaysia, the Philippines, Singapore, Taiwan and of course Thailand.

TAC supplies 60 per cent direct. The balance is procured by Exotic Siam Ltd in the UK from other importers.

A catalogue of the full range of products and prices is available in all stores, and telephone ordering is actively encouraged by Exotic Siam sales staff, although the host retail organization receives 20 per cent commission on all sales as an inclusive payment for floor space rental, sales administration and overheads.

Windsor Stores has outlets in France and the USA. Exotic Siam has been offered retail concessions in both countries.

Both John Redwood and Alan Rees-Jones require your advice as an international marketing consultant on:

1 The potential impact of culture in the selected markets of France and the USA upon sales of their product ranges.
2 Detailed considerations that Exotic Siam should assess before proceeding further with international expansion.

Section 1   The potential impact of culture in the selected markets of France and the USA upon sales of Exotic Siam product ranges

1.1   COUNTRIES UNDER CONSIDERATION

Both within and between France and the USA cultural divergence exists. Yet it is necessary to identify and exploit areas of cultural affinity to maximize product sales.

In-depth research by means of focus groups will assist in discovering areas of contention, so that these may be avoided in the company's marketing mix strategy. Product sales will not depend upon Exotic Siam product profile and positioning alone, but upon the surrounding elements of the company's market presentation and related mix variables. Ultimately adjustment may need to be made to accommodate international differences.

1.2   SELECTED DIVISIONS OF CULTURE

This subject is most complex and often dismissed by the practitioner until embarrassing mistakes are made, followed by the cost of lost business. It may be wise for Exotic Siam to explore the main factors as between South East Asian products in the UK market and UK trading practices, and the markets for exploitation in France and the USA, thus:

- 1.2.1   Language
- 1.2.2   Religion
- 1.2.3   Values and attitudes
- 1.2.4   Education
- 1.2.5   Social organization
- 1.2.6   Technology and material culture
- 1.2.7   Law and politics
- 1.2.8   Aesthetics

1.2.1   Language
Although trading will proceed under the Windsor Stores banner, the spoken, written and official languages will differ from that of the UK.

In France the level of linguistic pluralism is low, and therefore the language hierarchy favours French as the national spoken language. English, though an international language, will not assist with trading at local level or in dealing with French employees. In the short term French-speaking expatriate staff will be needed to assist in the transition to international status for Exotic Siam's retailing operations. In addition, local advertising must use the language of the mass media, again French.

In the USA there is of course close linguistic affinity between English and American. Only minor adjustments to colloquial and business linguistics will be required.

1.2.2 Religion

In certain nations with developed and developing economies, sacred objects, philosophical systems, beliefs and norms, prayer, taboos, rituals and holidays pose a cultural network which must not be offended. This is not the case in either France or the USA and would not affect the marketing of the Exotic Siam range of products in either country.

1.2.3 Values and attitudes

Throughout the world values and attitudes towards a multitude of intangibles differ, often markedly. For example, the dimensions of time, levels of achievement, the work ethic, wealth, attitudes towards change and risk-taking must be assessed by the international marketer.

The purchase of Exotic Siam products will require a change in attitude by buyers to bring into their homes goods of South East Asian origin. The adoption process will depend upon the level of open innovation within the buyer group. It would be wise for Exotic Siam to conduct motivational research among likely target groups to assess the attitude towards their product ranges and the way in which such products are valued.

1.2.4 Education

In the developing countries of South East Asia formal, vocational, primary, secondary and higher educational systems are very different from those in the UK, France and the USA. However, the movement of products is from east to west, and therefore few difficulties will arise.

As in the UK, Exotic Siam must check all labelling and instructions attached to products. Translations must not only be accurate but embrace the idiomatics of the spoken language/educational levels in the countries of end-use application.

1.2.5 Social organization

One marked difference in culture between East and West is social organization and the forms this takes: kinship, social institutions, authority structures, interest groups, social mobility, social stratification and status systems. These are less marked between countries in the West. However, the importance attached to Exotic Siam products may be positively correlated with social stratification and hence status systems. Again this should be researched to ensure that market targeting of (a) the company profile and (b) the ranges of products is conducted on a scientific basis by Exotic Siam.

1.2.6 Technology and material culture
The difference here again is between East and West. Within France and the USA transportation and communications systems and associated infrastructure are well established and do not pose a threat to the marketing of Exotic Siam products.

1.2.7 Law and politics
The realms and multitudes of dimensions surrounding the home country laws in France and the USA, plus the further dimensions of foreign and international laws and the regulations at trade and product level, *must* be examined fully before Exotic Siam can proceed with international expansion. It is unlikely, however, that political ideology, as such, will pose a threat in either country.

1.2.8 Aesthetics
This single dimension of culture itself has many sub-systems which *will* impact upon the effective marketing of the Exotic Siam product ranges. The area of perceived aesthetic value should be linked with the motivational research programme previously identified to examine cultural differences between countries. In turn this will assist the determination of an 'international product range' schedule in the UK, France and the USA, so that economies of scale can be achieved.

The perceptions of beauty, good taste, design, the use of colour and textures far outstrip the meaning of a brand name for the Exotic Siam range of merchandise. These perceptions must be tested against social stratification and the potential reasons for purchase.

Natural products from the Far East normally will need to harmonize with what exists in the household, whether they are bought for the family unit or as gifts for friends and relations.

It is anticipated that purchase motivations will also be different for each product range. Cane and rattan furniture may be purchased as a daily used consumer durable or as occasional furniture for use in the garden or conservatory, whereas oriental fashion jewellery may have only a short-term novelty value.

Therefore it is deemed essential to determine purchase motivations for all product ranges by social stratification so as to enable the launch of Exotic Siam in either France or the USA to be correctly positioned.

Section 2   Detailed considerations that Exotic Siam should assess before proceeding further with international expansion

2.1   A CORPORATE PRIORITY STATEMENT

The success achieved to date in the UK has been outstanding, at approximately one store opening each month on average for the past 4 years. Can this growth be maintained within the UK or should Exotic Siam seek retail expansion overseas?

A policy statement is required, and the associated level of priority for such expansion overseas must be specified. Such expansion must be proactive and not reactive to opportunities presented by Windsor Stores.

There is an inherent danger in having too much investment/activity in one area, i.e. the Windsor Stores retail concessions. It would be wise to consider the longer-term implications for Exotic Siam if relations between the two companies became soured.

2.2   FINANCIAL AND MANPOWER CONSTRAINTS

Growth must be financed. Sources of finance from within the Exotic Siam corporation and beyond must be found to take on further expansion. It is unlikely that growth on an international scale will be financed from retained earnings alone.

The cost of finance must be assessed against the return on the investment and the period of the expected return. Opportunity cost must be considered, i.e. the cost of other alternatives foregone should the Exotic Siam venture with Windsor Stores extend to France and/or the USA.

One major factor which governs international expansion is the manpower resources available and required.

It is assumed that the London head office controls retail operations centrally, with a level of decentralization at store level. Once the horizons for retailing spread to two different countries logistically removed from the UK, new management control operations will be needed. New staff, new structures, new communication systems will be required, and all will require a significant level of financial investment.

2.3   MARKET INFORMATION REQUIREMENTS AND REVIEW

A fact-finding mission to compile a dossier of market-related information for both the selected areas within France and the USA is needed. Market profiles, forecasts, competitor profiles and an identification of target markets within each country are required in relation to many environmental market factors. The following list is not exhaustive but serves to indicate the nature and importance of these considerations when trading between parts of South East Asia and France/USA.

Information type:

- Market size, volumes, values and cyclical, secular and seasonal trends and forecasts
- Level and positioning of competition
- Prevalent trade practices
- Attitudes towards products/company/host retail organization
- Political, economic, social, cultural stability
- Prevailing government intervention/deregulation
- Barriers to trade, tariff and non-tariff business
- Profit repatriation restrictions
- Constraints on future trade
- Channels to be used
- Need for and availability of facilitating agencies
- Levels of visible risk
- Advice available from trade/government sources
- Buyer behaviour
- Need to adjust to local customs
- Price sensitivity
- Areas of development potential through future segmentation of markets, i.e. the development potential beyond Exotic Siam's existing product provisions.

The information-gathering process will need to be conducted through desk and field research and must be subjected to internal management appraisal by means of an objective evaluation system before further progress is made.

2.4 MARKETING AUDIT

A comprehensive marketing audit is now required. It must assess the internal strengths and weaknesses of the company in relation to the opportunities and threats it faces in the UK, USA and French markets.

2.5 RISK ASSESSMENT

The audit, plus a full financial appraisal should collectively aim to assess the level of corporate and financial risk Exotic Siam faces with regard to:

1 Staying and expanding within the UK
2 Venturing into France with Windsor Stores
3 Crossing the Atlantic to markets within the USA

2.6 TIME-SCALES

It may be a time to advise caution. The company's growth track record to date has been outstanding. It may be wise to reflect upon progress to date before expanding yet further overseas. Assuming that the intention will be to pursue a path of internationalization, then a time-scale for the expansion plan must be set to harmonize with UK retail and Thai sourcing and procurement operations.

2.7 A REVIEW OF CORPORATE OBJECTIVES

Assuming these considerations have forced the company to reflect and reconsider the potential presented by Windsor Stores, a full review is required of Exotic Siam corporate objectives with reference to all existing operations. French and USA retailing operations cannot simply be 'added on'.

To pursue a path of international expansion will impact upon the company as a whole. This must be anticipated and planned for in advance, by means of a full review of corporate and hence marketing objectives.

2.8 REVIEW MARKET AND ORGANIZATIONAL CONTROL

In light of the redefining of objectives, the company will have considered the financial and manpower resource constants outlined in Section 2.2. This assessment now needs new reference points, i.e. the market place and the organization as a corporate entity, so that objectives can be set with realism and, above all, those that are achievable and capable of measurement are set within identified constraints.

2.9 JUSTIFICATION FOR MARKET ENTRY

A clear defensible statement, one easily communicable to many 'publics', must lay down 'which market Exotic Siam is to enter and why'. Rationality must prevail – this is no time for emotionally based decisions.

2.10 ASSUMPTIONS ABOUT THE SELECTED MARKET

In order to proceed with a detailed strategic marketing plan it will be necessary in the light of incomplete or uncertain knowledge to make some assumptions. The fact-finding mission and risk assessment may have, however, reduced the need to make too many guesses for the future.

2.11 ADDITIONAL MARKET INFORMATION PLUS THE NEED TO ESTABLISH A MANAGEMENT-INFORMATION SYSTEM

The assumptions made may identify gaps in essential knowledge. Additional market information must then be gathered to reduce the level of management and corporate risk.

Controlling overseas operations is a perennial problem with most international companies. At the start of Exotic Siam's expansion plans it *is* necessary to establish and maintain an effective information system and the specific reporting mechanisms within it.

Assuming one or both markets are to be considered for exploitation, then it is necessary to outline and review changes that are required in existing marketing operations to embody the international market(s) selected.

Each section of the following plan must be reviewed against specified time scales:

Outline marketing plan

2.12   Marketing objectives
2.13   Marketing-mix strategy
      2.13.1   Products
      2.13.2   Prices
      2.13.3   Marketing communications
      2.13.4   Distribution, transportation and documentation
2.14   The sales plan
2.15   Staffing
2.16   Contingency plans
2.17   Controlling the international marketing plan
2.18   Budget implications

A main problem Exotic Siam will face is in achieving a balance within the plan and thereby matching marketing operations to markets.

One common principle of international marketing, standardization, must be considered seriously to achieve economies of scale between international markets to be penetrated.

Planning and control : 'Gabrielle'

All world-famous designers are influenced by their times and the everyday world around them, so that today's experience may be harnessed to anticipate tomorrow's mood. Gabrielle was one of that rare breed who excelled in the world of fashion until about 90 years of age.

Born in the 1880s in the French Loire Valley of peasant stock, she was nurtured by her father, Jean Pierre Mondin, who paid for her education at a convent near Paris. Girls at the convent were taught to sew especially well, so her first job was as a seamstress, sewing dresses for the French aristocracy; but, to make extra money, she sang in respected cafés and music-halls under her father's name 'Mondin'.

She gained rapid fame as a singer and distinction for wearing eye-catching hats. Her first business venture started as 'Mondin the milliner' in 1910 with a small boutique, 'Mondin Modes'. Her instinct for fashion quickly led her on from hats to dresses – revolutionary ones for the times – and again to fashion jewellery based upon the variety of contacts made in the international world of fashion of those times.

In the early 1920s Gabrielle launched her first perfume, again using her father's name – Mondin No. 1. The fragrance was unlike any of those times, combining some eighty spices and flowers. Today the perfume is still respected as one of the finest on the worldwide market. It was not until 1970, some 50 years later, that Mondin No. 2 was launched, just before Gabrielle's death.

Today the Mondin Fashion House is stronger than ever. World-renowned fashion designers have carried on the Mondin heritage.

As a tribute to its founder, the House of Mondin now wishes to introduce a new perfume called 'Gabrielle', which conveys the very style of a most remarkable lady of fashion. 'Gabrielle' will eventually be available in the Mondin boutiques throughout the world as well as from the many exclusive retailers of women's perfumes. Initially, however, 'Gabrielle' will be offered in Paris and London before the Mondin international sales team targets wider international markets.

QUESTION

As a marketing consultant to the House of Mondin, you have been asked to specify the management functions that would be performed by a newly proposed post of marketing director, based in London. You have also been requested to outline the stages necessary for developing 'Gabrielle' to full-scale commercialization.

Section 1 The management functions to be performed by a person occupying the proposed position of marketing director

The concept of managing at any level includes planning, organizing, directing and controlling the activities of subordinates to achieve set objectives.

1.1 PLANNING

It will be the responsibility of the marketing director to design, implement, monitor and assess the marketing plan for the House of Mondin.

Initially, a full audit of company marketing activities should be undertaken, to assess the company's position in world markets, the internal strengths and weaknesses and the external opportunities and threats which exist. The audit will assist in the determination of where the company is now and where it should be within a specified time period.

The marketing director therefore should determine what needs to be done, by whom, by when and in what order to fulfil the requirements of the appointment.

To comply with the requirements of planning the following elements must be considered.

1.1.1 Marketing objectives
Both qualitative and quantitative, measurable and realistic objectives must be set as a series of goals to be achieved over specified time-scales.

1.1.2 Forecasts
Predictions must be made about what will happen by a specified time in relation to the achievement of specified objectives within the context of a competitive market environment.

1.1.3 Marketing policy
Before strategic and tactical plans are finalized, general guidelines for individual and group action must be established to guide decision-making. Policy statements will relate to all facets of the marketing spectrum.

1.1.4 Marketing strategy
The responsibility of the post extends to design and the programming of major actions that must be taken to achieve the objectives specified. The scope of this strategy is normally considered to embrace all elements of the marketing spectrum, which is more normally defined as the marketing mix.

222

1.1.5 A schedule of tactical operations

This will include a plan detailing when individual or group activities will need to be started and when they should be completed to show how individual events relate to the whole tactical plan. Timing and the ability to plan effectively under time constraints is critically important for effective marketing.

1.1.6 Procedures

At a more detailed level (and these will take time to develop) methods for implementing company policy at strategic and tactical levels will need to be determined.

1.2 ORGANIZING

The marketing director must arrange personnel within departmental control so that they relate effectively to each other to complete the work assigned to them. This means that it will be necessary to develop an organization structure to achieve marketing orientation within the House of Mondin.

Part of the directorial responsibility will be delegated, so that work will be assigned, along with responsibility and authority, to develop the abilities of subordinates into a marketing team. The marketing director must act as a catalyst to assist in establishing relationships by creating the necessary conditions whereby objectives are achieved by mutual co-operation.

1.3 DIRECTING

The status of an executive director within the UK has legal implications depending upon the company composition. One of the marketing director's functions is directing the team to carry through approved plans. Other functions include the following.

1.3.1 Training

To ensure that individuals know how to fulfil the duties and responsibilities expected of them. The marketing director should identify training needs within the team and arrange for these to be dealt with either internally or by means of an external agency.

1.3.2 Staffing

To ensure that job specifications are developed for each position and that suitably qualified personnel are appointed to them. To develop commitment within the team the marketing director should be in at the appointment stage, especially if the positions are to be filled internally.

1.3.3 Counselling

Personal development programmes will be needed for each member of the team and performance appraisals conducted; but in many companies there are periodic reviews at convenient times within a busy work schedule. Counselling by the marketing director should comprise private discussions with subordinate members of the team on how output may be improved and ambitions realized, and, if necessary, acting as a confidant to help with personal problems.

1.3.4 Motivating

As a team leader, the marketing director is responsible for staff motivation. The position will set the climate within the department and an organizational culture for the fulfilment of tasks through appealing to team needs.

1.3.5 Supervising

To demonstrate and reinforce the position assigned, the marketing director must be capable of giving instructions, guidance and setting the 'discipline levels' for members of the team. Support given to the team will be support returned to the team leader. The position of marketing director will be as strong as the strength of the subordinate team.

1.4 COMMUNICATING

Responsibilities at board level may take the marketing director away from the team and away from the physical boundaries of the organization. As it is vital that this management function is performed conscientiously, effective delegation will have to be practised. In addition, information must be exchanged with subordinates, peers and the managing director about progress, development plans and key problems to be anticipated or encountered.

1.5 CO-ORDINATING

Marketing cannot be viewed as one isolated operational area within the House of Mondin. Marketing embraces all business functions, and the success of the new position will depend upon the holder's ability not only to communicate but co-ordinate activities with other internal business functions and externally appointed agencies.

1.6 CONTROLLING AND EVALUATING

The role of the marketing director must be viewed within a system which requires inputs to cause change in a conversion process to produce marketing activity. Such an open-ended approach to management is not complete without a feedback control mechanism to enable marketing activities to be assessed against the achievement of intended goals and objectives.

Management control therefore is a necessity. The marketing director must be capable of measuring progress, evaluating what is to be done, when and by whom to ensure objectives are met. Controlling comprises the following activities.

1.6.1 The setting of standards

It is the responsibility of the marketing director to determine levels of individual and team performance within the marketing division.

1.6.2 Monitoring

Once a framework of qualitative and quantitative standards has been established, it must be used. The monitoring process is designed, often through the company's marketing information system, to detect deviations from standards set. The monitoring system must be designed to respond in time for corrective action to be taken. In simple terms the marketing director and his team must keep their 'finger on the pulse' to assess what is happening now as well as being concerned about future developments.

Monitoring consists of measurement against prescribed standards. The measuring devices must be powerful enough, rigorous enough and sensitive enough to detect problems *before* it is too late to take corrective action.

1.6.3 Taking corrective action

When performance falls too far below the standards set, corrective action must be taken; and when variations from performance are better than anticipated, favourable trends must be successfully exploited.

1.6.4 Evaluation

The management control function and the function of evaluation are inextricably linked, and hence difficult to separate meaningfully.

The evaluation function, however, is intended to determine causation: why performance has deviated positively or negatively from standards set. Answers to the question may help to prevent such occurrences happening again and will also enable the organization to be better prepared in the future to maximize profit through customer satisfaction. Evaluation should lead to an understanding of ways in which the company can/should respond under conditions of deviation from anticipated norms.

The position of marketing director for the House of Mondin is a new post. We know little about the position or the team that exists or will be built to perform the necessary marketing activities to achieve effective marketing operation within the company.

The functions of management identified above will not all take equal amounts of time. Indeed, as the appointed person becomes settled in the post, the balance of time given to these activities will change, as delegation takes place with increasing levels of confidence in the team and its organization.

Section 2 The stages developing 'Gabrielle' perfume to full-scale commercialization

In outline the stages envisaged for this new product development programme will be:

1 Research at corporate level within the House of Mondin
2 Feasibility research for 'Gabrielle'
3 Development
4 Test marketing 'Gabrielle'
5 The international product launch through to full-scale commercialization

At the end of each stage a full management review will be necessary before the new-product development programme can proceed along the path to full-scale commercialization.

INTRODUCTION

In my role as marketing consultant to the House of Mondin it is my responsibility to ensure that steps are taken to achieve the full commercial potential of 'Gabrielle'.

The reasons for the product launch appear sentimental, yet the company will gain more from this initiative if the new perfume is successful on a worldwide scale. The memory of Gabrielle Mondin will then live on.

It is to be appreciated that Gabrielle used her father's name professionally and this is now synonymous with the world of fashion. The words 'from the House of Mondin' will help to promote the new perfume – 'Gabrielle'.

2.1 RESEARCH AT CORPORATE LEVEL WITHIN THE HOUSE OF MONDIN

Had senior management within the House of Mondin not decided out of sentiment to pay tribute to one of the world's leading ladies of fashion by introducing the new perfume, then a more formal process of corporate review would have taken place. Apart from reflecting upon how the new product fitted with existing corporate objectives and product strategy, the competitive position of the market place would have been taken into account.

A pool of other product ideas might well have been developed, appropriately screened along a set of predetermined criteria, so that the emerging idea or ideas received preliminary validation. Such research might have killed the intended initiative.

We must assume, however, at this stage that 'Gabrielle' is on stream for development.

2.2 FEASIBILITY RESEARCH FOR 'GABRIELLE'

Experimental technical research will be required to:

1 Establish the specifications of the new perfume so that it *is* distinctive and quite apart in fragrance from Mondin No. 1 and Mondin No. 2.
2 Conduct design studies and consider the technical alternatives of producing to a new perfume formula and then presenting this in an award-winning way through distinctive packaging.
3 Assess the feasibility of manufacture.
4 Estimate the development costs and time needed:

At this time market research should be conducted to:

5 Determine changes to the characteristics of the market, market size and prevailing trends for the purchase of up-market, high profile perfumes.
6 Establish the nature of competition and the threat that this may impose.
7 Relate packaging and fragrance to meet market requirements of the predetermined target group.
8 Confirm strategy for product placement and distribution, price levels and the psychological variables that will induce purchase.

(a) Time taken to get 'Gabrielle' to test market
(b) The real costs.
(c) The manpower required to design, develop, launch and follow through the new product
(d) The commercial potential of this tribute

2.3 DEVELOPMENT

Assuming that the House of Mondin has regarded the feasibility research favourably, then the following activities must take place within this development stage.

2.3.1 The technical development of 'Gabrielle'
A product prototype of the perfume and the packaging combined will need to be developed and modified to a stage of preliminary design finalization.

2.3.2 Production costing and planning

It is not clear whether this is an 'in-house' manufacturing function or external-ly sub-contracted. It is assumed that the producers of Mondin No. 1 and Mondin No. 2 will also produce 'Gabrielle'. In this case materials, labour, equipment and space must be assessed and difficulties discovered and resolved.

2.3.3 Market forecasting for 'Gabrielle'

At this development stage a detailed analysis of demand is required by the production planners. Together with demand analysis, an analysis of costs is required then to establish price levels.

2.3.4 Marketing Mix

The dynamics and balance between the elements of the marketing mix must now be planned, so that a clear vision appears on product formulation and presentation, pricing, promotional support and the eventual distribution profile. At the end of this development stage a further comprehensive managerial review is required to establish break-even positions and associ-ated cost/volume/profit relationships.

A decision must now be taken, based on the findings to date, whether to treat 'Gabrielle' as a one-off promotional gesture or as a serious product for worldwide distribution. It is assumed that the latter option would be the preferred choice.

2.4 TEST MARKETING 'GABRIELLE'

The technical differences between a pilot launch programme and a test market are beyond the requirements of this assignment. The company intends to 'offer the product initially in Paris and London' in the Mondin boutiques before proceeding with full-scale commercialization.

This exercise will be treated therefore as a test market in two different geographic areas and countries. It will serve to give a good assessment of market take-up, because the exclusive Mondin boutiques are targeted at the very groups of buyers who will (or will not) respond favourably to 'Gabrielle'.

The test-market planning will need to be synchronized, scheduled and appropriately budgeted, so that an accurate assessment of market response can be made at fixed time intervals. Based on experiences in the 1970s with Mondin No.2, standards can be set against which to measure market re-sponse.

Experimental production runs must be planned for the test and final production planning begun.

Following the introduction of 'Gabrielle' in the Mondin boutiques, with specialist press advertising, typical in-store positioning and point-of-sale displays, reaction to the product packaging, as well as customer reaction to the perfume and its presentation, must be assessed by the sales staff. Apart from sales responses, responses to all the marketing-mix variables should be assessed, with particular attention being paid to the perfume, the package design, and pricing, so that any necessary modifications can be made.

A general assessment of the test against forecasts and standards should be made periodically, as volume take-up is enjoyed. The ideal situation is to leave 'Gabrielle' 'in test' until a repurchase cycle is established but, for such a product, this may be far too long a period of time.

Assuming the test results are favourable and appropriate changes have been planned for and made, final plans for full launch and associated budgets must be determined. A final management review is now needed to put the House of Mondin seal of approval on the international launch of 'Gabrielle – a perfume of distinction from the House of Mondin'.

2.5 THE INTERNATIONAL PRODUCT LAUNCH THROUGH TO FULL-SCALE COMMERCIALIZATION

The main stages are the following:

1 The launch preparations
2 The launch
3 Follow up and review marketing activities

2.5.1 The launch preparations

This stage is a building-up process in preparation for the launch at international level. Production levels must be built up, so that adequate stock levels are held to supply the channels with sufficient stock to display and sell the perfume, with adequate buffering stock in hand to sustain continued demand.

Considerable investment is now needed, so the House of Mondin must be certain of market response. To reduce risk levels, the international launch programme can be rolled out on a progressive basis, concentrating initially on major population centres in countries in which Mondin boutiques are based.

It is anticipated, as with Mondin No. 1 and Mondin No. 2, that distribution of 'Gabrielle' will not be restricted to the Mondin boutiques as exclusive supply points, but to a wider base of enfranchised distributors and stockists in appropriate perfumery outlets. Therefore preliminary announcements must be made to the trade, to sales agents and the international sales force of the House of Mondin. The new product development programme must also be introduced to all international sales personnel.

Sample cases must be distributed to outlets. In selected Mondin boutiques the new perfume should, through the use of a respected PR agency, receive public showings to exclusive trade and customer groups.

Arrangements must be made for the distribution of promotional and advertising pre-print materials. Initial advertising should then be placed, with arrangements for good quality publicity through the PR agency.

An internal debate on the use of agencies must be held to ensure that the boundaries between PR and advertising activities are not crossed – a problem overcome by the use of one international agency with expertise in both areas. Existing experience can be called upon within the House of Mondin and reviewed for the launch of 'Gabrielle'.

2.5.2 The launch

A date must be set for the official launch, although the product will filter through to trade outlets over a launch period rather than on 'one day'.

First customer calls will be experienced and initial purchases made. In turn this will stimulate the order and re-order cycle throughout the distribution channels and form part of an ordering process for all Mondin products carried. In the initial months field reports and sales information feedback will be vital to assess sales take-up at an international level.

Monitoring performance internally is essential. Therefore efficient internal communication between outlets and head office is needed, so that problems can be overcome and, above all, measurement of sales and profit volume activity can be conducted against the controls set up for the launch programme.

Full-scale commercialization may take many months and maybe up to 2 years. The diffusion process may be slow and the House of Mondin may need to be patient in its expectations.

Eventually 'Gabrielle', like Mondin No. 1 and Mondin No.2, will be absorbed as an established product within the organization. The profit contribution will be assessed but will no doubt be related to the fact that 'Gabrielle' was established *primarily* as a tribute to a great lady of fashion, the founder of the House of Mondin.

Marketing communications : the Arthur Morrison Group

The following statement was made at a recent main board meeting by Jeremy Forbes, managing director of the manufacturing division, the largest division within the Arthur Morrison group of companies:

> I fully realize that we have been in business for over 100 years and I understand the problems and commercial risk of changing our corporate identity, but now *is* the time, gentlemen, to prepare ourselves for the 21st century.
>
> It is a natural assumption by the general public, our customers, finance institutions, the trade channels and various opinion leaders, that the Arthur Morrison Manufacturing Company is but a medium-sized, independent organization.
>
> Yet it *has* the backing of an entire multi-national corporation.
>
> It is time, gentlemen, that the *five* divisions of the Arthur Morrison Group came together as an integrated force in the international market place even though our headquarters is based in London.

Worldwide annual revenues of the group exceeds £500 million and yet companies within the group have traded as separate entities and not as one corporate unit. This has arisen because progress throughout the company history has been achieved more by mergers and acquisitions than from internal expansion.

Business development has been achieved from technical excellence, reliability, dependability, good quality products and services across the group divisions, which include geological exploration, mining, extraction, process manufacturing and research and development in worldwide chemical and allied industries. The Arthur Morrison Group has performed well to remain ahead in mature markets, although reported profits have not grown significantly in the past 5 years. The performance of the group as a whole has been principally influenced by the outstanding contribution of the manufacturing division. The marketing-oriented Jeremy Forbes carries considerable weight at main board level. As a vigorous individual, he constantly searches for new markets and makes full use of research agencies and outside marketing consultants.

Recent research had highlighted the lack of a group corporate identity, and he considers this is the next task for him to tackle. The main board has approved his proposals. Therefore the first task will be for the five operating divisions to trade under one corporate banner, 'Morrison Industries International'.

Jeremy Forbes has called in Adrienne Klein, a marketing communications consultant of distinction, to advise on how to modify corporate communications with a view to establishing a new corporate identity.

QUESTION

In the role of Adrienne Klein you are required to assist Jeremy Forbes to achieve the changes to corporate identity internally. Your specific brief is to present proposals for implementing changes to corporate identity and also to make recommendations on relevant aspects of marketing communications.

INTRODUCTION

To achieve the brief Jeremy Forbes has provided, the campaign must be scheduled into two parts:

Part 1   Internal campaign within the organization, to gain agreement to a new corporate identity.
Part 2   Communicating the new image to the specified target markets.

Market communication plan for the Arthur Morrison Group – a change in corporate identity

CORPORATE OBJECTIVES

1   To change the corporate identity of the operating companies within the Arthur Morrison Group to Morrison Industries International and thereby modify the projected corporate image.
2   To project this image to all opinion-leaders, publics and market segments, and thereby to build awareness and recognition for Morrison Industries International.
3   Convey the new image on *all* company communication instruments and to obliterate the independent logos and graphics of the operating divisions within the Arthur Morrison Group.
4   To achieve this transition as smoothly as possible, securing internal agreement to the new graphics and to convey the change of identity positively to existing customers in all appropriate ways.

Part 1 Internal campaign (Timing 6 months)

The following action must be taken to secure internal agreement to the proposals:

STAGE 1.1 TO COMMUNICATE INTERNALLY THE INTENTION TO CHANGE THE IDENTITY OF THE COMPANIES TO THAT OF THE GROUP

A meeting is held, both to explain the proposals and to seek ways to achieve the specified task. Those attending are Jeremy Forbes, Adrienne Klein and the heads of the divisions concerned.

The objective of the meeting is simply to announce the intention, gauge reaction and win initial support, though the decision for change has already been taken. To gain continued support, the group heads will then communicate the intention down the organization, seeking ideas from relevant key staff.

STAGE 1.2

Adrienne Klein briefs three creative design agencies on production of the graphics required, in terms of tone and appearance, to convey the group identity. In particular, this new identity should convey:

1 An established company in the chemicals and allied industries business
2 An internationally operating company
3 A progressive and forward-looking image
4 Achievement of a transition from what previously existed to what is to be adopted

STAGE 1.3

An internal meeting (as at Stage 1.1) is convened to obtain feedback and ideas to date (a political move).

STAGE 1.4

Presentations are received from the three design agencies. They are delivered to Adrienne Klein and Jeremy Forbes to prevent any internal conflicts at this stage, and to prevent existing advertising/PR agencies from seeing them.

STAGE 1.5

The design options are considered by the members of the original meeting at Stage 1.1, and any other ideas which may have been generated internally are looked at. A decision-making procedure is agreed and one design adopted (or the procedure repeated with modified designs until a generally acceptable design is generated).

STAGE 1.6

From the pool of designs tabled one has now been adopted, and it must be coverted into print, e.g. sample letterheads, compliment slips, visiting cards, etc. A house style must be conveyed in appropriate livery, i.e. corporate colours must be selected and adopted to support the design.

At this initial stage group divisional *names* should occur on the above communication instruments, together with Morrison Industries International to convey the linkage, e.g.

Morrison Industries International,
Group Companies,
Mining Division,
–
–

STAGE 1.7

When the design is approved, a PR agency must be appointed and briefed to prepare a corporate brochure explaining the change and promoting the range of products and services.

Part 2 Communicating the new image to the specified target markets
(Timing 6 months)

At the end of the Part 1 action a manual of graphic standards should be produced for use in Part 2.

2.1 MARKETING OBJECTIVES

To develop appropriate marketing strategies to permit the revised corporate objectives to be implemented.

In this case no specific products or services have been identified and hence no specific marketing objectives will be developed; but in practice, marketing communications objectives should be developed from the marketing objectives of the organization.

2.2 MARKETING COMMUNICATIONS OBJECTIVES

(a) To convey the new image to identified target market/publics and opinion-leaders and explain the rationale for this.
(b) To overcome or prevent concern that may arise from these target groups.
(c) To achieve the transition quickly with the minimum amount of fuss and within the budgetary constraints proposed.
(d) To test the reaction among key groups to the changes, particularly in the areas of graphic transfer.

2.3 TARGET GROUPS

The following target groups are to be considered as an immediate priority:

Home market

1   The City and finance houses
2   Existing customers and potential customers
3   Trade associations
4   The distributive trades used
5   Competitors
6   Internal personnel within the division and the total group
7   The general public within a defined catchment area of each company site from which workers/employees are drawn
8   Shareholders

Overseas market

Following the introduction of the changes on the home market, overseas markets should be tackled.

9   Existing and potential customers and distributive trades to be contacted

2.4 COMMUNICATIONS STRATEGY

To achieve the objectives specified the following strategy is proposed.

2.4.1 *Creative strategy*
The theme to be adopted will be low key but aim to project the company positively into the twenty-first century, so that the idea of a forward-thinking, progressive organization is conveyed. This will be handled visually and supported by a corporate brochure and limited media exposure.

2.4.2 *Media selection and justification*

The advertising task has been specified within the marketing communications objectives. The task is essentially to convey the changes cost-effectively. Products are not being advertised; therefore the campaign is to be visualized purely as corporate advertising.

To meet target audience	*Media*	*Form of usage/rationale*
Employees and shareholders	In-house journal	Editorial announcements
Employees	Letter to all employees	Announce the change and reason for it, to offset any adverse employee reaction
Distributive trade	Trade directories and limited trade magazines	Revised advertising format for corporate advertising
	Direct-mail shot containing the new brochure	To build confidence for the change
Existing customers	As above	As above
Potential customers	All communications letterheads, compliment slips, etc.	To convey the organization's corporate image to potential customers
General public	Local press advertisement/ editorial support	To convey the change and boost local opinion
Competitors	Trade press/directories	To convey the changes covertly and thereby create awareness for them

To meet target audience	*Media*	*Form of usage/rationale*
The City, finance houses and shareholders	*Financial Times* editorial and supporting full page advertisements	To create awareness and interest for the organization and to boost image
The overseas market and distribution channels	International trade press which carries corporate advertising and trade-directory advertising	This activity may become an incremental process (depending upon company priorities in this area)

The above outline strategy includes media advertising and non-media 'promotional activity' as well as PR action.

THE SALES PLAN

Conveying the new image has an interpersonal dimension. All salespersons must attend a national conference to be briefed fully on the new corporate stance, so that any dissonance, both among them and their customers, can be reduced to the minimum. The brochure and selective give-aways carrying the new company logo should be used at all appropriate sales calls during the 6-month period specified.

CONTINGENCY

Where an organization is associated with intangibles, such as change in corporate identity, the following problems may arise:

Problem	Actions to be taken
Adverse reaction from customers and employees	Retrenchment – to revert would be very costly in management time alone as well as wasteful in budgeting terms. Effort must be made to win over areas of resistance.
Time-delays creating confusion	The schedule of the change can only be implemented when all print runs are completed. Therefore the launch of the new image should be delayed until these are completed.
Confusion arising from lack of sustained marketing communications	Beyond the 6-month planning period and the 6-month implementation period, a planned and sustained programme of marketing communications is vital. This will be supported and supplemented in subsequent company *product advertising*.

BUDGET APPROPRIATION FOR THE ABOVE MARKETING-COMMUNICATIONS ACTIVITY

A budget has not been specified in the case study. Clearly for a company with an annual turnover in excess of £500 million, funds of a sufficient level will be found to achieve the communications tasks specified.

The following initiatives must be budgeted for: graphic design, print runs of letterheads and associated stationery, the corporate brochure, public relations activity, media advertising, promotional give-aways, a contingency reserve, advertisement production and consultants' fees.

Index

Above the line (promotion), 100, 120
Adoption process, 47–8
Advertising, 31, 100, 113, 125, 156
    agencies, 130
    budget, 115–19
    evaluation, 118–19
    expenditure, 115, 188
Affordable method (advertising budget),
    116
Agent (commission), 170–2
Attitudes, 42–3, 118
Audience measurement, 118
Automatic vending, 161
Awareness (in adoption process), 47

Banded pack, 99
Below the line (promotion), 99, 115,
    130
Branch office (export), 177
Brand image, 99
Brand loyalty (reinforcement), 101, 130,
    156, 197
Brand name, 99
Brand management, 199
Brand penetration, 78
Brand rationalization, 93
Branding, 29, 114, 156, 158, 198–200
Break even, 105, 112–13
British Overseas Trade Board, 172–3
Budgeting, 185–9, 192
    advertising, 115–19
    export, 166–7
Business analysis (in new product
    development), 82
Business format (franchising), 150–1
Buyer behaviour, 41–5, 196
Buying process, 45, 52, 154

Central Office of Information (COI), 173
Chain of supply, 23–4
Channel conflict, 144
Channel of distribution, 141–4
Channel intermediaries, 142, 154
Channel length, 142
Channel selection, 142–3
Clubs (book/record/tape), 161
Commercial TV areas (in marketing
    research), 62
Commercialization (in product
    development), 83–4
Commission agent, 170–2
Commodity markets, 148
Communication stage models, 118
Competitive parity (advertising budgets),
    117
Confirmation (in diffusion theory), 47
Consumer choice, 205
Consumer durables, 36
Consumer panels, 57–9, 118
Controls (in marketing), 185–9
Co-operative societies, 155
Copy (advertising), 118
Corporate advertising/promotion, 151
Corporate budget, 119
Corporate identity, 150
Cost plus pricing, 105
Culture (and marketing), 25, 44–5, 169, 170,
    179
Customer liaison, 122
Customer orientation, 18
Customer service, 140

Decision making unit (DMU), 52, 196
Decline (in PLC theory), 49, 94
Demand (in pricing), 104

Department stores, 155
Depth (of product mix), 86–8
Depth interviews, 76
Desk research, 72
Development (new product), 82–3
Differentiated marketing, 195
Diffusion (of innovations), 46–50
Diminishing utility, 103
Direct mail, 161
Direct marketing/selling, 31, 144, 159–62
Direct response advertising, 161
Discount stores, 159
Discounts, 30
Discrimination (price), 109–11
Display, 123
Disproportionate sampling, 60
Distribution, 91, 140, 208
    channels, 141–4
    physical, 146
Documentation (export), 167
Domestic (purchasers), 51–3
'Door to door' selling, 143, 160

Early adopters (in diffusion theory), 47
Early majority (in diffusion theory), 48, 92
Economic factors (affecting marketing), 25, 40–1, 99, 102–5, 201–5
Elastic demand, 103
Environmental influences, 22–7, 210
Ethics (and marketing), 201–5
Evaluation:
    in adoption process, 47
    of advertising, 119
Examination technique, 1–5
Examiners' reports, 5–9
Exhibitions, 132
Experimentation, 55, 73–4
Export Credits Guarantee Department (ECGD), 173
Exporting, 163–7, 173, 176–7
Extended product line, 148
External information (sources), 72–3

Family (in buying behaviour), 44
Fast moving consumer goods (FMCGs), 36, 57–8, 61, 99, 121, 144, 147, 154–8, 198, 200
Flexible planning, 189
'Four Ps', 19, 29–32
Franchising, 149–53

Gaps (in product mix), 87–8
Global marketing, 180
Goals:
    advertising, 116
    distribution, 147
    marketing, 183, 208
Goodwill, 110, 152
Government (and marketing), 25, 172–4
Group discussions, 76–7, 118
Growth (in PLC theory), 49, 91–2

Hall tests, 82
House image, 157
Hypermarkets, 157, 159

Idea generation (in new product development), 80–1, 122
Imitative products, 93
Independent retailers, 155
Industrial marketing, 38, 39, 198
Industrial purchasing, 51–3
Inelastic demand, 103
Information (in adoption process), 47
Innovation/innovators (in diffusion theory), 46–50, 91
Intermediaries (channel), 142
Internal information (sources), 65–7, 72
International trade, 175–80
Introduction (in PLC theory), 49

Job title (in recruitment), 135
Joint venture, 178

Laggards (in diffusion theory), 48
Late majority (in diffusion theory), 48
Latin square design, 55–7
Learning:
    buyer behaviour, 43
    for examinations, 2–4
Licensing, 178
Lifestyle, 25, 50, 196
Likert scale, 77
Luxury products/items, 26, 158

Macro environment, 24–6
Mail order, 155, 160
Market niching, 197
Market Research Society, 63
Market structure, 38–9

INDEX

Marketing:
  analysis, 65–6
  audit, 188
  channels, 23–7
  concept, 18, 202, 207–9
  defined, 17–21
  environment, 23–6, 126
  global, 180
  Information Systems (MkIS), 64–70, 80, 121–2, 188
  intelligence (in MkIS), 67–8
  management, 28–32, 140, 206–11
  mix, 19, 29, 32, 61, 104, 119, 138, 142
  planning/strategy, 50, 61, 88, 95–6, 104, 126, 163, 181–4, 185–9, 199
  research, 68–9, 75–8, 165, 169, 208, 209
  segmentation, 88
Mark-up pricing, 111–12
Mass marketing, 158
Maturity (in PLC theory), 49, 92–4
Merchandising, 121, 135, 156
Metro centres (in retailing), 162
Micro environment, 23–4, 202
Middlemen, 142–3
Models:
  advertising appropriation, 118
  buyer behaviour, 52–3, 78
Monitoring, 78
Motivation, 42, 171
Multi-nationals, 175–80
Multiple chains, 155–8
Multivariate analysis, 78

Natural environment (and marketing), 26
Negotiation, 135, 137, 156
Non-price competition, 145, 148
Non-random sampling, 59
Non-shop selling, 159, 162

Objective setting, 119, 146
Objective/task (advertising budget), 117
Objectives (marketing), 183, 199
Observation (in marketing research), 73–4
Offers (special/premium), 99
Oligopoly, 203
'On pack' promotions, 131
One-stop shopping, 114, 157
Opinion leaders, 44
Overseas marketing, 164, 175–80

'Own label', 144, 156, 157, 158, 199–200

Packaging/packing, 30, 98, 101, 106
Panels (consumer), 57–9
'Pareto' analysis, 67
Party plans, 143, 159–60
Peer groups (in purchasing), 49
Penetration (pricing), 91
Percentage of sales (advertising budget), 116
Perception, 42
Physical distribution, 146
Place (in four Ps), 29–32, 141
Planning:
  marketing, 50, 88, 104, 167, 181, 185–9, 191
  promotional, 132
  strategic, 19, 34, 104
Point of sale (POS), 131
Population (in sampling), 60
Positioning, 107
Power (in channels), 141–4, 154, 156, 199–200
Press release, 126
Price/pricing, 30, 91, 92, 94, 102–5, 106–8, 109–14
  discrimination, 109–11
  mark-up, 111–12
  prestige, 113–14
  target, 112–13
Primary research, 73–4
Probability (sampling, 59–61
Problem solving (in purchasing), 45
Product:
  development, 82–3
  differentiation, 101, 107–8
  in four Ps, 29
  ideas, 79–84
  imitative, 93
  innovative, 47, 91
  life cycle, 48–9, 89–97, 105, 144
  line, 85–8, 107
  line pricing, 106–8
  mix, 85–8
  planning/strategy, 88, 90–1, 182
  prominence, 121
  screening, 81–4
Promotion, 30, 98, 100–1, 132–3, 172
Proportionate sampling, 60

Public relations, 122, 125–8
Publicity, 31, 125–6
Pull (strategy), 156

Qualitative (methods in marketing
   research), 68, 74, 75–7
Quality, 29–30
Quantitative (methods in marketing
   research), 77–8
Quota sampling, 59
Quotas (sales), 136

Random sampling, 59–61
Recall, 118
Recognition tests, 118
Recruitment, 134–7
Reference groups, 43, 49
Remuneration, 170
Reports (examiners'), 5–9
Representative, 121–2
Retail chains, 144, 155
Retailing, 154–8, 159
Return on investment (ROI), 104
Revision process, 2–5

Sales force, 120–4, 134–7
Sales forecasts, 117, 122, 187, 190–3
Sales leads, 122
Sales promotion, 129–33
Sales/selling orientation, 20, 33–7
Salesman (export), 168–70
Sampling:
   disproportionate, 60
   probability, 59–61
   proportionate, 60
   quota, 59
   random, 59–61
Scientific change (and marketing), 25
Screening, 81
Secondary research, 72–3
Segmentation, 88, 99, 108, 110, 143, 194–7
Selection (personnel), 134–7, 171
Self concept/image, 41–2, 113
Selling/salesmanship, 122, 156
Semantic differential scale, 77
Service level/support, 145–8, 172

Shipping (export), 166
Situation analysis, 182–3
Skimming (in pricing), 91
Social stratification, 50
Special offers, 99
Sponsorship, 152
Stockholding, 140
Strategic planning/marketing, 19, 34, 90–1,
   95–6, 104, 156–7, 176, 181–4, 188, 198–200,
   210
Stratified sampling, 60
Supermarkets, 121, 157, 159
Superstores, 157, 159
Supply chain, 23–4
Supply (pricing), 104
Surveys (marketing research), 73–4
Symbol shops, 152
Syndicated research, 57
Systems approach, 139–40

Tactical objectives, 186
Target:
   marketing, 90, 99, 142, 197
   pricing, 112–13
Targets (sales), 136
Test marketing, 60–2, 83
Testing (in the revision process), 3–4
Total cost approach, 139, 147
Total distribution concept, 138–40
Total product concept, 148
Trade marketing/promotion, 110, 131
Trade shows, 132
Training, 134–7
Transportation costs, 140
Trial (in adoption process), 47

Unbranded goods, 205
Undifferentiated marketing, 195

Vertical integration, 143
Voluntary chains/groups, 152, 156

Wholesalers, 144, 156
Width (of product mix), 86–8